Midterm

TRANSFORMING AMERICAN POLITICS
Lawrence C. Dodd, Series Editor

Dramatic changes in political institutions and behavior over the past three decades have underscored the dynamic nature of American politics, confronting political scientists with a new and pressing intellectual agenda. The pioneering work of early postwar scholars, while laying a firm empirical foundation for contemporary scholarship, failed to consider how American politics might change or to recognize the forces that would make fundamental change inevitable. In reassessing the static interpretations fostered by these classic studies, political scientists are now examining the underlying dynamics that generate transformational change.

Transforming American Politics brings together texts and monographs that address four closely related aspects of change. A first concern is documenting and explaining recent changes in American politics—in institutions, processes, behavior, and policymaking. A second is reinterpreting classic studies and theories to provide a more accurate perspective on postwar politics. The series looks at historical change to identify recurring patterns of political transformation within and across the distinctive eras of American politics. Last and perhaps most importantly, the series presents new theories and interpretations that explain the dynamic processes at work and thus clarify the direction of contemporary politics. All of the books focus on the central theme of transformation—transformation in both the conduct of American politics and in the way we study and understand its many aspects.

FORTHCOMING TITLES

Revolving Gridlock, David Brady and Craig Volden

Congress and the Administrative State, Second Edition, Lawrence C. Dodd and Richard L. Schott

Governing Partners: State-Local Relations in the United States, Russell L. Hanson

The Divided Democrats: Ideological Unity, Party Reform, and Presidential Elections, William G. Mayer

Seeing Red: How the Cold War Shaped American Politics, John Kenneth White

New Media in American Politics, Richard Davis and Diana Owen

Extraordinary Politics: Dissent and Collective Action in the American System, Charles C. Euchner

Irony of Reform: Roots of American Political Disenchantment, G. Calvin Mackenzie

The Tragic Presidency, Robert L. Lineberry

The Collapse of the Democratic Presidential Majority, David G. Lawrence

Midterm

The Elections of 1994 in Context

EDITED BY
Philip A. Klinkner
Hamilton College

FOREWORD BY
Charles O. Jones

WestviewPress
A Division of HarperCollinsPublishers

To Honorine

Transforming American Politics

All rights reserved. Printed in the United States of America. No part of this publication may be reproduced or transmitted in any form or by any means, electronic or mechanical, including photocopy, recording, or any information storage and retrieval system, without permission in writing from the publisher.

Copyright © 1996 by Westview Press, Inc., A Division of HarperCollins Publishers, Inc.

Published in 1996 in the United States of America by Westview Press, Inc., 5500 Central Avenue, Boulder, Colorado 80301-2877, and in the United Kingdom by Westview Press, 12 Hid's Copse Road, Cumnor Hill, Oxford OX2 9JJ

Library of Congress Cataloging-in-Publication Data
Midterm : the elections of 1994 in context / edited by Philip A. Klinkner
     p. cm. — (Transforming American politics)
  Includes bibliographical references and index.
  ISBN 0-8133-2818-7. — ISBN 0-8133-2819-5
  1. United States. Congress—Elections. 1994. 2. United States—
Politics and Government—1993–   I. Klinkner. Philip A.
II. Series.
JK1968 1996c
324973'0929–dc20   95-48812
                                                                                                         CIP

The paper used in this publication meets the requirements of the American National Standard for Permanence of Paper for Printed Library Materials Z39.48-1984.

10   9   8   7   6   5   4   3   2   1

Contents

Foreword, Charles O. Jones ... ix
Acknowledgments ... xi

1 The 1994 House Elections in Perspective
    Gary C. Jacobson ... 1

2 Eight More in '94: The Republican Takeover of the Senate
    Franco Mattei ... 21

3 "Permanent Minority" No More: House Republicans in 1994
    John J. Pitney, Jr., and William F. Connelly, Jr. ... 47

4 Court and Country in American Politics: The Democratic Party and the 1994 Election
    Philip A. Klinkner ... 61

5 Money in the 1994 Elections and Beyond
    Theodore J. Eismeier and Philip H. Pollock III ... 81

6 The 1994 Electoral Aftershock: Dealignment or Realignment in the South
    Paul Frymer ... 99

7 The Politics of Pragmatism: The Christian Right and the 1994 Elections
    J. Christopher Soper ... 115

8 In Search of the Angry White Male: Gender, Race, and Issues in the 1994 Elections
    Grant Reeher and Joseph Cammarano ... 125

9 Re-exploring the Weak Challenger Hypothesis: The 1994
  Candidate Pools
   *L. Sandy Maisel, Elizabeth J. Ivry, Benjamin D. Ling,
   and Stephanie G. Pennix*   137

10 Innovative Midterm Elections
   David R. Mayhew   157

References   171
About the Book   183
About the Editor and Contributors   185
Index   189

Foreword

CHARLES O. JONES

It is a measure of the progress made in studying elections that most of the time we can predict the outcome. Every so often, however, we are startled by the results and scramble to search for deeper meanings. Forevermore, the 1994 congressional elections will be classified among those events marking important change. Special features abound: the Contract with America, a bold party platform signed by a huge majority of House Republican candidates; the end of 40 years of Republican minority status in the House of Representatives; a candidate for Speaker of the House essentially campaigning for the job; the only newly elected Democratic president in this century to lose both houses of Congress at the midterm; and the continuing transformation of the South from a Democratic to a Republican stronghold.

These developments have encouraged a stronger-than-usual policy reading of the election that has enhanced, even amplified, Speaker-designate Newt Gingrich's plans for taking charge of the national agenda. The contract and the media event of its signing in late September were ridiculed by most analysts. Many Democrats, including the president, appeared delighted to campaign against the document. It was widely believed that the Republicans had made a strategic blunder since they were bound to do well in the election and the contract could be used by Democrats against Republican candidates. One Democratic political consultant, Paul Begala, was quoted as saying, "There is not a night that I don't thank God for the contract."

On November 8, the Republicans won control of both houses of Congress, as well as control of several statehouses and state legislatures. No Republican incumbent governor, representative, or senator was defeated. The net gain of 52 House seats exceeded the expectations of the most optimistic Republican. It was the greatest net gain for Republicans since 1946 and was the basis for interpreting a mandate for the new Speaker. Imagine—a policy mandate for a leader of the House of Representatives! Not all congressional leaders would know what to do with such a charge. Gingrich, however, had the clear intention of bringing each of the contract's ten proposals to a vote in the House within a 100-day period. He proceeded to make organizational changes to achieve this goal, to set the House to work early in the new session (and late into each working day), to maintain strong party unity, to attract substantial Democratic support on several bills, and to pass all but one of the proposals (a constitutional amendment for term limits that requires a two-thirds majority). It was a stunning performance, if not exactly the recommended method for legislating.

Meanwhile, the new Republican Senate was deluged by the legislative product of the House. It performed its historical role of retarding the pace, with the minority Democrats employing all of the delaying tactics relied on by the Republicans to thwart President Clinton's program in the 103rd Congress. Still, there was no question that the agenda was being set on Capitol Hill in the Gingrich-led House of Representatives. And it was an agenda of such scope and weight as to occupy the Senate through the first session of the 104th Congress.

President Clinton was hardly a player in the early months of the new Congress. He was widely viewed as having lost an election without being on the ballot. Having to forgo a traditional policy function of the presidency, agenda setting, he was forced to rely on a veto strategy. This option was problematic for Clinton for two reasons. First, in an effort to avoid so-called gridlock and to build support for his program among Democrats, Clinton had not vetoed any bill in his first two years in office. A veto strategy is effective primarily as a credible threat. Because Clinton had not used the veto, the viability of a threat to do so had yet to be established. Second, the veto is not the preferred option for a policy-ambitious president like Clinton. Great presidents are not those who say "no" but are those who formulate new ideas for meeting urgent needs. Therefore, the 1994 congressional elections produced high anxiety in the White House as Clinton's staff searched for the means by which he might regain the initiative of his early months in office.

It is not too soon to begin analyzing this historic election. We will, of course, know much more about its impact with the passage of time. For example, it is said that the true test of the Contract with America will be the number of bills enacted into law, a reasonable basis for evaluation, to be sure. But we already know that the Republicans did better than expected in the 1994 elections, finally achieving majority status in the House of Representatives. What is the explanation? And it is a fact that there has never been a 100-day period in the House led by the Speaker to match that in the early months of 1995. How did it happen? Nor have Democratic presidents typically had to cope with such challenging political conditions. What are Clinton's options? A recounting of the special nature of what has happened and advance appraisals are clearly in order.

Philip Klinkner has identified exactly the right topics for treating the 1994 elections and their effects, and he has chosen an impressive group of scholars to analyze the results and explain what they mean. This collection offers historical perspective, contemporary context, and implications for the immediate future. It examines developments in voting behavior (including the "angry white male" and the Christian right), effects on the party system, regional shifts (with special emphasis on the South), and the ever-important subject of campaign finance. Political scientists will pay heed to this election for decades to come. *Midterm: The Elections of 1994 in Context* offers students a splendid beginning in their endeavors to comprehend the significance of one of the most startling and engaging political events in the post–World War II era.

Acknowledgments

This book had its origins in the stunning events of November 1994, when it dawned on me that midterm elections are rarely given the same thorough analysis as presidential elections, even when they are as obviously important as the elections of 1994. This view was echoed by Jennifer Knerr and Larry Dodd at Westview Press, whose support and encouragement made this project possible. I would also like to thank the contributors to this volume, since it is their ideas and research which provide its value. Special thanks should also go to David Mayhew; not only did he contribute a chapter to the volume but seven of the other authors in this book were his students at Yale University. This book was not intended as a Festschrift. Instead, as he would put it, if you throw a brick into a room full of scholars interested in midterm elections, you are bound to hit a few Mayhew students. Finally, this book is dedicated to my wife, Honorine, who never ceases to amaze me with her love and support.

Philip A. Klinkner

1

The 1994 House Elections in Perspective

GARY C. JACOBSON

The 1994 elections set off a political earthquake that will send aftershocks rumbling through national politics for years to come. For the first time in 42 years, Republicans captured the House of Representatives. The 52-seat gain that gave them a 230–204 majority was the largest net partisan swing since 1948.[1] Republicans also took control of the Senate, taking 8 seats from Democrats and immediately adding a party-switching opportunist (Richard Shelby of Alabama) to end up with a 53–47 majority. After a two-year hiatus, the United States again has divided government—one party controlling the presidency, the other party controlling the Congress. But in a startling reversal, this time the White House belongs to the Democrats while Congress belongs to the Republicans. The Republican congressional triumph led a national sweep for the party. Indeed, the only reason the election brought divided government rather than unified Republican control is that President Clinton was not on the ballot.

Clearly, the *results* of the 1994 elections—particularly the House elections, which are the focus of this Chapter—were extraordinary. The question for political scientists who study elections, however, is whether the *process* that produced them was also extraordinary. That is, does the Republican victory mean that the electoral world depicted by the conventional literature changed fundamentally in 1994? Or can we account for the Republican success within the framework of currently accepted ideas about congressional elections? These are the questions I begin to address here. Although answers must be far from definitive at this early date, before all the relevant data are in hand for analysis, the evidence available so far suggests that although the electoral processes shaping 1994 differed in important respects from those of recent decades, most of the familiar patterns held for 1994. Although House elections were, as the post-election commentary emphasized, nationalized to a greater extent than they have been in several decades, local variation was as pronounced as ever and for the usual reasons: incumbency, the quality of challengers, campaign spending, and the interaction of national issues with local circumstances.

I begin by presenting a stylized account of the Republican victory in the 1994 House elections, with special attention to how the nationalization of local contests contributed to the party's success. Marketable national campaign themes did not by themselves give the Republicans their House majority, however. National issues needed effective local sponsors to influence House voters; to win House seats, Republicans still needed plausible candidates with enough money to get the messages out to district voters. How the effects of national issues were mediated by candidates and campaigns in what continued to be predominantly an electoral process with local focus are shown in the second section part of the Chapter.

WHY DID THE REPUBLICANS WIN THE HOUSE?

Why did Republicans, after four decades of futility, suddenly win a clear majority of House seats? The short answer is that they won by inverting political patterns that gave Democrats comfortable House majorities despite a generation of Republican superiority in presidential elections. In my earlier work on divided government, I offered this summary explanation for the Republicans' inability to win control of the House:

> Republicans have failed to advance in the House because they have fielded inferior candidates on the wrong side of issues that are important to voters in House elections and because voters find it difficult to assign blame or credit when control of government is divided between the parties (Jacobson 1990a: 3).

In 1994, the Republicans won the House by fielding (modestly) superior candidates who were on the right side of the issues that were important to voters in House elections and by persuading voters to blame a unified Democratic government for government's failures.

Until 1994, Democrats were able to maintain House majorities despite Republican dominance of presidential contests by persuading electorates to use different criteria for making presidential choices than for making congressional choices. Most Americans want low tax rates, low inflation, a less-meddlesome government, a strong national defense, and law and order at home. Republican presidential candidates capitalized on their party's superior reputation on these issues to win five of the last seven presidential elections. But most Americans also oppose cuts in middle-class entitlements and many other social programs and fear unemployment, greater exposure to market forces, and greater environmental risk. Democrats held on to their congressional majorities in part by promising to protect popular programs, benefits, and safeguards.

House Democrats also promoted and thrived on a candidate-centered election system in which, as Tip O'Neill famously put it, "All politics is local." As the party believing in the value of government and thus of governmental service, Democrats fielded a higher proportion of ambitious, experienced, and talented candidates who were willing to do the hard work to build and maintain personal followings in their districts. House Democrats became adept at building local majority coalitions out of whatever material was at hand. The party's fractious diversity, which frustrated its presidential candidates' efforts to construct majority coalitions, was no barrier to success in local politics. Democrats ran as staunch friends of organized labor, civil rights activists, feminists, or the environmental movement when doing so attracted votes, and they avoided such alliances when it did not. Southern Democrats, for example, were able to portray themselves as fiscal and social conservatives despite their national party's image. By keeping the electoral focus local in districts where the national party's liberal reputation was a millstone, Democrats were able to capture and retain House seats that otherwise had distinctly Republican coloration (Jacobson 1990a).

All politics was *not* local in 1994. Republicans succeeded in framing the local choice in national terms, making taxes, social discipline, big government, and the Clinton presidency the dominant issues. They did so by exploiting three related waves of public sentiment that crested simultaneously in 1994: The first was public disgust with the politics, politicians, and government in Washington. The second was the widespread feeling that American economic and social life was out of control and heading in the wrong direction. The visceral rejection of Clinton by a crucial set of swing voters, the "Reagan Democrats" and supporters of Ross Perot, was the third.

An Angry Public

Public contempt for members of Congress as a class has been growing for more than two decades. All of the regular polling questions measuring attitudes toward government have found an increasingly angry and distrustful public. Disapproval of Congress's performance reached an all-time high of 79 percent in one 1994 poll, but this was only the latest, incremental extension of a long-term trend.

Rising distrust and anger were fed by several streams. One major stream flowed directly from the politics of divided government during the Reagan-Bush years. Divided government encouraged the kind of partisan posturing, haggling, delay, and confusion that voters hate whenever Republican presidents and Democratic Congresses faced major policy decisions. It also guaranteed that voters would wind up feeling betrayed by the inevitable compromises that made agreement possible, as they did in 1990 when George Bush and the Democratic Congress cut a deal to reduce the deficit through a combination of tax increases and program cuts (Jacobson 1993a).

The formal end of divided government in 1992 was supposed to end gridlock. It did not. Many of the Clinton administration's most ambitions plans—health care reform, for example—had died in an agony of conflict and partisan recrimination. The truth, revealed early in the 103rd Congress when Bob Dole led a successful Republican filibuster against Clinton's economic stimulus package, was that, as Krehbiel's insightful analysis made clear, divided government did not end at all (Krehbiel 1994). Divided partisan control of *policy making* persists as long as the minority party holds at least 40 seats in the Senate and can therefore kill any bill it wants to kill.

The illusion of unified government put the onus of failure on the Democrats; the reality of divided government let Senate Republicans make sure that the administration would fail. Clinton was elected on a promise of change; but Senate

Republicans could prevent change, and they did. It was not difficult, for although everyone may agree that change is desirable, rarely is there ready consensus on *what* changes to make. The health care issue is Exhibit A. If voters did not get change with Clinton—or if they did not like the changes he proposed—the alternative was to elect Republicans.

Public anger at a government paralyzed by gridlock was intensified by the widespread sense that the problems the political establishment failed to address are indeed serious. The benefits of economic growth during the Reagan years went largely to families in the top income decile. The broad middle class has, by many measures, made little economic progress for two decades; even the most upbeat observers admit that the incomes (including fringe benefits) of the families in the middle half of the distribution were nearly flat over the two decades between 1973 and 1992.[2] Moreover, middle-class incomes have become more volatile from one year to the next, so that even if middle-income people have not done worse on average, their level of uncertainty about the economic future has been appreciably greater.

Although the economy grew during the first two years of the Clinton administration, the fruits of growth again went largely to families at the upper end of the economic scale. Hence, in an October 1994 *Los Angeles Times* poll, 53 percent of the respondents thought the economy remained in recession. The economic discontent that elected Clinton in 1992 had barely faded by 1994, and this time it helped to elect a Republican Congress. In 1992, 79 percent of the voters (in the national exit poll) thought the economy was in bad shape, and 62 percent of them voted for a Democrat for the House. In 1994, 75 percent said they were no better off financially than they were two years ago; 57 percent thought the economy was still in bad shape, and 62 percent of this group voted for the Republican (Langer 1994).

Economic prosperity, moreover, is not the only measure of the quality of life. The public institutions that serve ordinary people—for example, public schools, police, and courts—seemed to be in trouble. The issues of crime, illegal immigration, and unmarried teenage welfare mothers that dominated the 1994 campaigns in many places were not new, but they gained new urgency as signs that American society was out of control. For millions of Americans, government had delivered neither physical nor economic security, failing conspicuously to reverse what was seen as moral and cultural decline. The large majority that believed the nation was on the wrong rather than the right track (i.e., 57 percent compared to 37 percent in the 1992 exit poll) indicated that the longing for "change" that put Clinton in the White House was not satisfied. Two-thirds of those who thought the nation was on the wrong track voted for Republican House candidates, compared to only 29 percent of those who thought the nation was on the right track.

Stagnant incomes, declining public services, and the rising fear of crime leave large segments of the population with poorer lives and diminished prospects. It is in this context that the perks and peccadilloes of politicians—scandals involving senior leaders in the House and the Keating Five in the Senate, bank overdrafts, unpaid restaurant bills, post office shenanigans, and pay-raise subterfuges—were so damaging to members of Congress. The image of representatives as self-serving, easily corrupted, and indifferent to the needs of the average citizen or the good of the nation pervaded the 1992 elections and helped produce the largest turnover in the House since World War II. Members were unable to shake that image in the 103rd Congress, and when Democrats were ostensibly in full control of the government, they became the principal targets of popular wrath and disappointment. In 1992, angry and dissatisfied voters voted Democratic in House elections 56 percent to 44 percent; in 1994, they voted Republican, 64 percent to 36 percent (Langer 1994).

The Clinton Problem

Clinton's reputation as a leader was, of course, the chief target and victim of the Republicans' gridlock strategy. But this was not the only problem Clinton posed for congressional Democrats. Although his overall performance ratings were not, comparatively speaking, all that bad, he thoroughly alienated important groups of swing voters: the so-called Reagan Democrats and much of the largely male Perot constituency. The cultural symbolism portrayed by many of the administration's actions was anathema to socially conservative white men, especially in the South. The conspicuous attention to race and gender diversity in making appointments called to mind the affirmative action programs they detested. Support for gays in the military, gun control, appointees like Lani Guinier (failed) and Joycelyn Elders (successful), and the role and style of Hillary Rodham Clinton reminded these swing voters of the cultural liberalism that was at the core of what they did *not* like about the Democratic party. Clinton's reputation with this segment of the electorate probably was worsened by one of his most notable successes: the passage of the North American Free Trade Agreement (NAFTA), which put him at odds with traditional blue-collar Democratic constituents.

Exit polls revealed that only 40 percent of southerners approved of Clinton's performance, compared to 51 percent in the Northeast and 45 percent elsewhere. Among white southern men, Clinton's approval stood at a dismal 27 percent. Moreover, the relationship between presidential approval and the House vote was notably stronger in 1994 than in other recent midterm elections. According to the exit polls, about 86 percent of House votes were consistent with presidential ratings (that is, for the Democrat if the respondent approved of Clinton's performance, for the Republican if the respondent disapproved). The comparable figure for 1990 was 68 percent, for 1986, 72 percent; only in 1982 did consistency ratings approach the 1994 level (82 percent). Clinton's low level of approval was thus more damaging than usual to his copartisans and was concentrated among swing voters. Support for Democratic House candidates among white southerners was 12 points lower in 1994 than it was in 1992 (35 percent compared to 47 percent). Fully 44 percent of the white southern males said that their House vote was a vote against Clinton (20 percent said it was a vote for Clinton); for non-southern males, the comparable figures were 33 percent and 24 percent. The House vote of white males nationally was 11 points more Republican in 1994 than it was in 1992; Perot supporters, who split their House votes evenly between the parties in 1992, voted 2 to 1 Republican in 1994 (Langer 1994; *New York Times*, November 13, 1994: A15).

In short, voters in 1994 were angry with government; Democrats were the party of government not only because they were in charge but also because their party believes in government. Republican candidates, who liked to claim that they did not, offered themselves as vehicles for expressing antigovernment rage by taking up the banner of structural panaceas—term limits, a balanced budget amendment, and cuts in congressional staff and perks—that were broadly popular and had special appeal to the alienated voters who supported Perot. The policy issues that resonated best with voters in 1994—crime, immigration, welfare dependency, taxes, and big government—were also Republican issues. Recognizing Clinton's unpopularity, especially in the South and especially among white males, Republican candidates sought to portray their opponents as Clinton clones; many of them used TV ads that had pictures of their opponents' face digitally "morphing" into Clinton's face.

Republicans were thus able to frame the choice in many swing districts as one not between an accomplished provider of pork and diligent servant of district interests and a challenger whose ability to deliver the goods was at best doubtful but between a supporter of liberal elitist Clinton, big government, high taxes, and politics as usual and a challenger opposed to these horribles. The House Democrats' customary strategy of emphasizing the projects, grants, and programs they brought to the district and the value of their experience and seniority not only failed but was turned against them. The more they reminded people of pork and clout, the more they revealed themselves as insiders, that loathed class of career politicians. With the choice framed this way, the old ploy of running for Congress by running against Congress—joining the chorus of criticism to put oneself apart from, and above, the institution (Fenno 1978)—was rendered threadbare as well. The Democrats were unable to duck individual responsibility for the House's collective shortcomings.

Ironically, the Republicans' Contract with America, which became so prominent in setting the Republican agenda after the election, had, in itself, little impact on the voters. On September 27, more than 300 Republican House candidates signed pledges on the steps of the Capitol to act swiftly on a grab bag of proposals for structural and legislative change, including constitutional amendments requiring a balanced budget and imposing term limits on members of Congress, major cuts in income taxes, and reductions in spending on welfare programs for poor families. Although the contract got some attention in the media and was a target of Democratic counterattacks, most voters went to the polls blissfully unaware of its existence. The *New York Times*/CBS News poll of October 29–November 1, 1994, found that 71 percent of respondents never heard of the contract and another 15 percent said it would make no difference in how they voted. Only 7 percent said it would make them more likely to vote for the Republican House candidate, while 5 percent said it would make them less likely to do so. The most prominent Republican effort to nationalize the campaign thus remained almost invisible to voters. This does not mean that individual parts of the contract were not used effectively by Republican campaigners; they were. But the contract itself had far more impact on Republican candidates (before and after the election) than on voters.

Nationalizing the Vote

Although the contract had little impact, Republicans did succeed in nationalizing the elections to a much greater degree than was usual in recent elections. They won the House by tying congressional Democrats to Clinton, to a discredited government establishment, and to a deplorable status quo. In effect, Republicans ran a set of midterm congressional campaigns that mirrored their successful presidential campaigns. As a result, their House victories echoed their presidential successes far more clearly than they did at any time during the last 40 years.

Most of the seats Republicans took from Democrats were in districts that leaned Republican in presidential elections. A serviceable measure of a district's presidential leanings can be computed by taking the average division of its two-party vote between the presidential candidates in 1988 and 1992.[3] The national mean for this measure of district presidential voting habits is 49.9 percent Democratic; its median is 48.3 percent Democratic. As Table 1.1 shows, Republican gains in 1994 were heavily concentrated in districts where the Democrats' vote, averaged over the two elections, fell below 50 percent. For example, 31 open seats formerly held by Democrats were at stake. Republicans won all 16 open Democratic seats in districts where Bush's share of the two-party vote, averaged together for 1988 and 1992, exceeded 50 percent; they won only 6 of the 15 seats where the Democrat's presidential average exceeded 50 percent. Republican challengers defeated 21 of 73 (28.8 percent) incumbent Democrats in districts where Bush's average exceeded 50 percent, but only 13 of 152 (8.6 percent) where Bush's average fell short of this mark.

The handful of switches to the Democrats followed the same pattern: Democrats took 4 of 5 open Republican seats where the Democrats' average share exceeded 50 percent; they won none of other 16 open Republican seats and defeated no Republican incumbents. The net effect of seats changing party hands in 1994 was a closer alignment of district-level presidential and House results than we have seen in any election since 1952—all the more remarkable because no presidential candidates were on the 1994 ballot. Notice, however, that alignment was much closer when incumbency did not intervene; of the open seats 88 percent went to the same party as the district's presidential majority, compared with 79 percent of incumbent-held seats. The simple correlation between the district's 1988 and 1992 presidential vote (averaged) and the 1994 two-party House vote was .88 for open seats, .73 for seats with Democratic incumbents, and only .47 for seats with Republican incumbents.

Republicans won the House in 1994 because an unusually large number of districts voted locally as they voted nationally. The same is true, necessarily, of individual voters. According to 1994 exit polls, 89 percent of those who voted Republican for president in the previous election voted for the Republican House candidate in the 1994 midterm elections; the comparable figures for 1982, 1986, and 1990 were 69 percent, 65 percent, and 63 percent, respectively. This change arose from a sharp increase in party loyalty among self-identified Republicans; in 1994 only 7 percent of Republican identifiers reported voting for a Democrat, compared to 15 percent in 1992 and 23 percent in 1990. Democratic candidates lost the support of Republican defectors who, in the past, helped them win Republican-leaning districts. Democratic identifiers were also more loyal in 1994 than they were in recent elections (10 percent defected, compared to 11 percent in 1992 and 21 percent in 1990), so the 1994 elections divided the electorate on a more strictly partisan basis than was typical in recent years.[4]

The Republican party's strong organizational effort to nationalize the campaign was helped enormously by new national networks of conservative talk-show hosts and conservative Christian activists. Conservatives in general and evangelical Christians in particular turned out at notably higher rates than other voters did and composed a significantly larger proportion of the electorate than in 1992.[5] Republican leaders did an outstanding job of organizing and mobilizing the groups

TABLE 1.1 District Partisanship and Electoral Outcomes in 1994 House Elections (percentage of Republican victories)

	District Leans				
	Republican		Democratic		
	Number of District Seats	Republican Victories (%)	Number of Districts Seats	Republican Victories (%)	Statistical Significance
Seats Held by Democrats					
Incumbents	73	28.8	152	8.6	$p < .001$
Open seats	16	100.0	15	40.0	$p < .001$
Seats Held by Republicans					
Incumbents	141	100.0	16	100.0	n.s.
Open seats	16	100.0	5	20.0	$p < .001$
Total	246	78.9	188	19.1	$p < .001$

NOTES: Republican-leaning districts are defined as those in which the two-party vote for Bush, averaged across 1988 and 1992, was greater than 50 percent; Democratic-leaning districts are those in which this average fell below 50 percent; n.s. means not significant.

in their coalition and of coaching their candidates in the art of using the party's themes effectively against Democrats. Newt Gingrich earned his speakership.

Still, the Republican most responsible for Gingrich's ascension to Speaker of the House in 1995 was not Gingrich but Bush. The termination of divided government in 1992 was essential to its return, transposed, in 1994. Bush's failure to win reelection put the full force of public anger and frustration with gridlock, policy failure, and the president behind Republican House candidates. Republicans have always done best in House elections when an unpopular Democrat sits in the White House (Jacobson 1990a). Robert S. Erikson once offered the tongue-in-cheek argument that losing the presidency was the Democrats' rational strategy for maintaining control of the House (Erikson, 1989). Congressional Democrats may well wish that they were as shrewd as Erikson supposed.

THE HOUSE ELECTIONS IN PERSPECTIVE

If the key to the Republican victory in 1994 lay in nationalizing the House elections, does this mean that the candidate-centered, locally focused electoral politics of the textbooks (mine included) went by the boards? The evidence suggests otherwise. Contests for open seats have always reflected national forces—including district presidential preferences—more accurately than have contests for seats held by incumbents (Mondak 1993). The connection was unusually strong in 1994, to be sure, but that reality alone is insufficient to argue that the conventional understanding of House elections is (at least temporarily) obsolete. Moreover, by all of the familiar aggregate indicators, local variation was as prominent as ever, and for all the usual reasons; national issues mattered in 1994, but the degree to which they mattered depended on how effectively they could be turned into local issues by the candidates and their campaigns.

Thus, first, the 1994 elections were not nationalized in the sense that electoral forces operated more consistently across districts than they have in other recent elections. Although the mean district vote swing to Republicans was by recent historical standards quite large (5.9 percentage points, which was the largest since 1974), it was no more *uniform* than the recent norm.[6] The standard deviation of the swing serves as a straightforward measure of electoral heterogeneity among districts (there are others; see Jacobson 1990a; Stokes 1965). Figure 1.1 plots over the postwar period the standard deviation of the swing for all contests and for contests involving incumbents only (years ending in "2" omitted because of redistricting). The 1994 observations are by no means out of line with those of the rest of the post–1964 electoral era (1966 conventionally marks the beginning of the modern era of highly candidate-centered congressional elections). The standard deviation of the swing for all contests in 1994 was 7.9, compared with the post–1964 average of 8.4; for contests involving incumbents, it was 7.0, compared with the average of 7.7 for the post–1964 period; in neither case is the difference statistically significant.[7]

FIGURE 1.1
The Standard Deviation of the Mean District Vote Swing in House Elections, 1946–1994

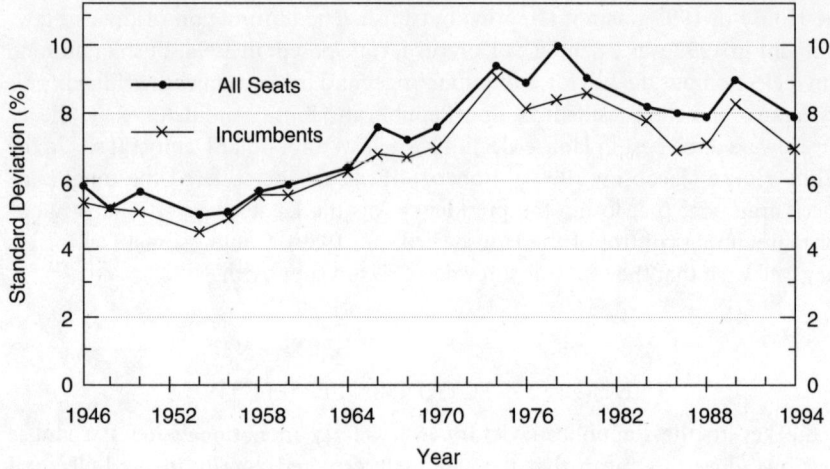

NOTE: Data for years ending in "2" are omitted because of redistricting.

Second, the electoral value of incumbency remained at a high level in 1994. The Gelman-King index puts it at 10.1 percentage points, though its value was higher for Republicans (11.9 points) than for Democrats (7.1 points).[8] Figure 1.2 traces the Gelman-King index over House elections since 1946. The 1994 elections were, on this dimension, again entirely normal. It was lucky for the Democrats that they were; the pattern of results displayed in Table 1.1 suggests that, without the incumbency advantage, the Democratic minority in the 104th Congress would be considerably smaller.

Third, strategic behavior both reflected and magnified election year trends. Democrats behaved as if they expected it to be a bad year for their party and helped to make it so. Strategic Democratic retirements (Jacobson and Kernell 1983) clearly hurt their party's overall performance. Although about the same proportion of House Democrats and Republicans retired (i.e., 11 percent), most of the Republicans left to run for higher office (13 of 20, or 65 percent), while most of the departing Democrats (20 of 27, or 71 percent) did not. Among retirees who did not leave to pursue another office, age is the only variable with any predictive power for Republicans, while age, previous vote margin, and district presidential partisanship all contributed significantly to Democratic retirements; the closer the margin in 1992 and the more Republican the district in presidential voting, the more likely a Democrat was to retire. In simple percentages, 18.0 percent of the Democrats in districts that leaned Republican in presidential elections retired, compared with only 7.2 percent of the Democrats in districts that leaned Democratic in presidential elections ($X^2 = 6.94$, $p < .001$). The retirements of the former group proved disastrous for the Dem0ocratic party; as noted earlier, Republicans took every one of the 16 seats thereby exposed.

FIGURE 1.2
The Incumbency Advantage in House Elections, 1946–1994 (Gelman-King index)

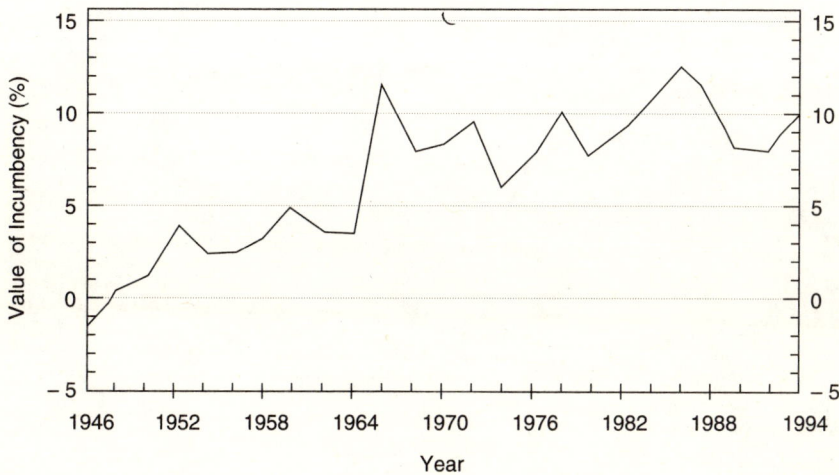

Another sign of the Democrats' strategic responses to expectations was the unusual distribution of uncontested seats. Observe in Figure 1.3 that for the first time in the entire postwar era, Democrats conceded more seats to Republicans (i.e., 35) than Republicans conceded to Democrats (i.e., 17) in the general election. The principal explanation for the long-term trend displayed in Figure 1.3 is of course the rise of the Republican fortunes in the South, but the circumstances prevailing in 1994 certainly contributed to the striking inversion of the usual pattern.

The quality of challengers also reflected rational career strategies, though as usual, potential Democratic challengers were much more sensitive to election-year expectations than were Republicans (Jacobson 1990a). Democrats have long enjoyed a stronger "farm system" that supplies experienced House candidates because they hold more of the lower-level offices (particularly in state legislatures) that form the typical stepping stones to Congress. Normally, therefore, Democrats have a substantial advantage in experienced challengers. On average over the previous 24 postwar congressional elections, 26 percent of the Republican incumbents, but only 16 percent of Democratic incumbents, faced challengers who previously held elective public office. Prior to 1994, Republicans fielded the more-experienced crop of challengers only twice: in 1966, when they picked up 47 seats, and in 1992, when they picked up 10 seats while losing the White House. They did so again in 1994, but mainly because so few experienced Democrats were willing to take the field; only 14 percent of Republican incumbents faced experienced Democratic challengers, the second lowest proportion in any postwar election.

The Republicans' proportion of experienced challengers (15 percent) was merely average for them, but then many of their most highly touted challengers were unapologetic amateurs running as antigovernment outsiders. Despite all

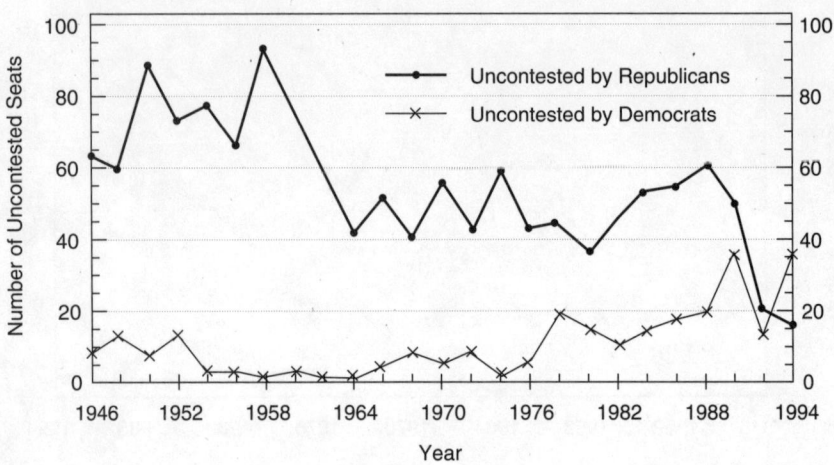

FIGURE 1.3
Uncontested House Seats, 1946–1994

of the rhetoric condemning career politicians, however, experienced Republican challengers greatly outperformed the novices, picking up significantly more votes and victories. Experienced Republican challengers won 44 percent (15 of 34) of the races they entered, compared with 11 percent (19 of 174) for inexperienced Republican challengers. Naturally, experienced challengers were more common in districts with Republican presidential leanings. But even controlling for local partisanship and other relevant variables, experienced challengers did significantly better on election day, as we shall see in the following analysis.

One reason experienced Republican challengers did better than the amateurs is that, as always, they raised and spent much more money. The distribution of campaign funds in 1994 followed the expected pattern in a year when campaign activists expected a strong partisan tide (Jacobson and Kernell 1983). The preliminary data reported in Table 1.2 show that Republican challengers were significantly better funded than Democratic challengers. Not only was their average spending higher, but more of them were financed beyond the threshold usually required for a competitive campaign. Experienced Republican challengers were especially well funded, spending an average of $471,564 compared with $199,837 for the other Republican challengers. Democrats, on the defensive, channeled relatively more money to incumbents; Republican incumbents had far less to worry about and could get away with lower spending. As usual, both parties generously funded their candidates for open seats who were remotely competitive regardless of national trends.

The strategic allocation of Republican campaign funds was also strongly influenced by local conditions. Republican challengers raised and spent more money in districts that leaned Republican in presidential elections, particularly in districts

TABLE 1.2 Campaign Spending Patterns in 1994

	Democrats	Republicans	Statistical Significance
Incumbents			
Average Expenditure	$608,443	$460,393	$p < .001$
More than $500,000	50.2%	36.3%	$p < .01$
More than $700,000	32.0%	15.3%	$p < .001$
More than $1 million	13.8%	1.9%	$p < .001$
Challengers			
Average Expenditure	$152,659	$244,042	$p < .01$
More than $300,000	18.9%	31.1%	$p < .05$
More than $500,000	6.3%	17.8%	$p < .01$
Open Seats			
Average Expenditure	$557,660	$597.655	n.s.
More than $500,000	50.0%	60.4%	n.s.

NOTE: N.S. means not significant.
SOURCE: Computed from data reported in Federal Election Commission, 1995. News release, "1994 Congressional Fundraising Climbs to New High," April 28.

where Democratic incumbents made themselves vulnerable by supporting their party and president on key roll-call votes. For this analysis, the measure of party support on key votes is a simple additive index of support for the Clinton administration's position on three major issues in the 103rd Congress. The votes were (1) on the 1993 Omnibus Reconciliation Bill (HR 2264), which attacked the deficit by cutting programs and raising taxes (thus opening members who voted for it to the charge of supporting "the biggest tax increase in history"); (2) on the North American Free Trade Agreement (NAFTA) Implementation Bill (HR 3450), which had bipartisan support but was opposed by the Perot constituency; and (3) on the 1994 Omnibus Anti-Crime Bill (HR 3355), attacked by Republicans for including what they charged were pork barrel projects and opposed by the gun lobby for its ban on assault weapons.[9] The index is the number of times the Democrat voted with the Democratic administration; it thus takes values from 0 to 3.

Table 1.3 shows that the vigor of a Republican challenge, at least as measured by campaign spending, was strongly related to both the local political climate and the Democratic incumbent's degree of party loyalty on tough votes. Democratic loyalists in Republican-leaning districts were the principal targets of the most lavishly funded Republican challenges. Not surprisingly, the data show that they were most likely to lose the election as well.

Table 1.3 makes it plain that the fates of Democratic incumbents in 1994 were shaped by their own behavior as well as by the strength of their opposition and the district's political leanings.

To further clarify how these variables worked, I estimated some regression models of their effect on the Democratic incumbent's share of the two-party

TABLE 1.3 The Democrats' Party Loyalty on Key Votes and
Republican Challengers' Campaign Spending Averages and Percentage of Victories,
by District Presidential Leanings

Party Support on Key Votes	All Districts	District Leans Democratic	District Leans Republican
Index value of 0			
Republican spending averages	$156,564	$42,378	$185,111
Republican victories	0.0%	0.0%	0.0%
Number of districts/seats	5	1	4
Index value of 1			
Republican spending averages	$180,885	$70,258	$300,361
Republican victories	13.5%	7.4%	20.0%
Number of districts/seats	52	27	25
Index value of 2			
Republican spending averages	$220,696	$145,739	$417,806
Republican victories	15.3%	7.0%	37.0%
Number of districts/seats	98	71	27
Index value of 3			
Republican spending averages	$355,327	$292,115	$519,677
Republican victories	22.6%	15.8%	40.0%
Number of districts/seats	54	39	15

NOTE: Democratic-leaning districts are those in which the Democratic presidential candidate's share of the vote, averaged over 1988 and 1992, exceeded 50 percent; the others are defined as Republican-leaning districts.
SOURCE: Spending data are from the Federal Election Commission, 1995. News release, "1994 Congressional Fundraising Climbs to New High," April 28.

vote. The independent variables include the Democratic candidate's vote in 1992, district presidential partisanship, the challenger's experience, campaign spending, and the incumbent's support for the administration's position on key votes. District presidential partisanship is estimated by the average district share of the two-party vote that went to the Democratic candidate in 1988 and 1992. Experienced candidates are defined as those who have previously held elective office. Campaign expenditures are entered as the log of total spending, with a minimum of $5,000 assumed for all candidates (spending below this total need not be reported to the Federal Election Commission). The results appear in Table 1.4.

The values for variables for four regression equations are shown in columns one through four in Table 1.4. According to values for the first two equations, campaign spending, challenger experience, and district voting patterns all had their expected large effect on the results of these races. The challenger's level of

TABLE 1.4 Party Support on Key Roll-Call Votes and the Vote for Democratic Incumbents in the 1994 Election

Constant and Independent Variables	All Districts		South	Non-South
	Equation 1	Equation 2	Equation 3	Equation 4
Constant	36.37[a]	41.98[a]	68.57[b]	35.17[b]
Standard error	9.90	9.70	25.78	10.72
Democrat's vote in 1992	.39[a]	.38[a]	.32[b]	.39[b]
Standard error	.05	.05	.11	.07
District presidential partisanship	.29[a]	.13	.10	.16
Standard error	.05	.07	.15	.09
Challenger has held elective office	−1.87	−1.91[c]	−4.40	−1.47
Standard error	.97	.93	2.62	1.03
Log of challenger's spending	−2.31[a]	−2.29[a]	−1.41[c]	−2.43[a]
Standard error	.29	.28	.69	.31
Log of incumbent's spending	.97	1.23	−1.10	1.62[c]
Standard error	.66	.65	1.77	.70
Voted for 1993 budget	−2.30[c]			
Standard error	1.06			
Voted for NAFTA	−1.86[c]			
Standard error	.72			
Voted for crime bill	−1.15			
Standard error	.79			
Party support index		−7.23[a]	−8.45[c]	−5.83[c]
Standard error		2.10	4.31	2.60
Party support index X District presidential partisanship		.10[b]	.12	.08
Standard error		.04	.08	.05
Adjusted R^2	.80	.81	.70	.84
SER	4.54	4.44	4.71	4.37
Number of cases	194	194	53	141

[a] $p < .001$
[b] $p < .01$
[c] $p < .0$

NOTE: The dependent variable is the Democrats' share of the two-party vote.

spending was strongly related to the vote (the incumbent's spending was not, but at least its coefficient displays the expected sign, which is by no means always the case in Ordinary Least Square (OLS) regressions of this sort). Other things equal, the presence of an experienced Republican challenger reduced the incumbent's vote by nearly 2 percentage points, a figure comparable to other recent election years (Jacobson 1990a). District presidential partisanship and the Democrat's performance in the previous election were also strongly linked to the Democrat's vote.

The values in equations 1–4 in Table 1.4 also demonstrate that the Democratic incumbents' own behavior affected their electoral fates in a major way. Not only did support for the party's (and administration's) positions hurt Democrats indirectly by stimulating better-funded opposition (recall Table 1.3), it hurt them directly as well. Equation 1 shows that each of the key votes was individually damaging. By this evidence, House Democrats did not suffer across the board in 1994 for the alleged sins of their party and president; their difficulties were proportional to their support for the administration on the most visible issues before the 103rd Congress. Put another way, the Republicans' national campaign themes were evidently effective to the degree that individual Democrats were vulnerable to the charge of supporting the administration on controversial issues. If this is so, we would also expect national campaign themes to have been more effective in districts with a stronger inclination toward Republicans in presidential elections and where Clinton was especially unpopular—the South.

Regression equations 2 through 4 test these hypotheses. Equation 2 examines the interaction between party support (here entered as the additive index to avoid proliferating interaction terms) and district presidential partisanship. The positive coefficient on the interaction term indicates that the Democrat's level of support for Clinton's policies affected different constituencies differently, costing more votes the more Republican the district voted in recent presidential elections. Equations 3 and 4 estimate the same model separately for southern and non-southern districts. Regressions with interaction terms can be opaque, so Table 1.5 reports the effect of different levels of support for the party for a range of values of district presidential partisanship estimated by three regression equations.

Although not all the key coefficients meet the conventional standard of statistical significance, the results are consistent with the view that the incumbent Democrat's roll-call record had a larger impact in the South, where its effect was also more strongly mediated by the district's level of support for Democratic presidential candidates. Both the impact of the voting record and the mediating effect of presidential partisanship were considerably smaller outside the South. In non-southern districts, local political conditions—as measured by the incumbent's vote in 1992 and district presidential partisanship and campaign spending—were more strongly related to the vote. Notice that the coefficient on the Democratic incumbent's spending in districts outside the South is both positive and significant; the only other subset set of incumbents for which this has been true since reliable campaign spending data have become available were the Republican incumbents in 1974. In extraordinarily adverse circumstances, incumbents appear to get some benefit from spending money, even according to OLS models.

In sum, although all politics was not local in 1994, the electoral effect of national issues varied across districts and regions, depending on incumbency, the quality of candidates, the level of campaign spending, the partisan makeup of the district, and the behavior of the incumbent. Wielding potent campaign themes drawn from national issues, Republicans needed only reasonably attractive and

TABLE 1.5 The Electoral Penalty Paid by House Democrats for Voting with the Party on Key Votes

Range of District Presidential Partisanship (%)	Number of Times Voting with President		
	1	2	3
All districts			
40	−3.1	−6.2	−9.3
50	−2.0	−4.1	−6.1
60	−1.0	−2.0	−3.0
70	0.0	0.1	0.1
80	1.1	2.1	3.2
South			
40	−3.8	−7.5	−11.3
50	−2.6	−5.2	−7.8
60	−1.4	−2.9	−4.3
70	−0.3	−0.5	−0.8
80	0.9	1.8	2.7
Non-South			
40	−2.6	−5.1	−7.2
50	−1.7	−3.5	−5.2
60	−0.9	−1.9	−2.8
70	−0.1	−0.2	−0.4
80	0.7	1.4	2.1

NOTES: Entries are the difference in the Democrats' predicted vote percentage under the alternative conditions as estimated from the equations in Table 1.4. District presidential partisanship is measured as the two-party vote for Dukakis and Clinton, averaged over the 1988 and 1992 elections. Frequency of party support is determined by the number of times a member voted with the president on the following key votes: the 1993 budget reconciliation act, NAFTA, and the 1994 crime bill.

well-financed candidates to take seats from Democrats in districts that leaned Republican in presidential elections. Democratic retirements from such districts created a host of open-seat opportunities that well-funded Republican candidates exploited to the hilt. Against incumbent Democrats, Republicans did best where they fielded experienced, well financed challengers against Democrats whose votes tied them to the Clinton administration in districts where the president (and his party more generally) were relatively unpopular—where, in other words, the local campaign could give national themes the most extensive publicity and the local context gave these themes their greatest resonance. Poorly funded Republican challengers were largely unsuccessful even in districts where Democrats should have been vulnerable.[10] The central issues in the 1994 House elections may have been national, but how they played out depended strongly on local circumstances.

1996 AND BEYOND

Whether the nationally focused local campaigns of 1994 set a precedent for future House elections is uncertain. Irrespective of that question, however, the election will have profound consequences, for the Democrats' loss of majority status in the House has altered the strategic environment in a way that leaves Republicans in better shape than they have been at any time since the New Deal realignment.

First, Democrats have little prospect of taking back many of the seats lost to the Republicans in 1994, particularly in the South, and they are quite likely to lose more of them. The logic of electing conservative Democrats rather than Republicans to protect local (southern) interests no longer prevails now that Democrats have lost the special influence wielded by members of the majority party. The same is true in districts outside the South where Democrats have held on through their ability to deliver the goods despite being out of ideological or partisan sync with their constituents.

Second, and equally important, the Democrats will no longer have their majority status and committee power to attract Political Action Committee (PAC) contributions from business interests. The pragmatic corporate and trade association PACs that were happy to make a marriage of convenience with Democrats as long as Democrats were running the show are now free to pursue a love match with the ideologically more-compatible Republicans. Their fondness for Democrats has never extended to challengers, and now they have less incentive to contribute to incumbents as well (Jacobson 1989a). They also have less reason to worry about contributing *against* incumbent Democrats, whose ability to retaliate against PACs that fund their opponents has diminished. Because such groups supply about 60 percent of all PAC donations, Democrats face the prospect of a severely unfavorable imbalance of campaign resources in future elections.

Third, despite the Republican gains in 1994, Democrats still have more House seats at risk by at least two measures. Although the parties won a similar number of the most marginal seats (those won with less than 55 percent of the two-party vote) in 1994, 36 of the 44 marginal Democrats were incumbents, whereas 38 of the 41 marginal Republicans were newly elected and so can expect the sophomore surge to raise their margins next time. Furthermore, only 36 Republicans represent districts that, on average, voted Democratic in 1988 and 1992, whereas 52 Democrats represent Republican presidential districts, 26 of them in the South. If, as is likely, the insults of minority status inspire an additional round of Democratic retirements, Republicans are poised to pick up even more seats.

Finally, all of these developments come on top of the boost given to Republicans by the redistricting that followed the 1990 census. In my earlier work on divided government, I took pains to show that, contrary to Republican allegations, gerrymandered districts were not to blame for their inability to make headway in the House (Jacobson 1990a). Their problem was not the way Republican voters were distributed but that Republican candidates simply did not attract enough voters. In 1994, they finally did attract enough voters. For the first time since 1952, Republicans won more House votes than Democrats (53.6 percent of the two-party House vote went Republican), and they won more House seats than the Democrats. Still, there is no question that reapportionment and redistricting did contribute to their victory. The states in the South and Southwest that gained seats after the 1990 census are notably more Republican in their voting habits than the states in the Northeast and Midwest that lost the seats. The drawing of minority-majority districts has also strengthened Republicans by packing African-American voters (who vote overwhelmingly Democratic) into minority districts (Hill 1995). The effects of reapportionment were muted in 1992 because Bush was a drag on the whole Republican ticket, but the potential was evident in the party's gain of ten House seats that year despite losing the White House. In 1994, Republicans more than fulfilled that potential.

Taken together, these circumstances suggest that despite the Republicans' relatively narrow majority (narrower than any of the Democrats' majorities during their 40 uninterrupted years of control), the Democrats face an uphill battle to take the 14 or more seats they need to regain control. On the other hand, House Republicans so far seem bent on the high-risk strategy of tying their fates to their party's collective performance in delivering on the Contract with America under the singular leadership of Gingrich. If they succeed and voters like the results, then Republicans will pick up additional seats in 1996. Neither success nor voter approbation is remotely guaranteed, however. Republicans cannot cut taxes, spend more on defense, and balance the budget without slashing middle-class entitlements and terminating entrenched programs supported by powerful constituencies. Devotion to the contract will ensure that in the 104th Congress, Republican members will be the ones casting politically dangerous roll-call votes, forcing the familiar tradeoff between individual responsiveness and collective responsibility.

CONCLUSION

During the decades of Democratic control, individual responsiveness to local interests almost always trumped collective party responsibility (Mayhew 1974a; Arnold 1990). Adopting the contract as a focus and delegating more power to party leaders than any House majority since the revolt against Republican House Speaker Joseph (Uncle Joe) Cannon in 1910, the Republicans have tried to commit themselves to a far greater degree of collective responsibility. Whether they hold to that commitment against pressures from district interests targeted to bear the immediate costs of carrying out the contract's fiscal promises will do much to shape future House elections. If they hold fast, then the heightened impact of national issues observed in the 1994 House elections should continue; the 1996 elections will turn into a referendum on the Republican Congress as well as on the Clinton administration. If they do not, the diffuse, locally focused electoral politics of the recent past could reemerge, with individual members saving their own skins but weakening their party collectively in the process. What happens will depend on how many Republicans give high priority to reelection (not a few of those in their first term deny interest in congressional careers) and whether those who care about reelection believe they would be hindered more by their party's falling short on the contract or by voting to inflict the pain required when enacting key parts of the contract. For students of the electoral connection, the 104th should turn out to be the most interesting Congress in years.

NOTES

1. Bernard Sanders of Vermont, the lone independent, survived.
2. See Paul Richter, "It Just Seems We're Worse Off," *Los Angeles Times* (January 26) 1995, A25.
3. The 1988 district presidential vote was recomputed for each district to adjust for redistricting after 1990; the data are from Barone and Ujifusa (1993).
4. *New York Times*, November 13, 1994.
5. According to a survey sponsored by the Christian Coalition, 33 percent of the 1994 voters were "religious conservatives," up from 24 percent in 1992 and 18 percent in 1988 (*Congressional Quarterly Weekly Report*, November 19, 1994, 3364); in the 1994 exit poll, 38 percent identified themselves as "conservatives," compared with 30 percent in 1992 (*Hotline*, November 12, 1994).
6. The swing is defined as the change in the division of the two-party House vote in the district from 1992 to 1994.
7. I omitted elections in years ending in 2 from these comparisons because of redistricting.
8. Gelman and King estimate an unbiased measure of the incumbency advantage by regressing the Democrats' share of the two-party vote on the Democrats' vote in the previous election, the party holding the seat, and incumbency (which takes a value of 1 if the Democrat is the incumbent, −1 if the Republican is the incumbent, and 0 if the seat is open). The coefficient of the incumbency variable estimates the value (in percentage of votes) of incumbency for the election year (Gelman and King, 1990).
9. Initially, I also included the Brady bill (a gun control measure), but it provided no additional explanatory punch so I excluded it. I substituted *Congressional Quarterly*'s presidential support score (averaged for 1993 and 1994) for the key vote index in the following reported regression analyses (*Congressional Quarterly Weekly Report*, December 18, 1993, 3476–78; *Congressional Quarterly Weekly Report*, December 31, 1994, 3656–57), but it had much less explanatory power than this three-vote index.
10. Against incumbent Democrats in Republican-leaning districts, 49 percent (19 of 39) of the Republican challengers who spent in excess of $300,000 won, whereas only 6 percent (2 of 32) of the challengers who spent less than this sum managed to defeat incumbents. If analysis is further confined to Democratic incumbents who supported the Clinton administration on at least two of the three key votes, the respective percentages are 52 percent (14 of 27) and 13 percent (2 of 15).

2

Eight More in '94: The Republican Takeover of the Senate

FRANCO MATTEI

In the words of several media commentators, the stunning Republican success in the 1994 midterm elections had the disruptive and shocking force of a "meteorite," an "earthquake," a "tectonic shift," a "tsunami," a "deluge," even a "neutron bomb."[1] The reach of the partisan landslide that on November 8 shook the political landscape was largely unexpected; it created the conditions for important transformations in the internal organization of the 104th Congress and a radical reorientation of the legislative agenda. Although most prognosticators anticipated changes in Senate membership, the Republicans' takeover of the House, after an unprecedented four decades in the minority, appeared to be a cosmic event that broke the gravitational pull of Democratic control and eclipsed other aspects of the midterm elections. In the "historic power shift" of 1994, the outcome of the Senate elections was but one wave of the Republican tide washing many Democrats from state and national offices.

In an election year in which the slogan "Cut their pay and send them home" seemed to capture effectively the public's discontent and dissatisfaction with the performance of Congress, with the operation and the size of the federal government, and with the behavior of career politicians,[2] the midterm vote was expected to be driven by the desire for political change and to challenge the reelection prospects of several incumbents. In its spring preview of the 1994 campaigns, the *Congressional Quarterly Weekly Report* asked "whether the buds of anger and frustration that burst into bloom in 1992 were annuals, limited to a single season of glory, or perennials that will return again this election season" (Connolly 1994: 937). On election day, voters' unrest did translate into change, albeit of a different nature from that of two years before. Although the 1992 congressional elections "departed dramatically from recent historical patterns" by combining very large membership turnover (through retirement and incumbent defeat) with a quite modest partisan change (Jacobson 1993b: 153), the 1994 midterm elections delivered a radical, across-the-board partisan readjustment, coupled with significant membership replacement. Republican candidates scored impressive gains in national, state, and local contests, and for the first time since 1954, the GOP gained control of both chambers of Congress; not since 1948 had a Democratic president shared power with a Republican Congress.

The contrast between the two most recent election years was quite evident in the Senate. In 1992, the two parties each lost two seats held by incumbents and retained all open seats, and the overall partisan split was not altered (57–43). In 1994, the GOP won all open seats, none of its incumbents was defeated, and it regained the 54-seat majority it held in 1980 and 1984.[3] In addition, for the first time since the direct election of senators in 1914, the freshman class was composed entirely of Republicans.

This chapter analyzes the results of the Senate elections and reviews considerations that appear to be useful in explaining and predicting Senate outcomes. The first section deals with the national conditions that forecast Senate results, including the "midterm penalty" typically suffered by the incumbent's party, the risks caused by seat exposure, the image of the parties, the popularity of the president, and the perception of the state of the nation. The following section provides a more detailed overview of the outcome of Senate races. The final section attempts to place the 1994 Senate elections in perspective by focusing on the skills and the resources of the candidates running for office and the type of campaigns they were able to mount.

NATIONAL CONDITIONS

The results of congressional elections are routinely affected by three main features: timing in the presidential cycle (that is, whether they are on- or off-year elections), the number of seats a party holds (that is, exposure), and the mood of the electorate.

The Midterm Penalty

The loss of representation for the president's party in off-year (midterm) elections is well established in the conventional political wisdom. Thus, the Democratic party was "due" to lose some of its support in November as a midterm penalty to be paid for its success in the previous presidential election. Indeed, a writer has paraphrased Benjamin Franklin, "While not as perfectly certain as either death or taxes, the loss of seats by the president's party in the U.S. House of Representatives as a result of midterm elections is a remarkably dependable event" (Campbell 1993: 5).

Automatic seat losses cannot be expected in Senate contests because losses have not occurred with the same regularity as in House elections. In midterms since 1934, the president's party has always lost seats in the House but has lost Senate seats in 11 of 14 elections, giving up, on average, 4 seats. However, the parties of the seven presidents since Eisenhower have suffered a combined net loss of just 3 seats in their first midterm elections. Moreover, in 5 midterm elections following a change in party in the White House (that is, in 1954, 1962, 1970, 1978, and 1982), the president's party has won seats twice, lost twice, and come out even once, for a net *gain* of one seat. In 1978, the last time the Democrats controlled both the White House and Congress, the party broke even in the open-seat category and lost three incumbent-held seats. Thus, in average midterm elections, whether the analysis is based on all prior off-year election results or just those during a president's first term, one would have ruled out a Republican takeover of the Senate. The problem for the Democrats, of course, was that 1994 appeared to be anything but an "average" midterm election year.

Exposure and Open Seats

Although the midterm penalty imposed upon the in-party did not create clear-cut opportunities for Republicans to pick up a large number of seats in the Senate, the Democrats' disadvantage in terms of exposure offered the GOP additional and better chances to score partisan gains. Democrats had to defend 22 of the 35 Senate seats at stake, including 6 of 9 open seats; in this respect, the 1994 midterm elections were unlike most previous off-year elections. In the 14 elections held after 1964, the number of seats exposed and the number of seats lost by the in-party have been much more closely related, yielding a correlation of $-.84$. During this period, in only three instances did the incumbent party have more than 20 exposed seats, and on these occasions, it suffered an average loss of 8 seats—a shift that would have been sufficient to change control of the Senate in 1994. Indeed, the last time a party had 22 exposed seats was in the 1986 midterm elections; the Republicans lost 8 seats and the Senate majority.

The high number and lopsided distribution of open seats also appeared to slightly favor the Republicans' chances of gaining ground. Nine Senators chose not to run in 1994, and the 6 seats opened up by Democratic departures, were the most in at least 60 years (Ornstein et al. 1994) and created conditions favorable to Republican inroads. Between 1954 and 1992, 146 Senate seats have changed party hands, 94 after incumbent defeats, and 52 in open-seat races; GOP candidates have won only 42.6 percent of the former but 51.9 percent of the latter.

In general, the political environment in the states and the profiles of the politicians competing for office introduced important variations across Senate races. However, in contrast to the usual specific mix of *local* context and concerns, in 1994 Republican candidates, especially in open-seat contests, seemed to ride a powerful *national* tide promising to submerge regional differences, lift all party boats, and sought to shrink or sink the Democratic majority. Voters' choices made in special elections held in 1992 and 1993 and the public's mood during the election year indicated that 1994 might turn into a large swing year.

The Mood of the Electorate

In 1994 at the July 21–23 meeting of the Republican National Committee (RNC), Party Chairman Haley Barbour sounded very confident about the November election as "the best environment I've seen for Republicans since I became involved in politics" (Von Drehle 1994: 15). The GOP saw favorable omens in the results of several special elections held since the 1992 presidential contest. In December, Republican Paul Coverdell beat first-term incumbent Wyche Fowler, Jr., in a runoff election for the Georgia Senate seat, a seat the Republican party won in the 1980 sweep but lost just six years later in the Democratic comeback to majority status. In a landslide in June 1993, Texas State Treasurer Kay Bailey Hutchison won the seat vacated by Senator Lloyd Bentsen, giving the Republican party control of both Texas Senate seats for the first time since Reconstruction. Victories in 1993 in high-profile mayoral elections (Los Angeles and New York) and gubernatorial elections (New Jersey and Virginia) produced net Democratic losses and were the prelude to the success of Republican candidates in two 1994 special House elections in Kentucky's second district and Oklahoma's sixth.

In the Kentucky race, the Republican candidate, anticipating the 1994 campaign's focus on the president and the Democratic Congress, linked his Democratic opponent to Clinton. In an apparent effort to shift the focus away from such national considerations and neutralize their effects in the fall campaign, White House pollster, Stanley Greenberg, advised Democratic candidates to localize their elections by emphasizing their independence and their personal commitment to represent and protect the interests of their states when he said, "Democrats make gains in this race running on their accomplishments and their agenda to help people at home. There is no reason to highlight these as Clinton or Democratic proposals" (Merida 1994: 12).[4]

But, by nationalizing the midterm races, the GOP set the stage for the *interpretation* of the election results as a wholesale rejection of the president and the Democratic party's control of the political agenda. Students of congressional elections have used the president's popularity and an evaluation of the incumbent party's competence to derive expectations about Senate aggregate outcomes (Abramowitz 1988; Abramowitz and Segal 1986, 1992; Lewis-Beck and Rice 1992). To the extent that behavior of these two variables predicts election results, directly or indirectly, both hinted at Democratic losses in 1994.

In 1994 Clinton was a remarkably unpopular incumbent, despite a growing economy at home and the absence of explosive crises abroad.[5] During 1993, Clinton averaged an approval rating of just 49 percent, the lowest level of first-year support for an elected president and higher than only Ford's. Among sociodemographic groups, southern whites expressed the most negative evaluations of the president, suggesting the special need for Democratic candidates in that region to avoid too close an association with the incumbent. Furthermore, supporters of Ross Perot, a key swing-vote group courted by Democratic and Republican candidates, showed no sympathy for Clinton; of Perot supporters 53 percent disapproved and only 37 percent approved of his handling of the presidency.[6] Unfortunately for Clinton, his popularity declined even more as the election drew near. Between mid-August and mid-October 1994, at least 50 percent of the people interviewed by Gallup voiced disapproval of Clinton's handling of his job, the highest and longest-lasting negative rating among the seven most recent presidents facing first midterm elections.[7]

As the president became increasingly less popular with the public and less welcomed by Democratic candidates on the campaign trail, several polls showed a corresponding erosion of support for the Democratic party. By July, for the first time in three years, the GOP was perceived as the party better able to handle the most important problem facing the nation.[8] In October, people expressed more confidence in the Republican party's ability to handle foreign affairs, the economy, crime, creating jobs, taxes, and the deficit; the Democratic party was ranked above the GOP on only the issue of poverty. At the same time, in perhaps the most revealing sign of an exceptional 1994 election year, the generic congressional vote showed Republican candidates ahead of Democrats for the first time since 1950.[9] Beginning in the late summer and early fall of 1994, several polling organizations showed a consistent Republican edge among registered voters and an even bigger advantage among those most likely to vote.[10]

Perhaps in an effort to galvanize and mobilize the Democratic party's base, the president decided to join the Republicans in framing the election as a national referendum on his administration or a return to the "flawed policies and easy promises" of the 1980s proposed again by the Contract with America. According to prominent Democratic strategists, the contract represented a turning point in the campaign and a major tactical mistake by Republicans. In the words of Democratic campaign consultant Paul Begala, "There is not a night that I don't thank God for the contract. It is the greatest gift to the Democratic party since Medicare." For Tony Coelho, an advisor to the White House during the 1994 campaign, the contract "was our break. We think we can win on it. . . . It has given us something to go to our base with and get our base voter, who was not motivated before, to come out. . . . Our base voter is now motivated, and I think it will make the difference. This is the beginning of the campaign. We are engaged" (Seelye 1994).[11]

During the final weeks of the campaign, a rise in Clinton's approval rating following foreign policy successes in Haiti, Iraq, and the Middle East; the criticism directed at the central items of the contract; and the adjournment of Congress allowing the mostly Democratic incumbents to go home and reconnect with their constituents led several Democratic leaders to argue that the momentum of the campaign had shifted. These events, however, did not change the predominant outlook about the election. Despite the arguments made, nearly all predictions pointed to significant Republican gains and the takeover of the Senate. It seemed no longer a matter of whether the Republicans would gain a majority; the questions, rather, were by what margin and at the expense of which Democrats. In an unprecedented show of confidence, Bob Dole and Newt Gingrich appeared on the *News Hour* on October 20 to discuss the GOP agenda as Senate majority leader and Speaker of the House of the yet-to-be-elected 104th Congress. Unlike in 1980 and perhaps to a larger extent than in 1986, the change in the control of the Senate appeared a very likely, if not a foregone, result.

THE NEW REPUBLICAN MAJORITY

On election day, Republican candidates received 53.3 percent of the two-party vote in the 35 Senate contests and took 60 percent of the seats—all of those defended by the party and 8 of the 22 seats previously held by Democrats (see Table 2.1). The GOP victory seemed to have both breadth and depth. Helped by the favorable circumstances of the election year, the party picked up seats in all regions

TABLE 2.1   1994 Senate Election Results

State	Candidates	Percentage of Vote Received
Arizona*	S. Coppersmith (D)	39.5%
	J. Kyl (R)	53.7
California	D. Feinstein (D)•	46.8
	M. Huffington (R)	44.8
Connecticut	J. Lieberman (D)•	67.0
	J. Labriola (R)	31.0
Delaware	C. Oberly (D)	42.5
	W. Roth Jr. (R)•	55.8
Florida	H. Rodham (D)	29.5
	C. Mack (R)•	70.5
Hawaii	D. Akaka (D)•	71.8
	M. Hustace (R)	24.2
Indiana	J. Jontz (D)	30.5
	R. Lugar (R)•	67.4
Maine*	T. Andrews (D)	36.4
	O. Snowe (R)	60.2
Maryland	P. Sarbanes (D)•	59.1
	W. Brock (R)	40.9
Massachusetts	E. Kennedy (D)•	58.1
	W. Romney (R)	41.0
Michigan*	B. Carr (D)	42.7
	S. Abraham (R)	51.9
Minnesota*	A. Wynia (D)	44.1
	R. Grams (R)	49.1
Mississippi	K. Harper (D)	31.2
	T. Lott (R)•	68.8
Missouri*	A. Wheat (D)	35.7
	J. Ashcroft (R)	59.7
Montana	J. Mudd (D)	37.6
	C. Burns (R)•	62.4
Nebraska	B. Kerrey (D)•	54.8
	J. Stoney (R)	45.0
Nevada	R. Bryan (D)•	50.9
	H. Furman (R)	41.0

(continues)

TABLE 2.1 *(Continued)*

State	Candidates	Percentage of Vote Received
New Jersey	F. Lautenberg (D)•	50.3
	G. Haytaian (R)	47.0
New Mexico	J. Bingaman (D)•	54.0
	C. McMillan (R)	46.0
New York	D. Moynihan (D)•	55.2
	B. Castro (R)	41.5
North Dakota	K. Conrad (D)•	58.0
	B. Clayburgh (R)	42.0
Ohio*	J. Hyatt (D)	39.2
	M. DeWine (R)	53.4
Oklahoma*	D. McCurdy (D)	40.0
	J. Inhofe (R)	55.2
Pennsylvania	H. Wofford (D)•	46.9
	R. Santorum (R)	49.4
Rhode Island	L. Kushner (D)	35.5
	J. Chafee (R)•	64.5
Tennessee "A"	J. Sasser (D)•	42.1
	B. Frist (R)	56.4
Tennessee "B"*	J. Cooper (D)	38.6
	F. Thompson (R)	60.4
Texas	R. Fisher (D)	38.3
	K. B. Hutchison (R)•	60.8
Utah	P. Shea (D)	28.3
	O. Hatch (R)•	68.8
Vermont	J. Backus (D)	40.6
	J. Jeffords (R)•	50.3
Virginia	C. Robb (D)•	45.6
	O. North (R)	42.9
	J. M. Coleman (I)	11.4
Washington	R. Sims (D)	44.3
	S. Gorton (R)•	55.7
West Virginia	R. Byrd (D)•	69.0
	S. Klos (R)	31.0
Wisconsin	H. Kohl (D)•	58.3
	R. Welch (R)	40.7
Wyoming*	M. Sullivan (D)	39.3
	C. Thomas (R)	58.9

NOTES: States in *italics* are states where seats were last held by Democrats; an asterisk * denotes an open seat; the bullet • indicates incumbent; R denotes Republican and D, Democrat.
SOURCE: Election results are from *Congressional Quarterly Weekly Report*, April 15, 1995: 1090–1097.

of the country: 1 in the West, 2 in the Midwest, 3 in the southern and border states, and 2 in the East. At the same time, the electoral performance of Republican candidates was affected by the ideological leanings of the states' electorate as measured by CBS/New York Times polls (Erikson, Wright, and McIver 1993). The correlation between state ideology and the vote was .46 ($n = 33$). As expected, both variables were also related to Clinton's job rating as measured in the exit polls conducted by the *Voter News Service.* In the 25 races for which data are available, the state's ideological orientation and the president's disapproval level showed an $r =.72$; the bivariate correlation between Clinton's disapproval level and the percentage of the two-party vote received by Republican candidates was .43.

The Republican success also appeared to be more decisive than that of the winning party in each of the two most recent Senate takeovers. In 1980, Republican candidates won a *minority* of the major party vote (47.5 percent) but carried two-thirds of the Senate seats, taking 11 of the 14 races won with no more than 52.1 percent of the vote (Mann and Ornstein 1994). In 1986, Democratic candidates received a thin majority of the two-party vote (50.8 percent)—lower than in 1980—but won 9 of the 11 closest contests, taking 59 percent of all races. In 1994, Republican candidates gathered a higher percentage of the major party vote (53.3 percent), and of the 8 most competitive races (those where candidates received from 45 to 55 percent) only 3 ended up in the Republican column while 5 broke the other way. In the 4 contests—those in California, New Jersey, Pennsylvania, and Virginia—won with less than 52 percent of the two-party vote, Democrats were successful in all but 1. On the other hand, 11 of the 14 winners with at least 60 percent of the major party vote, were Republicans.

In the 33 races where seats were at stake in both 1988 and 1994, the aggregate two-party swing toward the Republican party was 5.8 percent (from 47.2 percent to 53 percent).[12] In the 7 open races, the percentage of the two-party vote received by Republican candidates moved up by 10.2 percent.[13] The support enjoyed by Republicans increased in 23 states while it decreased in the remaining 10. Four of these 10 seats were defended by Democratic freshmen (Joe Lieberman, Herb Kohl, Richard Bryan, and Daniel Akaka), for whom the vote surged above the margins achieved in their first victories, and 2 were open Republican seats (Missouri and Minnesota) where retirement "slumps" could be expected. In Texas, Hutchison could not match her record performance of June 5, 1993, against appointed incumbent Bob Krueger, but she won her race with a very comfortable 60.8 percent of the total vote. Four-term incumbent William Roth, with 56.8 percent of the vote, had a median showing, doing worse than he did in 1988 and 1970 but better than he did in 1976 and 1982. First-term incumbent Jim Jeffords was the only Republican who experienced a sharp decline of support as he won reelection with 55.4 percent of the vote, 14 percent below his 1988 tally. Robert Byrd was the only nonfreshman among the 5 Democratic incumbents who increased their margin of success. The other 12 Democratic incumbents lost, on average, 7.9 percent of their most recent level of support. Jim Sasser and Charles Robb led the list with deficits of 22.5 and 19.8 percentage points, respectively; Frank Lautenberg, Paul Sarbanes, and Bob Kerrey contained their losses at less than 3 percent.

Member and Party Turnover

The GOP pickup was propelled by a sweep of the 6 open seats, the largest in 40 years, and was completed by the defeat of two Democratic incumbents, Harris Wofford in Pennsylvania and Sasser in Tennessee. Wofford was perceived to be in a precarious position throughout the election year, and his defeat was not entirely unexpected. His victory in the 1991 special election was a surprising come-from-behind success over former Governor Richard Thornburg, who advertised himself in a climate marked by growing political cynicism and distrust of politicians, as someone who "walked the corridors of power" in Washington. Wofford won the race with 55 percent of the vote to become only the second Democratic senator to represent the state since Joseph Clark's election in 1956 with 50.2 percent of the major-party vote and his reelection in 1962 with 51.2 percent. By most accounts, in 1994 Wofford conducted a lackluster campaign against a qualified and well-financed challenger who outspent him while repeating the core message shared by most Republican campaigns across the country: lower taxes and a smaller, less-expensive government. As a Democratic incumbent, Wofford had to face the problems experienced by most fellow partisans in a pro-Republican year, and his image and political reputation suffered, probably more than any other Democrat's, from the administration's failure to deliver on health care reform and from the growing opposition to the president's plan, which was increasingly identified as an example of an overreaching federal government. In 1991 perhaps the most memorable slogan of Wofford's campaign was, "If criminals have the right to a lawyer, I think working Americans should have the right to a doctor. That's why I'm fighting for national health insurance in the Senate." In 1994, after the collapse of health care reform in the Senate, Wofford had no similar clear-cut platform to run on.

The Wofford race in Pennsylvania mirrored one interesting pattern of the national congressional vote. According to exit poll data, Democratic candidates had their best performance in 10 years among liberals and moderates, carrying 82 percent and 58 percent of their vote, respectively; Republican candidates received 80 percent of the conservatives' vote, their highest share since 1984 (Ladd 1995a). In Pennsylvania, as in many other states, the percentage of self-identified conservatives was higher than it was in 1992, and they provided the Republican candidate with the necessary base to climb to electoral success. Moderates and liberals supported Wofford, but their numbers were not large enough to guarantee victory; only self-described conservatives—more than twice as many as liberals—preferred Santorum, and they made him the winner. Had the distribution of voters based on ideological orientation stayed the same as it was in 1992 when Arlen Specter edged out Lynn Yeakel, Wofford would have succeeded (Madonna and Yost 1995).

The defeat of Sasser in Tennessee was less predictable, especially early in the campaign. Elected in 1976 with 52.7 percent of the major party vote, Sasser achieved reelection in 1982 and 1988 with larger shares of support—61.9 percent and 65.3 percent, respectively. In 1994, even though he appeared to lead the race to succeed George Mitchell as Democratic leader, Sasser became the victim of the tide that swept Tennessee as well as the nation. In the governor's race, Representative Don Sundquist, Republican, beat his Democratic opponent Phil Bredesen by a margin of 54 to 45, and Republican candidates won the three contests for House open seats. With 42.3 percent of the vote, Sasser did only marginally better than Representative Cooper, who was preferred by 39 percent in his bid for Gore's seat. In his race with Sasser, Bill Frist, one of several GOP challengers who in 1994 personally contributed relevant sums of money to their campaigns, exploited the public's dissatisfaction with Clinton and displeasure with professional politicians. Sasser was painted as Clinton's "water boy" and as a perennial fixture of Washington politics. In his campaign ads, Frist introduced himself as an outsider and a new face, almost in a Carteresque mode: "Bill who? Never heard of him. He must be somebody new." At the same time, he castigated veteran incumbents: "Bill Frist supports term limits to stop career politicians, and the death penalty to stop career criminals."

Nationally, with only two incumbents losing, the 1994 Senate elections displayed a unique combination of partisan change and incumbents' resilience (see Tables 2.2 and 2.3). Before 1994, partisan shifts normally were produced by incumbent defeats rather than by pickups in open-seat contests.[14] In the majority-switching elections of 1918, 1932, 1946, 1948, 1952, 1954, 1980, and 1986, the average success rate of incumbents was 63.8 percent, almost 30 points lower than it was in 1994 when it reached 92.3 percent—a reelection rate higher than occurred in the House and the fourth highest since direct election. Among Democrats, the reelection rate of 87.5 percent was much greater than it was in 1980, when only 53 percent of party incumbents survived the Republican onslaught; in 1986, marking the return of Senate Democrats to majority status, 63 percent of GOP incumbents won their reelection bid. Fewer casualties among incumbents are associated with smaller classes of newcomers; in 1994, the number of freshmen members of the new party majority was the lowest on record. On the other hand, only in 1994 and in the realigning elections of 1932 and 1934 did all freshmen share the same party affiliation.

Despite the high reelection rate, incumbents did slightly worse than expected in one respect. Between 1970 and 1992 about 50 percent of all senators were reelected with at least 60 percent of the major party vote (Krasno 1994); in 1994 less than 40 percent of incumbents (10 out of 26) defeated their challengers with at least 60 percent of the vote—the lowest share since 1978. The result, of course, was affected by the relatively high number and poor performance of Democratic incumbents; out of 16, 3 won with at least 60 percent of the vote, while 7 of 10 GOP incumbents were successful with more than three-fifths of the vote.

Finally, Table 2.3 shows the historical anomaly of the elections held between 1976 and 1980 when the Senate incumbents' plunging reelection rates appeared to produce "vanishing incumbents" while the House experienced "vanishing marginals" (Hinckley 1980: 442). In the 1990s, we may still be witnessing the rapid disappearance of incumbents as a result of retirement rather than defeat; in several instances, voluntary departures may simply anticipate the verdict of the general election (Box-Steffensmeier and Franklin, 1995). As of this writing, 10 incumbents, 8 Democrats, and 2 Republicans have already announced they will not seek reelection in 1996.

Regional Distribution of Senate Seats

A comparison of the regional bases of the Senate Republican majorities in 1947, 1953, 1981, and 1995 shows a dramatic shift from midwestern and, to a lesser extent, eastern states toward southern and western states (see Table 2.4). The post-election switch by Richard Shelby (Alabama) and Ben Nighthorse Campbell (Colorado) further reinforces this electoral pattern. For the first time in this century, Republicans in the Senate drew a majority from southern states—where the party won its first seat since Reconstruction in 1961—*and* a minority from midwestern states—the party's traditional stronghold and now the only region represented by a majority of Democratic senators. Republican gains across the country reduced the number of states with split Senate delegations to its lowest level since 1966. However, relative to 1980, the count of divided states in 1994 decreased in all regions except the Midwest, where four states were represented by pairs of Democratic senators and only two states had a Republican delegation.

Ideological Change

Regional shifts in the makeup of the Republican membership have been tied to its ideological orientation; the ascendancy of the southern and western wings of the party has coincided with the rise of its most conservative component. For instance, calculated by the Americans for Democratic Action (ADA), the average ADA score, an indication of how liberal or conservative a senator's voting record is based on key votes designated by the ADA (0 being most conservative while 100 being most liberal), for southern Republican senators in the 103rd Congress was 8.1; Republican senators from border and western states received averages of 18.2

TABLE 2.2 Member Turnover in Senate Elections, 1914–1994

Year	Seeking Reelection	Not Renominated	Not Reelected	Reelection Rate	Size of Freshman Class Total	GOP
1914	24	2	0	91.7%	10	3
1916	29	4	9	55.2	18	10
1918	29	4	5	69.0	16	10
1920	30	4	8	60.0	17	13
1922	29	3	10	55.2	18	5
1924	30	5	5	66.7	12	9
1926	33	4	8	63.6	13	5
1928	32	2	5	78.1	10	9
1930	30	5	8	56.7	18	4
1932	32	5	9	56.3	16	0
1934	32	2	8	68.8	13	0
1936	27	1	5	77.8	15	2
1938	31	4	5	71.0	13	8
1940	32	5	3	75.0	12	7
1942	33	4	7	66.7	13	10
1944	30	5	4	70.0	14	6
1946	29	6	7	55.2	19	15
1948	25	2	8	60.0	18	4
1950	32	5	5	68.8	13	7
1952	31	2	9	64.5	15	9
1954	32	2	6	75.0	14	7
1956	29	0	4	86.2	10	4

(*continues*)

and 19.8, respectively. Senators from eastern states were the least conservative with a score of 39.7, followed by their colleagues from the Midwest, with a score of 22.2.

The 1994 elections, combining 3 party replacements and 8 party switches, moved the Senate to the right. The 3 Senate Republican retirees came from different areas of the ideological spectrum, but their replacements were considered to be more conservative overall. David Durenberger represented a moderate voice within the party; he, John Chafee (Rhode Island), Mark Hatfield (Oregon), and Jim Jeffords (Vermont) earned ADA scores above 50 (absences were not counted) in both sessions of the 103rd Congress. Durenberger was also 1 of only 3 Republicans who more often voted for rather than against Clinton's positions in both 1993 and 1994. The ideological difference between Durenberger and his replacement, Rep. Rod Grams, is quite striking for members belonging to the same party. Grams, nominated and elected with the backing of the Christian coalition, was 1 of 19 Republican representatives (and only 11 non-southerners) to receive a score of 0 in the ADA rankings in both 1994 and 1993. In 1994, only 35 Republicans voted against Clinton more often.

Retiring Senator Malcolm Wallop was one of the most consistent opponents of Clinton's positions and among the most conservative Republicans. He received a

TABLE 2.2 (Continued)

Year	Seeking Reelection	Not Renominated	Not Reelected	Reelection Rate	Size of Freshman Class	
					Total	GOP
1958	28	0	10	64.3	18	3
1960	29	0	1	96.6	5	2
1962	35	1	5	82.9	10	2
1964	33	1	4	84.8	7	2
1966	32	3	1	87.5	7	5
1968	28	4	4	71.4	14	9
1970	31	1	6	77.4	11	5
1972	27	2	5	74.1	13	5
1974	27	2	2	85.2	10	2
1976	25	0	9	64.0	17	8
1978	25	3	7	60.0	20	11
1980	*29*	*4*	*9*	*55.2*	*18*	*16*
1982	30	0	2	93.3	5	3
1984	29	0	3	89.7	7	2
1986	*28*	*0*	*7*	*75.0*	*13*	*2*
1988	27	0	4	85.2	10	5
1990	32	0	1	96.9	4	3
1992	28	1	4	78.6	12	5
1994	*26*	*0*	*2*	*92.3*	*11*	*11*

NOTE: Freshmen exclude gubernatorial appointees, winners of special elections not held in November, senators appointed earlier in the election year who won election in November; the 1922, 1936, and 1970 freshman classes each include one minor party senator; information in *italics* denotes change in partisan control of the Senate.
SOURCES: U.S. Congress, *Congressional Directory*.

mean ADA score of 6 in the 103rd Congress. According to congressional vote ratings by the *National Journal*, Wallop headed its list of conservative senators every year of his last term in at least one of three issue areas (economic, social, and foreign) considered by the analysis, and in 1989, 1990, and 1993 he led the Senate as the most conservative member in all three areas. His replacement, three-term Representative Craig Thomas, has had a similar ideological profile. Since he joined Congress in 1989, Thomas has topped the *National Journal* list of conservatives in at least one issue area in four of his six years of service; his average ADA score for 1993 and 1994 was 8. In 1990, he was one of only two House members to receive a perfect rating from the U.S. Chamber of Commerce and a 0 from the AFL-CIO COPE (American Federation of Labor-Congress of Industrial Organizations Committee on Political Education).

John Danforth of Missouri was the most moderate among fellow Republican senators elected by southern and border states; he was placed ahead of 34 and 33

TABLE 2.3 Member Turnover by Class in Senate Election, 1914–1994

Year	Seeking Reelection	Not Renominated	Not Reelected	Reelection Rate	Size of Freshman Class	
					Total	GOP
1914	24	2	0	91.7%	10	3
1916–1920	88	12	22	61.4	51	33
1922–1926	92	12	23	62.0	43	19
1928–1932	94	12	22	63.8	44	13
1934–1938	90	7	18	72.2	41	10
1940–1944	95	14	14	70.5	39	23
1946–1950	86	13	20	61.6	50	26
1952–1956	92	4	19	75.0	39	20
1958–1962	92	1	16	81.5	33	7
1964–1968	93	8	9	81.7	28	16
1970–1974	85	5	13	78.8	34	12
1976–1980	79	7	25	59.5	55	35
1982–1986	87	0	12	86.2	25	7
1988–1992	87	1	9	87.4	26	13
1994	26	0	2	92.3	11	11

NOTE: Freshmen exclude gubernatorial appointees, winners of special elections not held in November, senators appointed earlier in the election year who won election in November; the 1922, 1936, and 1970 freshman classes each include one minor party senator.
SOURCE: U.S. Congress, *Congressional Directory*.

of his party colleagues in ADA rankings in 1994 and 1993, respectively. Former Missouri Governor John Ashcroft is considered more conservative than Danforth.

Of course, the most significant change came from seats lost by Democrats, especially in Ohio and Pennsylvania. The Ohio seat of Howard Metzenbaum, one of the fiercest liberals in the Senate with perfect ADA scores in 1993 and 1994, was taken by former Representative Mike DeWine, who compiled a conservative record in his four terms in the House. As previously mentioned, Wofford was replaced by a two-term representative, Santorum, a senator who is more conservative than Specter or his Republican predecessors from Pennsylvania. Former Majority Leader Mitchell and Don Riegle, former chairman of the Banking, Housing, and Urban Development Committee, were the other two Democratic retirees with ADA scores above the party average in the 103rd Congress. Mitchell was replaced by Representative Olympia Snowe, a moderate (she was outscored in the 1994 and 1993 ADA rankings by only 9 and 5 returning Republican House members, respectively; she was also among the 10 Republicans least likely to vote with a majority of their party against a majority of Democrats) but certainly less liberal than Mitchell or former Representative Thomas Andrews, who logged a perfect ADA score in 1993 and 1994 but lost to Snowe.

TABLE 2.4 Regional Distribution of Senate Republican Majorities, 1947–1994

1947

Region	East	Midwest	West	South	Border
Percentage Republican	75	95	45	0	50
Percentage Democratic	25	5	55	100	50
Number of seats	20	22	22	22	10

1953

Region	East	Midwest	West	South	Border
Percentage Republican	75	86	55	0	30
Percentage Democratic	25	14	45	100	70
Number of seats	20	22	22	22	10

1981

Region	East	Midwest	West	South	Border
Percentage Republican	50	59	65	45	30
Percentage Democratic	50	41	35	55[b]	70
Number of seats	20	22	26	22	10

1995

Region	East	Midwest	West	South	Border
Percentage Republican	50	41	65[a]	59[a]	50
Percentage Democratic	50	59	35	41	50
Number of seats	20	22	26	22	10

[a]Includes Richard C. Shelby (Alabama) and Ben Nighthorse Campbell (Colorado) who switched party affiliation after the November 8 election.
[b]Includes Harry F. Byrd, Jr. (Virginia) who was elected as an independent in 1970 and 1976.
NOTES: East: Connecticut, Delaware, Maine, Massachusetts, New Hampshire, New Jersey, New York, Pennsylvania, Rhode Island, Vermont
Midwest: Illinois, Indiana, Iowa, Kansas, Michigan, Minnesota, Nebraska, North Dakota, Ohio, South Dakota, Wisconsin
West: Alaska (1981 and 1995), Arizona, California, Colorado, Hawaii (1981 and 1995), Idaho, Montana, Nevada, New Mexico, Oregon, Utah, Washington, Wyoming
South: Alabama, Arkansas, Florida, Georgia, Louisiana, Mississippi, North Carolina, South Carolina, Tennessee, Texas, Virginia
Border: Kentucky, Maryland, Missouri, Oklahoma, West Virginia

Retiring Senators David Boren, Harlon Mathews, and Dennis DeConcini and defeated Senator Jim Sasser had a more moderate voting record than other Democratic senators—below the ADA party averages in 1993 and 1994—reflecting the difference between Democrats from the southern, border, and western states on the one hand and the more liberal group elected from the East and the Midwest on the other. Jon Kyl and James Inhofe came from the House with very solid conservative records; Bill Frist and Fred Thompson were both newcomers to Congress and considered very likely to contribute to the Republican agenda to introduce radical changes in pursuit of downsized federal government and balanced budgets.

Membership Experience

Only 4 senators in the 103rd Congress were first elected without prior political experience in either an elective or appointed capacity (they were Bennett and Hatch from Utah, and Bradley and Lautenberg from New Jersey). Thirty-two members served in the House, 16 were governors of their states, 13 held some other statewide office, 12 were state legislators, 15 held a local office, and 8 were political appointees, party officials, or Senate candidates (Herrnson 1995).

Unlike their House counterparts, the 11 Senate newcomers had rather impressive political résumés. Seven served in the House (6 served in the 103rd Congress; and DeWine retired in 1990 after four terms and was elected as Ohio's lieutenant governor), 1 was a two-term governor and two-term state attorney general, 2 had previous political experience (Abraham as state party chair in Michigan, as cochair of the NRCC, and as a deputy chief of staff for Vice President Dan Quayle; and Thompson as the chief minority counsel on the Senate Watergate Committee). Only Frist had very limited political experience; for example, first voting in 1988, Frist was appointed in 1992 by the governor as chairman of the Tennessee Task Force on Medicaid.

The backgrounds of the new senators were consistent with data showing that a governorship and service in the House have provided the primary stepping stones to the Senate (Canon 1990); since 1913, more than half of the members elected to the Senate were previously elected to the House or a governorship. In particular, having held a House seat has become increasingly important to being a successful Senate candidate. The percentage of senators who served in the House was 32.7 percent between 1913 and 1959, and 36.9 percent between 1960 and 1987; on the other hand, the percentage of Senators with previous gubernatorial experience declined from 23.2 percent between 1913 and 1959 to 13.7 percent from 1960 and 1987. Of the senators elected between 1988 and 1994, 42.1 percent had legislative experience in the House and 13.2 percent had executive experience as governors.[15]

In the last two elections, transformations in House and Senate membership have shown different patterns. The 1992 House freshman class contained a greater share of elected officials (72 percent) than the holdover class (68 percent); the Senate freshman class, on the other hand, was relatively inexperienced with only four of its members (33 percent) coming from "manifest offices" (that is, Representative and governor). In 1994, more than half of the freshmen representatives were inexperienced while 73 percent of the rookie Senators moved up from positions in the House or as governors. This difference in backgrounds, of course, applied to Senate and House Republicans since they made up the entire rookie Senate class and 85 percent of the House freshmen; among them, only 51 percent of new members belonging to the GOP had prior elective experience. The Senate and House Republican majorities were also different in terms of length of Congressional service; 60 percent of House Republicans but less than 38 percent of Senate Republicans have been elected since 1990. An increase in amateurism may be expected in landslide elections or periods of high electoral opportunity (Canon 1990). Thus, although the change in the experience of House freshmen between 1992 and 1994 follows the anticipated direction, the change in the Senate does not.

In one respect, Republican representatives found themselves in 1994 where Republican senators were in 1980: they were a majority without any experience in that role *but* with a specific and aggressive agenda to pursue—Reagan's program in 1981 and the contract in 1995. In the 104th Congress, 120 of 230 Republicans in the House (52.2 percent) had been elected in the previous two years; in the 97th Congress, 27 of the 53 Republicans in the Senate (51 percent) had been in office two years or less. Furthermore, like the 1994 House freshmen, the 1980 newcomers did show a rise in amateurism; only 6 of the 16 GOP freshmen (37.5 percent) served in the House, and none were previously elected governor. In 1994, 22 Republican senators were veterans of the 1981 Senate. It can be anticipated that the combination of the seniority system, conferring to some veteran but moderate Republican senators the authority to chair key committees; Senate floor rules, giving every individual, as well as the minority, greater leverage than exists in the House; and the lack of a binding commitment of those on the Senate side to the contract pursued by a more disciplined House majority will slow down the pace of the legislative work and require some policy compromises.

CANDIDATE RESOURCES AND CAMPAIGN INTENSITY

After the 1976, 1978, and 1980 elections showed a dramatic difference between the reelection rates of Senate and House incumbents, several scholars argued that the greater electoral safety of Representatives was, to a large extent, the result of weak challenges posed by relatively unexperienced and underfinanced candidates. The advantage that has been enjoyed by House members "may be less a matter of what incumbents do right than of what challengers do wrong—or not at all. By a number of measures held to be important to the vote—visibility, campaign activity, positive reputation—Senate challengers may be competitive with their opponents and House challengers not competitive" (Hinckley 1980: 442; see also Abramowitz 1980; Mann and Wolfinger 1980; Ragsdale 1981).

This distinction between Senate and House elections turned out to be overdrawn since slightly more than half of the campaigns challenging Senate incumbents were low-key events, similar to most House elections. In such an election "one of the candidates—by virtue of an inability to raise funds, to attract media coverage, or both—is unable to mount a forceful, stimulating campaign.... A low-key race may also occur as a result of candidate ineptitude, or because (despite candidates' energetic efforts) the press simply does not see a particular campaign as worthy of a great deal of attention" (Westlye 1991: 17–18; see also Krasno 1994). Campaigns for open seats have been much more likely to be hard-fought, with in excess of 80 percent of these elections defined as "high-intensity races—in which a great deal of information about both candidates is made available to, and presumably reaches, the electorate." (Westlye 1991: 17). In these races, candidates very often have held visible elective office or were well-known amateurs; they have had the opportunity to develop skills and establish connections necessary to wage effective campaigns and their financial resources have outstripped or were rather evenly balanced with those of their opponents. Unless incumbents are considered vulnerable, open seats typically offer better opportunities of political gain for "quality" candidates with prior elective experience, especially statewide and in the House; with widespread name recognition; and with the capability to attract the money needed to sustain credible, competitive, and hard-fought campaigns. Although occurring less frequently in races involving incumbents, hard-fought campaigns are more likely in Senate elections than in House elections, and "the high proportion of quality challengers and hard-fought campaigns—aspects that clearly differentiate Senate and House contests—creates senators' reelection difficulties" (Krasno 1994: 155). Furthermore, experienced candidates may provide early tests of incumbents' reelection prospects by mounting primary challenges.

Party Primaries

A party primary has offered an early indication about the vulnerability of an incumbent; several studies have shown that the presence of a strong challenge and the incumbent's margin of victory in his or her party primary are related to the general election results (Abramowitz 1988; Abramowitz and Segal 1992; Bernstein 1977; Kenney and Rice 1984; Maisel 1992; Squire 1989; Westlye 1991). Indeed, in recent election years, the emergence of a quality challenger has been a *sufficient* condition of an incumbent's loss of his or her seat at the hands of a primary opponent or of a challenger in the general election.[16] In 1992, appointed California Senator John Seymour was defeated by Dianne Feinstein after overcoming the challenge posed by conservative Congressman William Dannemeyer. In 1990 no incumbent faced a quality opponent; between 1982 and 1988 Republicans David Karnes (Neb.), James Abdnor (N.D.), Charles Percy (Ill.) and Howard Cannon (Nev.) lost the general election after defeating quality challengers with previous experience as U.S. Representatives or state governors. In 1980 Democrat Richard Stone (Fla.) lost the primary to State Insurance Commissioner (and former 1974 challenger) William Gunter; Democrat Herman Talmadge (Ga.) managed to win

TABLE 2.5   Challenges to Elected Incumbents in Senate Primaries, 1974–1994

Number of Challengers	Number of Races		Percentage of Uncontested Races	
	1974–1992	1994	1974–1992	1994
0	136	16	52.1%	61.5%
1	90	5	34.5	19.2
2	26	5	10.0	19.2
3	8	0	3.1	0.0
4	1	0	0.4	0.0
Total	261	26	100.1%	99.9%

NOTE: Challengers include candidates receiving at least 5 percent of the primary vote.
SOURCES: For 1974–1990, Abramowitz and Segal (1992); for 1992 and 1994, *Congressional Quarterly Weekly Report*.

his primary defeating Lt. Gov. Zell Miller in a runoff but lost the general election to Mack Mattingly; Democrat Donald Stewart (Ala.) lost his primary to Jim Folsom, Jr., state public service commissioner and son of a former governor. Only seven elected incumbents have been defeated over the last 20 years, and since 1980 just one (Alan Dixon D-Ill.) lost in the Democratic primary to a challenger.

The 1994 party primaries were uneventful and thus typical of recent elections. As shown in Table 2.5, in 1994 the proportion of uncontested primaries was higher than that of the average of the previous ten elections, that is, 61.5 percent versus 52.1 percent; no incumbent faced a quality challenger or ran a significant risk of losing. Two researchers (Abramowitz and Segal 1992) reported that between 1974 and 1990, the mean victory margin for incumbent candidates was 56.1 percent and that while in 1992, a comparatively competitive congressional election year, the margin dropped to 44.6 percent, in 1994 it grew to 62.6 percent. Not surprisingly, Robb, who faced a strong challenge, fared the worst, finishing first by "only" a 24-point margin in a primary attracting just 9 percent of Virginia's registered voters. Robb, the top vote getter (with 71.3 percent) among 21 senators defending seats they won in 1988 and long viewed as a rising political star inside and outside the state, was the most recent example of an incumbent made vulnerable by scandals (Peters and Welch 1980; Abramowitz 1988). Robb was singled out early in the election year as one of the most vulnerable Democratic incumbents. His reputation was tarnished by a long-lasting and well-publicized feud with Douglas Wilder (including the 1991 disclosure of illegally taped phone conversations), his alleged involvement in extramarital affairs, and his participation in parties at which illegal drugs were used. Wilder announced in January that he would not run against Robb in the Democratic primary, the selection method chosen by Democrats instead of a nominating convention in part to prevent an independent candidacy by the former governor.[17] Wilder, of course, would have posed a quality challenge to Robb, who was nonetheless the only incumbent opposed in the primary by a challenger with elective experience, state senator Virgil Goode, Jr. After entering the race in June as an independent and dropping out of it in September, Wilder formally (but coldly) endorsed Robb for the Senate seat on October 22. In November, Virginia voters narrowly reelected Robb, perhaps finding Lt. Col. Oliver North's personal shortcomings even more egregious than those of the incumbent.

Other incumbents drew less experienced challengers: among them, a minister, an appliance repairman, a sales consultant, an accountant, a retired clergyman, a company executive, a commercial fisherman, and a political activist. Chafee won his primary by 38 percentage points; Daniel Patrick Moynihan and Feinstein defeated their challengers, with subaverage performances, by 47 and 61 points, respectively. Sarbanes, Lautenberg, Hutchison, Byrd, Kohl, and Gorton achieved renomination with at least a 67-point margin.

The absence of an incumbent usually attracts higher levels of competitiveness. According to Westlye (1981), only 13 percent of the open-seat primaries held between 1968 and 1984 were uncontested races; and 15 percent were decided by a 60 to 99 percent margin; on the other hand, 42 percent of the winners of these primaries beat their closest opponents by no more than 25 points. Since 1984, open-seat primaries have shown a great deal of variation: while in 1986 all but one were either uncontested or won by at least 60 point margins, in 1992—again, a more competitive year—none was decided by a margin greater than 57 points, and all but three (73 percent) were carried by less than 25 points. The 1994 open-seat primaries displayed a polarized pattern of competitiveness. At one end, 6 of 18 candidates (who were evenly distributed between the parties) did not meet opposition, and another did not face a credible challenger (i.e., someone receiving at least 5 percent of the primary vote). At the other end, 5 candidates won their respective primaries with less than a 10 point margin, the same percentage observed between 1968 and 1984.

Democratic winners had more close calls than Republican winners, but no discernible relationship between primary and general election results have emerged from the data; in 1994, all Democratic candidates ran in a politically hostile environment. For instance, Jim Cooper was unopposed in the primary in Tennessee, Thomas Andrews was uncontested in the primary in Maine, whereas Sam Coppersmith won his primary in Arizona by a handful of ballots; all three were defeated in their efforts to keep their states in the Democratic column and received a very similar percentage of the vote. In races for Republican-held seats, Mike Sullivan was unopposed in the primary in Wyoming, while Alan Wheat narrowly won his primary in Missouri; like their fellow Democrats Cooper, Andrews, and Coppersmith, Republicans Sullivan and Wheat lost in the general election with less than 40 percent of the vote.

Candidates' Experience

Table 2.6 presents data about the political experience of candidates challenging incumbents and running for open seats between 1968 and 1984, and between 1986 and 1994.

TABLE 2.6 Candidates' Experience in Senate Elections, 1968–1994

Candidate's Experience	Percentage Running Against Incumbents		Percentage Running in Open Seat Elections	
	1968-1984 (N = 225)	1986-1994 (N = 136)	1968-1984 (N = 141)	1986-1994 (N = 66)
U.S. Senator or Governor	7%	6%	13%	12%
Other Statewide Elective Office or State/National	12	12	15	5
U.S. Representative	20	16	28	52
State Senator or Representative	21	20	13	9
Mayor, County or City Office	9	7	13	6
Nonelected Party Office or Other Nonelected Political Office	7	3	3	5
No Political Experience	22	32	14	12
Total[a]	98%	100%	99%	101%

[a]Totals may not add up to 100% because of rounding.
SOURCES: For 1968–1984, Westlye (1991); for 1986–1994, *Congressional Quarterly Weekly Report*, various issues.

With regard to races involving incumbents, the levels of experience of the challengers have been remarkably similar in the two time periods. The only change shown was the declining presence of those with experience as Representatives and a corresponding increase in inexperienced candidates among those willing to run against Senate incumbents. In the last two elections, there were only 6 House members (3 current and 3 former) in 53 contested elections involving incumbents. In 1994, one-term Representative Huffington and two-term Representative Santorum challenged two freshmen Senators, Feinstein in California and Wofford in Pennsylvania, respectively; both outspent the incumbents in hard-fought races decided by 2.5 percent of the vote or less. Former three-term Indiana Representative Jim Jontz, narrowly defeated in 1992, waged an imaginative campaign but was vastly outspent by Richard Lugar, a powerful incumbent who won a state record-breaking fourth term with two-thirds of the vote and later announced his candidacy for the Republican nomination for President. Although House members have had better-than-average success in displacing Senate incumbents since 1968,[18] Santorum became the first Republican representative to defeat a Democratic incumbent since the 1980 election. Likewise, Frist was the first political novice to beat a Democratic incumbent since the last Republican takeover of the Senate.

The absence of incumbents in elections held after 1984 has attracted a much higher proportion of members of the House than in recent years. With the exception of the election in 1992, at least half of the candidates in open-seat races gave up their offices in the lower chamber to try to join the Senate. In 1994, 12 of 18 candidates running for open seats were elected to the House previously, 11 were members of the 103rd Congress, and 1 served in the House between 1982 and 1990 before being elected lieutenant governor of Ohio. Unlike in 1992, when 5 of the 6 U.S. Representatives running were Democrats (and three of them won), in 1994 the two parties were equally represented as to House members running for the Senate.

Campaign Spending

The ability to raise adequate financial resources is a key element to mounting hard-fought campaigns and to achieving electoral success. In 1994, in only 5 of the 35 Senate elections did the loser outspend the winner. In these 5 instances, Democrats won if they were incumbents defending their seats but lost when they were running to win open seats. Feinstein in California and Robb in Virginia fought back the heavily financed challenges brought by Huffington and North, who came remarkably close to winning their races despite the considerable controversies surrounding their candidacies. In Maryland, incumbent senator Sarbanes was outspent but victorious over former Tennessee senator and RNC chair Bill Brock. Despite his financial prowess, Brock had the "wrong" background to campaign as an outsider against the Washington establishment. After an unimpressive win in the party primary, in which he was attacked for having only weak ties to the state, Brock never posed a serious threat to Sarbanes' reelection. In two open-seat contests in Tennessee and Minnesota, the difference between the money spent by winners and losers was narrow; the national partisan tide helped Republican candidates carry both races.

Table 2.7 shows that in 1994 well-financed Republican challengers forced incumbent Democrats to spend more than they had in the past four election cycles. The remarkable surge in the amount of money spent by GOP challengers was due to two main factors: the willingness and ability of some of them to bankroll their own campaigns and the success of North in Virginia in raising funds from individuals. Candidate contributions accounted for 18 percent of the funds raised by

TABLE 2.7 Average Expenditures in Senate Campaigns, 1986–1994 (millions of dollars)

Year	Incumbents ($ millions)		Challengers ($ millions)		Open Seats ($ millions)	
	Democrat	Republican	Democrat	Republican	Democrat	Republican
1994	$5.15	$3.26	$1.02	$5.71	$2.62	$3.37
1992	2.85	4.80	2.85	1.13	2.67	2.78
1990	3.61	3.47	1.39	1.99	.93	2.27
1988	3.46	4.11	2.16	1.55	3.20	2.57
1986	2.71	3.60	1.92	1.87	2.85	3.87

SOURCE: Federal Election Commission, press release, April 28, 1995.

Republican challengers, more than 5 times the share represented by PAC money and more than 15 times the proportion of funds Republican challengers gave themselves in 1992. Led by Huffington's personal disbursements or loans of $28.4 million, five other Republicans gave $500,000 or more to their campaigns: Mitt Romney in Massachusetts ($3.1 million), Brock in Maryland ($1.6 million), Frist in Tennessee ($1.265 million), Bernadette Castro in New York ($1.1 million), and Colin McMillan in New Mexico ($.5 million). Among Democratic challengers, only Richard Fisher spent more than half a million dollars on his campaign for the Texas seat held by Hutchison. North far outdistanced all other senate candidates by raising $20.5 million from individuals; Feinstein and Ted Kennedy followed North in this category with $9.3 and $8.2 million, respectively. Even removing the exceptional cases of Huffington and North, GOP challengers in 1994 still spent a record average of $2.9 million, forcing Democratic incumbents to raise their campaign expenditures to an average of $4.3 million. In light of the political climate of the election year, it is not surprising to find that Democratic challengers had very limited resources to sustain their efforts to unseat GOP incumbents; on average, both Democratic challengers and Republican incumbents spent less than they did in the last four elections. Finally, Republican strength is also conveyed by data on open-seat contests where GOP candidates outspent Democratic candidates in seven of nine races even though the Democratic party controlled six of the nine seats at stake.

Campaign Intensity

Despite several highly visible and controversial races, the 1994 Senate elections did not appear to deviate from previous ones in terms of their intensity. Slightly more than 50 percent of recent campaigns featuring incumbents have been rated low-key. In 1994, on the basis of reports published in The *Congressional Quarterly Weekly Report* and information about campaign spending, the percentage of low-key races was estimated to be at least 50 percent. The Pennsylvania and Tennessee "A" races that produced the only two incumbent defeats of the year were among the hard-fought campaigns; so were the most expensive races in California, Virginia, and Massachusetts. On the other hand, seemingly hard-fought campaigns did not necessarily lead to close contests; in Maryland, Brock outspent the incumbent but never came within 20 points of his opponent.

In 1994, all nine open-seat contests probably qualified as hard-fought, with the Arizona race being, perhaps, a somewhat low-key exception. Democratic first-term Representative Coppersmith barely survived the primary, beating by 59 votes Secretary of State Richard Mahoney. The closeness of the race triggered a recount that delayed by 17 days, to September 30, the official determination of the nominee to replace retiring Senator DeConcini. At that time, Federal Election Commission (FEC) data revealed that the Democratic candidate had about $109,000 in cash on hand whereas Jon Kyl, the five-term Republican Representative who ran unopposed in his own party, had more than $1.2 million on hand. Coppersmith consistently trailed Kyl in the polls and was outspent by a 2.6 to 1 ratio. On November 8, Coppersmith lost the election by about 15 points, joining in defeat his fellow party candidates for governor and all but one candidate for a House seat.

Other races for open seats appeared one-sided despite being, at least toward the end, hard-fought. In Missouri, six-term Representative Wheat, who reportedly spent about 2 months without airing advertisements due to sheer lack of funds, narrowly won a costly Democratic primary, carrying only 25 of the 115 state counties (Germond and Witcover 1994: 2363). Then, throughout the fall campaign, former Republican Governor Ashcroft enjoyed a comfortable lead in public opinion polls, although Wheat closely trailed him in the money race.[19] As anticipated, Ashcroft won in a landslide against an opponent who, in many respects, epitomized the ideal target in the political climate of 1994: a 12-year incumbent, a very liberal Democrat, somebody accused of being soft on crime and against the death penalty, and a member of Congress involved in the House bank scandal (Wheat wrote 86 overdrafts).

In Ohio Joel Hyatt enjoyed widespread name recognition and a sizeable war chest in his effort to succeed departing Senator and father-in-law Metzenbaum. Hyatt, however, had a lackluster performance in the May primary, which he won beating by less than 2 percent Mary Boyle, commissioner of Cuyahoga County (Cleveland). DeWine's steady, double-digit lead in virtually all polls taken during the summer and the fall was evidence of a race with very little movement.[20] As in most other states, DeWine's victory on November 8 was part of the broad Republican sweep. In Ohio, Governor George Voinovich won reelection with a stunning 72 percent of the vote, three GOP House incumbents faced no Democratic opposition, three Democratic freshmen Representatives lost their seats, and the Democratic party lost another open seat.

CONCLUSION

By electing Bill Clinton to the White House and confirming Democratic majorities in the House and the Senate, voters in 1992 sanctioned the return to unified government for the first time since 1980. Formal control of the executive and legislative branches of government gave the Democratic party an opportunity to redirect the national political agenda and pass legislation recently blocked by presidential veto. Change and the end of gridlock were major themes and promises of the 1992 election campaign, as well as expectations against which the performance of the 103rd Congress would be evaluated. At the same time, the unified partisan control of government provided a sharp distinction between Democratic incumbency and Republican opposition so that lack of legislative accomplishments and inability to deliver measurable change was to offer the sour and sullen voters of the 1990s a clear target for their continuing anxiety about the future and their frustrations about "politics as usual." Revolt against Congress could become fused with rejection of Democrats as the embodiment of the status quo; the voters' unabated quest for change could take on the partisan focus lacking from the 1992 outcome.

In light of the across-the-board Republican gains in 1994, in the Senate and elsewhere, the elections lend themselves to the kind of partisan interpretation that lost most of its appeal during the recent decades of split results and electoral fragmentation driven by voters' weakening party loyalties. In 1994, in addition to the flawless reelection rate of Republican incumbents, the "disjunction" between House and Senate races dating back to the early 1970s (Jacobson 1990a) disappeared in 1994, with the GOP controlling 53 percent of the seats of both chambers of Congress. Furthermore, 22 states held elections for senator and governor, and only 9 (41 percent) returned a split outcome; going into the election, 14 of these states elected governors and senators from different parties. Finally, the percentage of states with a split Senate delegation dropped to the lowest level since 1966.

The situation in 1994 was, to some extent, similar to the circumstances surrounding the 1980 election: "Whether or not it proves to have the makings of a realigning or critical election, 1980 certainly appeared to refute House Speaker Tip O'Neill's favorite aphorism that 'all politics is local.' The decisiveness of the results, the content of the campaign, the involvement of the national Republican party, all pointed to a national decision by voters that President Carter and his party had failed and that the Republicans—in the presidency and in Congress—deserved an opportunity to govern" (Mann and Ornstein 1981: 50). Although Clinton could not be on the ballot in 1994, early readings of the "message" sent by the midterm outcome include a mix of "dissatisfaction with President Clinton, with liberalism, with the Democratic party, and with Washington in general" (Apple 1994b). Analyst William Schneider (1994) put it more bluntly, "It was Bill Clinton, stupid. A massive anti-Clinton coalition came together and produced the revolution of Nov. 8." As in 1980, Republicans did have a blueprint for action; if implemented, it can radically change the current balance between local and federal government and deeply transform existing social and domestic policies. Whether 1994 will mark the beginning of a short-lived experiment or inaugurate a long-lasting political and partisan change depends, of course, on the congressional performance of the new Republican majority. The ability of House and Senate Republicans to agree on major initiatives, muster the necessary votes for them, and persuade skeptical and often confused voters of their soundness will be a key variable in the political equation of the 1996 elections.

NOTES

1. These descriptions can be found in the post-election reports of the *Washington Post National Weekly Edition*, *U.S. News and World Report*, *Time*, *USA Today*, *Congressional Quarterly Weekly Report*, and the *American Enterprise*. The last expression alludes to the voters' choice that turned out of office only Democratic incumbents.

2. The slogan was popularized by GOP presidential hopeful and former Tennessee Governor Lamar Alexander.

3. In the last 40 years, only four other times did a party successfully defend all its Senate seats; no Democratic seat was lost in 1958, and no Republican seat switched hands in 1960, 1966, and 1980. The election results put the Republican total at 52 seats, a gain of 8. Richard C. Shelby (D-Ala.) switched party affiliation the day after the election, and Ben Nighthorse Campbell (D-Colo.) did the same on March 3, 1995.

4. The advice was reminiscent of the suggestion offered to GOP Congressional candidates by 1990 National Republican Congressional Committee (NRCC) Co-Chair Ed Rollins that they run against Bush, if necessary, after he broke his pledge of "no new taxes".

5. Despite the expansion of the economy and the low rate of inflation, 69 percent of those interviewed for an ABC News poll taken on October 5–9 said that they "were working harder but earning less." On the other hand, Clinton received no credit for the reduction of the federal deficit during the first two years of his Administration: of those polled by CBS/New York Times on October 29–November 1, 65 percent believed that Clinton's economic plan had no effect or actually *increased* the deficit.

6. *American Enterprise,* January-February 1994: 82–4.

7. According to the *Gallup Report,* 53 percent disapproved of Truman's performance in office in September 1946. In a poll taken September 6–7, 1994, 54 percent of those interviewed disapproved of the way Clinton was handling his job, the lowest percentage for the President since his inauguration. Analyst Kevin Phillips remarked about Clinton's unpopularity that "if the Vegetarians were the sole party on the ballot opposing Clinton, they'd probably be winning too." (*Boston Globe,* September 25, 1994).

8. *Gallup Poll Monthly,* August 1994: 16–19.

9. *Gallup Poll Monthly,* October 1994.

10. In an October 20–24 poll conducted by the Times Mirror Center, the Republican advantage among all registered voters was 3 percent and 8 percent among likely voters.

11. Almost a week before the signing of the Contract With America on September 27, 16 Republican candidates for Democratic or open seats in the Senate introduced their own seven-point Agenda for the Republican Majority: it called for a balanced budget amendment, welfare reform, tougher anticrime legislation, a capital gains tax cut, and tax credits for families with children. The document received virtually no media coverage. Given the quite limited familiarity of America with the well-publicized contract, very few voters were probably aware of the Agenda.

12. These are the "Class 1" seats; Oklahoma and Tennessee "B" are thus excluded from computations in the rest of the paragraph.

13. In the two other open races for the Tennessee "B" and Oklahoma seats won in 1990 by Al Gore, Jr. and David Boren, the pro-Republican shift was a whopping 30.3 percent.

14. In 1986 Democrats regained the Senate majority by defeating 7 Republican incumbents and picking up only 1 open seat. In 1980 Republicans won a majority by beating 9 Democratic incumbents and taking 3 open seats. In the watershed election of 1958, Democrats gained 13 seats—11 from incumbent defeat and just 2 from open seats.

15. Of the 58 senators elected between 1984 and 1994, 29 have served in the House, and 9 (15.5 percent) have been previously elected governor.

16. Here, the definition of quality challenger follows Maisel's; it includes members and former members of Congress, officials elected statewide, former occupants of these offices, and celebrities (Maisel, 1992).

17. *Congressional Quarterly Weekly Report,* April 23, 1994: 958.

18. A challenger beat the Senate incumbent in 20 percent of the races held between 1968 and 1984, and in 13 percent of the races that took place since 1986. The success rate of House members in the two periods was 33 percent and 23 percent, respectively.

19. According to the final FEC report on the 1993–94 election cycle, Ashcroft spent about $4.1 million and Wheat about $3.5 million.

20. *Cook Political Report,* December 19, 1994.

3

"Permanent Minority" No More: House Republicans in 1994

JOHN J. PITNEY, JR.
WILLIAM F. CONNELLY, JR.

Earthquake, tidal wave, tsunami ... realignment? In winning 230 House seats in 1994, Republicans bested their 1992 total by 54 seats—and left pundits groping for the most vivid word to describe the outcome. Before suggesting that the GOP triumph was either permanent or inevitable, however, awestruck observers should have recalled that Republicans scored an even larger gain in 1946, only to lose it in the Truman comeback of 1948.

Erring in the other direction, presidential pollster Stanley Greenberg downplayed the outcome when he said, "Republicans took just over half the votes cast ... and the Republican majorities in Congress are narrow" (Democratic Leadership Council 1994: 5). In the same vein, a Confederate spin doctor might have dismissed the Battle of Gettysburg as a razor-thin Union victory in a small Pennsylvania town.

Though 1994 did not guarantee future GOP dominance, it did make history. In House elections, Republicans won nearly 9 million more votes than they did in the 1990 midterm elections, while the Democrats won 769,000 fewer than in 1990 and 3 million fewer than in 1982. The combination of a growing vote for the winners and a shrinking vote for the losers was unmatched since the Democratic ascent during the Depression (Cook 1995: 1076). The GOP's 1994 showing undercut the argument that the electorate was merely turning its back on the in-party. If that were the case, disgruntled voters could have stayed home—as they did in the Watergate election of 1974, when the GOP vote dropped by more than 3 million from its 1970 level while the Democratic vote rose by less than 1 million (calculated from Ellis 1989: 6). In 1994, people voted *for* Republicans, not just *against* Democrats.

More important, the Republican takeover ended 40 years of Democratic control of the House, the longest span of one-party rule that Congress had ever seen. Until the 1994 campaign, such a result seemed unreachable. Except for the most optimistic Republicans, the political community regarded the House GOP as a "permanent minority." In discussions with the authors, even the visionary Newt Gingrich called winning the House "the hardest problem in American politics" and said that 80 percent lay beyond the House GOP's control. In our 1994 study of House Republicans (Connelly and Pitney 1994), we likened this problem to a Rubik's Cube, a popular three-dimensional puzzle that challenges the player to align all similarly colored squares on the same sides of the cube. The roles of *ideas, interests,* and *institutions* correspond to the cube's three dimensions, and the actions of *individuals* constitute the hands twisting the cube. Throughout the Reagan and Bush administrations, one or more of these elements always worked against the House Republicans. During the 1990 budget debacle—which featured an idea-free administration, a tax-weary public, a divided congressional GOP, and a nest of personal feuds—*all* the elements turned the wrong way.

Four years later, as we explain below, the elements lined up in the House Republicans' favor. Although they profited from forces they did not fully control, they were hardly a group of Forrest Gumps, passive beneficiaries of destiny. Instead, they carried out shrewd strategic and tactical decisions, which paid off in November.

The extent of their victory became clear after the election, when President Clinton and House Democratic Leader Richard Gephardt virtually elbowed one other aside in racing to offer mild versions of GOP tax cut proposals. This me-tooism reversed Samuel Lubell's description of a pale Republican moon reflecting the Democratic sun (Lubell 1956: 212). But how long could the new solar system last? One leading theorist, A. James Reichley, answered with the title of his December 1994 *Wall Street Journal* essay, "Get Ready for 60 Years of GOP Rule." Arguing that "realignment lives," Reichley noted the elections of 1800, 1860, and 1932 each resulted in a majority party that remained dominant for six or seven decades. If American politics runs on 60- to 70-year cycles, then 1994 could well prove to be a turning point.

Realignments are not inevitable, and when they do occur, they are hard to discern until years later. Scholars will debate the meaning of the 1994 election well into the twenty-first century. Meanwhile, Speaker Tip O'Neill's law—"all politics is local"—now requires the Gingrich corollary, "except when it is national." The Republicans nationalized the 1994 election by raising a central issue for historic realignments, namely, the proper role of government. Therefore, a discussion of the 1994 campaign should start with the role of ideas.

IDEAS

The Contract with America, the centerpiece of the House Republicans' campaign, embodied two major ideas. The first was the very concept of a covenant between the party and the electorate, an idea that reflected the "responsible-party" school of political science. In 1950, the Committee on Political Parties of the American Political Science Association (1950: 18) endorsed a system in which "the party program becomes the work program of the party, so recognized by the party leaders in and out of the government, by the party body as a whole, and by the public"—a description nicely fitting the contract. The second major idea, closely related to the first, was that a Republican program should go beyond mere criticism of the Democratic administration and should offer a clear vision of conservative governance. The House Republicans would thus spell out how they would relimit the federal government and return power to the states and the people.

Although some observers described the contract as the spur-of-the-moment invention of political consultants, its roots actually stretched back to the 1980 campaign. On September 15, 1980—a day called Governing Team Day—Ronald Reagan and GOP candidates for the House and Senate gathered on the Capitol steps and pledged themselves to a policy agenda. The project manager for Governing Team Day was the secretary of the GOP freshman class in the House, a young Georgian named Newt Gingrich. In a House floor speech before the event, Gingrich explicitly invoked the responsible-party school when he said, "A wide range of political scientists including James MacGregor Burns, Frederick Sontag, Manning Dauer, Jack Saloma, and others, have urged steps to strengthen the party system. There is a growing consensus that a weak party system leads to irresponsibility, to single issue politics and to domination by special interests" (*Congressional Record* 1980: 24683). In his description of the 1980 event, he clearly foreshadowed the 1994 contract when he said, "Federal candidates for election or reelection from across the country will gather. We will sign a covenant to take five steps to improve the quality of American life. . . . We are also setting a yardstick for measuring us in 1982. 'Should you elect us, look at our covenant and measure our achievements against what we say we will do as a team'" (*Congressional Record* 1980: 24683).

Gingrich and company hoped that the covenant would include highly specific proposals, but the Reagan camp balked. As a result, the agenda consisted of such broadly worded items as "selective cuts in government spending" and "all-out efforts to encourage more private investment" (Dewar 1980). Despite the agenda's vagueness, which disappointed Gingrich, the press reacted favorably. Columnist David Broder said that the message of party responsibility "is an honest statement, and it is as commendable for the Republicans to dramatize it as it is risky" (Broder 1980).

A few years later, Jerry Lewis (R.-California), chair of the House Republican Research Committee, launched the Project on the First One Hundred Days, an effort to develop a GOP agenda for the start of the 99th Congress. In January 1985, the Research Committee issued its report, titled *Ideas for Tomorrow, Choices for Today*. If the Governing Team Day covenant suffered from sketchiness, the 70-page House Republican Research Committee report overcompensated by listing 252 legislative proposals. In striving for breadth and consensus, the report contained some contradictions, such as support both for a simplified tax *and* a set of new tax credits and deductions (Fuerbringer 1985). Nevertheless, *Ideas for Tomorrow, Choices for Today* set two important precedents: linking of a policy agenda to specified bills, and adaption of FDR's "hundred days" to a House GOP initiative.

At the time, the political community scarcely noticed. Until 1992, the House Republicans would labor in the shadow of GOP presidents who viewed them as a reliable bloc of votes, not a valuable font of ideas. While the election of Clinton unchained them from an often-burdensome loyalty to the chief executive, it also seemed to present them with a new problem: co-optation. Clinton campaigned as a New Democrat, eager to snatch innovative free-market ideas from reformist Republicans (Connelly and Pitney 1994: 170). But by early 1994, after Clinton secured passage of a tax-heavy budget and proposed an incomprehensible and bureaucratic health care plan, Republicans knew that they could plausibly tag him as an old-style liberal.

Some Republicans thought that the party should focus exclusively on an anti-Clinton strategy, warning that a clear-cut policy agenda would only expose the GOP to Democratic attacks. Gingrich, who was now House GOP whip and heir to retiring minority leader Bob Michel, argued that the party needed magnet issues as well as wedge issues; that is, it had to attract voters to its cause and not merely split them from the Democrats. At a February 1994 conference in Salisbury, Maryland, House Republicans sided with the Gingrich approach and agreed to the following principles for the upcoming campaign: "individual liberty, economic opportunity, limited government, personal responsibility, and security at home and abroad" (Gillespie and Schellhas 1994: 4). During the next few months, the House GOP leadership consulted with Republican House members and nonincumbent candidates, seeking to turn the general principles into specific proposals that would enjoy broad intraparty consensus. When they developed the proposals that would go into the contract, political consultants test-marketed the wording, order, and style of presentation (Koopman 1994: 5).

On September 27 the House GOP unveiled the contract at a Capitol Hill rally that resembled Governing Team Day, except for the absence of senators and presidential candidates. Among the contract's elements were a balanced budget/tax limitation amendment and legislative line-item veto, an anticrime package, welfare reform, a tax reduction, a ban on putting American troops under United Nations command, regulatory reform, overhaul of the tort liability system, and congressional term limits. All of these proposals had long been floating in the GOP's primeval policy soup; indeed, most appeared a decade earlier in *Ideas for Tomorrow, Choices for Today*. But the point of the contract was not to dazzle voters with novel ideas but to show that the Republicans stood for something. In his remarks on the Capitol steps, GOP Conference Chair Dick Armey said that, "running solely against an unpopular president would only deepen the public cynicism. . . . It's time for the Republican Party to accept the role of leadership the American people are demanding" (Armey 1994b). In describing the contract, Armey emphasized mediating institutions and decentralized government when he said, "[W]e propose to cede back power from the hallowed halls of Congress to the more hallowed kitchen tables of America. . . . Our contract recognizes the limits of government and the unlimited contribution of husbands, wives, mothers, fathers, children, and grandparents in a safe and prosperous America" (Armey 1994b).

Although the initial press reaction ranged from dismissive to hostile (Cannon 1995), the House Republicans had two advantages in airing their message. First, "alternative" media enabled them to bring the contract directly to party activists and potential supporters. Anyone on CompuServe or with access to the Internet could download the entire text of the contract, along with GOP talking points and other supporting materials. And talk radio, especially the Rush Limbaugh program, put Republican voices in millions of homes and automobiles.

The second advantage was Democratic error. For reasons that remain unclear, Democrats deliberately framed their internal poll questions so as to give reassuring results to the White House (Kelly 1994: 50). Despite public polls showing that the electorate spurned the Clinton health care plan, Democratic national chairman David Wilhelm proclaimed as late as August, "The vote on health care reform is the litmus test for change in 1994" (Wilhelm 1994). Democrats attacked the GOP for seeking to reduce government—even though public survey data showed strong public support for the limited-government ideas in the contract (Ladd 1995a: 10). In the final weeks of the campaign, pollsters Larry Hugick and Andrew Kohut wrote that "local influences on congressional elections" could still keep the GOP from capitalizing on the antigovernment mood of 1994 (1994: 6). But by accepting the GOP challenge to nationalize the election, the Democrats helped shift the campaign's focus to areas of Republican strength. Although a majority of voters paid little attention to the contract per se, the ensuing policy debate made a difference. On the question of which party could do a better job with the country's most important problem, a January poll gave the Democrats a 39 to 31 percent advantage, but by October the Republicans led by 41 percent to 37 percent (Ladd 1995b: 45).

"We're absolutely grateful for it [the contract]. . . . There is now a clear contrast in the 1994 race," said White House adviser George Stephanopoulos (Kelly 1994: 47). With a more acute understanding of this contrast, a Democratic consultant told the *New York Times* in October, "It's bleak, very, very bleak. We're in the soup up to our neck, and it's hot" (Apple 1994).

INTERESTS

During the 1980s, Tony Coelho (D.-California), chair of the Democratic Congressional Campaign Committee, spoke bluntly to political action committees, saying, "We're going to be the majority party (in the House) for a long time, so it doesn't make good business sense to give to Republicans" (Houston 1986). Thanks to their permanent-majority status and Coelho's blatant threats, House Democrats built a daunting advantage in PAC fund-raising.

In 1994, Coelho returned to serve as informal chief of the Democratic campaign, only to find a new psychology at work. At long last, Republican control of the House loomed as a real possibility—if not in 1994, then surely within the next election or two. Now it was House Republicans who were talking tough. Gingrich reportedly told PAC directors, "Don't pick a specific [race] out; just put your money in any or all of them, because when I become Speaker, for anybody that's not on board now, it's going to be the coldest two years in Washington" (Simpson 1994). While Gingrich's blunt words did not reverse the overall pattern of PAC giving, they did have some impact. PAC contributions to House Democratic incumbents increased 10 percent, from $64.3 million in 1992 to $71.1 million in 1994; meanwhile, contributions to GOP House challengers rose *48 percent,* from $4.4 million in 1992 to $6.5 million in 1994 (Federal Election Commission 1995).

The politics of interests encompassed much more than PAC contributions. In 1993 President Clinton staked his party's political fortunes on his health care plan, triggering an unprecedented array of grassroots lobbying efforts—mostly in opposition. Employing recent advances in databases and communications technology, groups such as the Health Insurance Association of America (HIAA), which was headed by former Republican House member Willis Gradison, and the National Federation of Independent Businesses (NFIB), attacked the Clinton plan in carefully targeted mailings and advertisements (Faucheux 1995). This effort succeeded in its primary goal of deluging Congress with letters and phone calls, and it also had the side effect of undermining support for the Democrats.

In 1994 appeals to economic interests helped the GOP. On the one hand, people at the lower end of the scale had yet to see any significant benefits from the Clinton economic program. In 1993, the last year for which data were available, the number of Americans in poverty reached a 30-year high at 39.3 million (U.S. President 1995: 21). On the other hand, higher-income voters absorbed hefty tax increases resulting from the 1993 budget package—which passed without a single Republican vote in either chamber. So when HIAA and NFIB told these voters that the Clinton plan would reduce the quality of their medical care and raise their taxes yet again, they were primed to act. In 1994, among voters with family incomes over $50,000, the GOP percentage shot up from 48 percent in 1990 to 57 percent in 1994, and turnout increased from 59.2 percent to 60.1 percent. Among those with incomes under $15,000, the GOP vote actually edged up from 34 percent to 37 percent, while turnout dropped from 34.3 percent to 27.7 percent (Ladd 1995b: 50; Taylor 1995).

Political analysis of interests has traditionally focused on economics, but in 1994 social interests came into play as well. In August Gingrich helped defeat the procedural rule on the administration's crime bill, thereby earning the gratitude both of social conservatives, who mocked the bill's social welfare provisions (e.g., midnight basketball), and the National Rifle Association (NRA) members, who vehemently opposed the ban on certain semiautomatic weapons. Gingrich then placated GOP moderates by letting them cooperate with Democrats on a compromise crime bill—but he had already succeeded in portraying the Democrats as soft on criminals and harsh on gun-owning citizens. "I managed the battlefield we had, with the forces we had, to maximize our opportunity," he said (Boyer 1994: 38).

Although polls showed widespread support for firearms restrictions, this sentiment was far less intense than the feeling on the other side, which had a powerful organization. In 1994 the NRA boasted 3.3 million dues-paying members, and its Political Victory Fund raised more money ($6.8 million) than any other trade or membership PAC (Federal Election Commission 1995). According to a

Fabrizio/McLaughlin post-election poll, 15.1 percent of reported voters called themselves members or supporters of the NRA (O'Leary 1995, 32).[1] In November, NRA backing helped a number of Republicans.

Religious conservatives accounted for another key element of the GOP. Since the early 1980s, they increasingly supplied something the Republicans long missed: grassroots volunteer labor. In 1994, the new House Republican leadership welcomed them as never before. Gingrich, who supported school prayer legislation throughout his career, had much stronger ties with religious conservatives than Bob Michel. Even Dick Armey, whose conservatism was grounded in such libertarian writers as Milton Friedman and Friedrich Hayek, took great pains to emphasize the common ground between economic and religious conservatives (Armey 1994a).

As if to confirm Armey's contentions, the Christian Coalition did not insist that the contract include social issues such as abortion. Instead, it praised a largely secular agenda (see Peyton 1994), knowing that a GOP House would be receptive to its views, even if many Republicans emphasized economic issues in their campaigns. Without formally endorsing any candidates, the Christian Coalition distributed 33 million voter guides that tended to put Republicans in the best possible light.

Once again, the Democrats delivered themselves unto their opponents. President Clinton alienated religious conservatives—particularly in the South— with his position on gays in the military. And Surgeon General Joycelyn Elders became a walking ammunition dump. Among other things, she described the Catholic church as "a celibate male-dominated church" whose antiabortion members should "really get over their love affair with the fetus," and she accused "the un-Christian religious right" of "selling our children out in the name of religion" (Hedges 1994). During the summer of 1994, congressional Democrats made a concerted assault against what campaign chairman Vic Fazio (D.-California) called "the fire-breathing Christian radical right" (Glasser 1994). This approach had limited appeal. In an age of drugs and drive-by shootings, evangelical Christianity hardly topped the list of America's worries.

The attacks boomeranged. Rep. Scotty Baseler (D.-Kentucky), worried about the loss of conservative Christian support, announced that he would accept no help from the Democratic Congressional Campaign Committee. As southern Democrats fretted, Republicans sped to the rhetorical high ground. William Kristol, chairman of the Project for the Republican Future, noted that the attackers described religious conservatives as "fervent" and further said, "In this context, 'fervent' is to evangelical Protestants what 'aggressive' is to Jews, a politely disguised expression of discomfort and disgust with the manners and mores of an entire social class. It is bigotry. . . . The Republican Party should say that the current smear campaign against its conservative religious allies is wrong, and it should hold those who are pursuing that campaign to account" (Kristol 1994).

In November, GOP support surged from its already high levels among white born-again Christians. And for the first time in history, a majority of white

Catholics voted Republican in House elections (Ladd 1995a: 23). Analyzing a variety of exit poll data, pollster Fred Steeper (1995) found a direct relationship between religiosity and likelihood of voting Republican in 1994, with religiosity having even more impact than income. This voting pattern had special force in the Bible Belt and helped Republicans win a majority of southern House seats for the first time since Reconstruction. It also offset their failure to make any headway among African-American voters.

INSTITUTIONS

In our Rubik's Cube metaphor, the concept of "institutions" incorporates such familiar components as the structure of elections, the organization of Congress, and the separation of powers. In our decentralized system, congressional elections have customarily emphasized parochial, concrete interests over broader, ideological patterns of thinking (Ceaser 1990: 201). Yet while lawmakers must answer to local constituencies, their institutions must address national concerns. Congress thus organizes along two conflicting lines. Congressional committees furnish economic interests and local constituencies with multiple points with which to veto legislation. Congressional parties, ideally, are vehicles for decisive change in the name of broad national principles. Party and committee organizations often compete, but in doing so they help Congress to balance party principles with parochial interests. Contrary to the common assumption that our constitutional system is biased against change, our political system fosters both friction and fission. The friction results from the obstacles to rash action posed by the system's branches and layers. The fission consists of the system's openness to an energetic politics of ideas. The system curbs the abuse of power while providing for its effective use; it limits change, yet permits constructive change.

Echoing the responsible-party school, some lawmakers seek grand ideological battles on the model of the New Deal and are attracted by the system's potential for energy, or fission. Others echo the "pluralist" school in welcoming the system's built-in friction. Throughout the 1980s, the Gingrich wing of the House GOP took the first approach by promoting a national strategy of confrontational opposition to legislation. Bob Michel's followers, who predominated among the ranking committee members, favored the accommodating all-politics-is-local, establishment approach.

Under Reagan and Bush, the separation of powers put House Republicans in a bind: their alliance with the president made them the party of government while the minority status in the House simultaneously made them the party of opposition. Both roles pained them. As the party of government, they had to curb their confrontational tactics for the sake of passing the president's program and they took the political heat when things went badly for the White House, as it did with the 1982 recession. But as the party of opposition, they usually waited on the outside as the president's agents made legislative deals with the majority Democrats. And they also had to grapple with a grim historical pattern: over time, the party holding the presidency has tended to lose ground in the House. Looking back at three downhill congressional elections in a row (1986, 1988 and 1990), some House Republicans in 1992 hinted in off-the-record interviews that they would not mind if Bush lost.

They got their wish. In several ways, the 1992 election dramatically altered the strategic playing field in their favor. First, House Republicans had a virtual guarantee of gaining strength in 1994; in every midterm election since 1938, the out-party picked up at least some seats.

Second, they no longer had to worry about the dilemma of government versus opposition. Now that the Democrats had to carry the president's program, the Republicans were free to throw as many rhetorical and parliamentary grenades as they wished.

Third, they enjoyed more unity than before. The large size of the freshman class of 1992, heavily conservative and confrontational, clinched Gingrich's hold on the House Republican Conference. And opposition to Clinton not only united Gingrich's young Turks with the "old bulls" who held ranking committee positions, but it also made it easier for the House Republicans to work with the Senate Republicans. Although they never did agree on a single deficit reduction plan or health care alternative, congressional Republicans helped kill "Clintoncare" and held the administration's budget plan to one-vote margins in each chamber. Every Democrat who supported the Clinton budget would thus face the charge that he or she cast the deciding vote for the largest tax increase in American history.[2]

Fourth, the Republicans now had the opportunity to make a government controlled by Democrats a clear target for voter dissatisfaction. Perhaps the best metaphor for House GOP efforts to nationalize the election was found in the typical House Republican campaign commercial in which the local Democratic candidate's image "morphed" into the president's face. Republican consultants wanted to morph every House Democrat into another Clinton.

These circumstances enabled Republican leaders to change their colleagues' perspectives on the 1994 elections. Instead of viewing them merely as 435 local races, Republicans now began to see them as a battle of two teams—a battle that they could actually win. On August 10, 1994, the Republican National Committee issued a memo titled "Why Participate?" which encouraged GOP candidates to sign the Contract with America with the following: "While it is true that congressional elections turn on local issues and concerns, participating in the 'Republican Contract with America' will enable a candidate to grasp the national Republican themes of reform and commonsense change, and to be part of a larger team, a unified national effort."

Thinking as a team, Republicans helped one another. Although disbursements by the National Republican Congressional Committee (NRCC) reached their lowest point in 16 years, the national GOP effort was quite strong. In previous years, a succession of top-heavy NRCC bureaucracies actually hurt the GOP by wasting party resources (Connelly and Pitney 1994: 137–142). In 1994, incumbent members bypassed the NRCC by sharing money directly with challengers and open-seat candidates (Wilcox 1995: 29–30). As suggested before, Gingrich and other party leaders persuaded PACs to back nonincumbent Republicans.

House Democrats were as vulnerable on the institutional side as they were with ideas and interests. Forty years in the majority dulled their sensitivity to institutional reform. In 1989, House Speaker Jim Wright and Majority Whip Tony Coelho both resigned in the face of burgeoning financial scandals. In the 1992 election cycle, the House Bank and Post Office controversies gave the GOP a good deal of ammunition (although some of it backfired as a result of Republican overdrafts). Many members of the Democratic class of 1992 campaigned as reformers, but the party leadership pressured them to shun like-minded Republicans and give up the idea of dramatic institutional change. "You have to have low expectations," said freshman Karen Shepherd (D.-Utah). "Institutions like this move at a glacial pace" (Calmes 1994).

The House Democratic leadership even managed to quiet the 1992 campaign's leading reform advocate, Clinton. At a post-election dinner, Speaker Tom Foley warned the president-elect not to "take on the Congress" (Drew 1994: 61). Clinton complied. When he made proposals for "reinventing government," he kept silent on the issue of congressional reform.

In mid-1994, a federal grand jury issued a 17-count indictment accusing House Ways and Means Committee Chairman Dan Rostenkowski (D.-Illinois) of defrauding taxpayers of more than half a million dollars over the course of two decades. This scandal was particularly damaging to the Democrats because it involved such a high-profile leader and such eye-catching accusations: among other things, Rostenkowski allegedly used taxpayer money to buy 60 crystal sculptures of the Capitol and 250 pieces of fine china. Many Republican candidates leapt on the case (Curran 1994). Gingrich called it "another example of the kind of arrogance of power that comes with one-party rule. What we're saying is that the Democrats are an arrogant party that likes to raise taxes and refuses to investigate how they spend your money. Rostenkowski will reinforce all that" (Gosselin 1994).

In perhaps the biggest individual upset of the 1994 elections, Rostenkowski lost his seat to a little-known GOP challenger. So did Speaker Foley, who joined a lawsuit to overturn in the state of Washington the term limits law, a fact that enabled his opponent to claim that Foley was suing his own constituents to keep his job. Karen Shepherd, along with a number of deflated Democratic reformers, also lost. One of these losers, Eric Fingerhut of Ohio, reflected bitterly, "My anger is directed at the Democratic Congressional leaders, some of whom were defeated on November 8 and some of whom were not. Rarely has a group of political leaders so richly deserved defeat" (Fingerhut 1994).

INDIVIDUALS

Individuals are not mere creatures of their environment: they can in turn shape the setting of interests, institutions, and ideas. In the case of the House Republicans, individual members and leaders can leave a mark on the party's overall fortunes.

During the 1980s, House GOP prospects reflected hundreds of decisions by potential candidates. The House Republicans suffered from serious retirement and recruitment deficits, which they overcame in 1994. Premature GOP departures, due in part to the frustrations of permanent-minority status, contributed to Democratic dominance in the House (Gilmour and Rothstein 1993). But in 1994, 28 Democrats—compared with only 20 Republicans—retired or sought other office. Most Democratic retirees probably recognized the difficulty of running as midterm candidates of the in-party, while prospects of majority status may have persuaded some potential GOP retirees to stay on.

Republicans also ran as strong challengers and as strong open-seat candidates. "In key seats, the Republicans did a masterful job of recruiting candidates," said former Democratic Congressional Campaign Committee (DCCC) Chair Beryl Anthony (D.-Ark.). "I expect they did out-campaign us in terms of candidate recruitment this year" (Rosenbaum 1994). Again, prospective GOP challengers may have hungered for the opportunity to run against a weakened Democratic president and been interested in the potential for majority status. Possible Democratic challengers found the same circumstances less inviting.

More than circumstance lay behind the GOP surge. Despite institutional constraints (Cooper and Brady 1981), leaders make a difference. Since arriving in the House in 1979, Gingrich tried to persuade House Republicans to heed not only their individual reelection interest but their long-term party interest in regaining a majority. To some extent, all House Republican leaders preached to their members about the party's well-being. In fundamental ways, however, Gingrich was different. Whereas other leaders dreamed vaguely of committee chairmanships and congressional perquisites, Gingrich spoke passionately about his vision of the whole society. In a series of long floor speeches and in his book *Window of Opportunity*, Gingrich 1984 addressed everything from reform of the National Park Service to the macroeconomy of the 21st century. Although his critics questioned the depth and consistency of his vision (e.g., Wills 1995), a growing cadre of House Republicans found him to be inspiring.

Just as important, he was not just addressing his message to his colleagues of the moment. His arrival in Congress coincided with the beginning of C-SPAN, and he helped pioneer the use of House floor proceedings to talk to the general electorate. In the short run, he used televised speeches to arouse public opinion on specific issues such as school prayer and the nuclear freeze. For the longer run, he was reaching the party's future elite. Many of the Republicans of the 1990s came of political age while watching Gingrich on C-SPAN. More than any other congressional leader, he molded the way they thought about politics.

In 1986, Gingrich assumed the chairmanship of GOPAC, a political organization founded several years before by Pete Du Pont. GOPAC's premise was that the Republican party's long-term national strength hinged on its "farm team" of state and local officeholders. Unlike traditional PACs, which concentrate on campaign contributions, GOPAC focused on recruitment and training. Through GOPAC-sponsored speeches, courses, and training tapes, Gingrich made contact with thousands of rising Republican activists (Kranish 1994). When Gingrich became Speaker in 1995, about one-fourth of House Republicans were graduates of GOPAC training, and more than half had listened to GOPAC tapes (Rosenstiel 1994).

So, whereas traditional legislative leaders have taken their followers' beliefs as they find them, Gingrich pursued a long-range plan to influence the thinking of House Republicans before they even entered Congress. One reason why the House Republican leadership could get so many candidates to sign the contract was that they had long been listening to Gingrich advocate its component ideas.

Gingrich, however, has not been Svengali. Despite his intellectual impact on the House GOP, the rank and file has had to respond to a diverse array of interest groups and constituencies. Gingrich has long recognized the need to accommodate different views and needs among the members. Christopher Shays (R.–Connecticut), among the most liberal House Republicans, has been a Gingrich fan and said, "Newt empowers people. When they come to him with an idea, he encourages them and gives them help. . . . I am one of countless numbers of people who have played a role in something far larger than all of us" (Cohen 1995: 66).

CONCLUSION

The 1994 election was good for political science: by ending the House Republicans' permanent-minority status, it gave scholars a chance to see how a GOP House would differ from a Democratic one. It also gave yet another twist to the Rubik's Cube. With Democrats in the White House and Republicans in control on the Hill, the strategic calculus for the two parties has changed. Which is "government," and which is "opposition"? With Gingrich proclaiming himself "Speaker of the Whole House" and the media treating him like a prime minister, the House GOP initially captured control of the political agenda. For the first time in decades, congressional Republicans eclipsed the White House. There was even talk of a return to the "congressional government" of the late 19th century.

Such speculation is premature: The Cube could turn again. True, House Republicans showed extraordinary unity in voting for the items in the Contract with America. But remember that those items became part of the contract precisely because they enjoyed a preexisting consensus within the GOP. Now the majority, the Republicans must face more divisive issues, which could allow the Democrats to split GOP ranks and score political points with the public. To take full advantage of this opportunity, however, the Democrats need attractive ideas of their own.

In early 1995, the politics of interests apparently took a decisive turn toward the GOP, as PAC money flowed in abundance. But the contributions could have their price. Jim Wright, Coelho, and Rostenkowski all ultimately hurt the Democratic Party by succumbing to the temptations of the political money game. Republicans may not be immune.

They must also beware the broader temptations of power. After 40 years in the majority, House Democrats came to rule in a high-handed manner, routinely squelching the minority party in committee and on the floor. On taking the majority, House Republicans promised a more open process, proclaiming that they sought reform, not revenge. Faced with an extremely combative Democratic minority, they could easily slip from deliberation to retribution.

The House Republican revolution still must contend with the Senate. Although shared minority status and opposition to the president helped bridge the gap in 1994, Senate Republicans did not sign the contract. In the majority, their differences with House Republicans stand out in even bolder relief. The GOP senators tend to be more entrenched in the ways of Washington, as 31 percent served before 1981, compared with only 12 percent of their House GOP colleagues. The Senate's procedures give more play to liberals in both parties, meaning slower action on conservative proposals that fly through the majoritarian House. And the relationship between Majority Leader Bob Dole and Speaker Gingrich remains chilly.

From the moment Gingrich took the gavel, House Democrats sought ethical and political issues with which to bring him down. "We have a long history with him, and you cannot dismiss that history," said John Lewis (D.–Ga.). "He's at risk of being consumed by some of the fires he helped start" (Toner 1995). Republicans reject the comparison between Gingrich's earlier efforts against Speaker Wright and the Democrats' current assaults. They cannot, however, ignore the possibility that these attacks could do damage.

If he survives, he may leave a major imprint on American politics. Through procedural changes, he has enhanced the power of the speakership within the House. Through the THOMAS website system, he has made congressional information accessible to millions of computer users. Through his post-contract address to the nation and his joint appearance with President Clinton in New Hampshire, he has raised the stature of his office in the eyes of the public. These developments did not happen by accident. In a 1981 article in *The Futurist*, he described the changes resulting from information technology and wrote that "it may be the legislator who helps the individual and groups communicate with each other and move toward a more holistic vision. . . . [T]here will be an increasing shift of power away from the executive branch and toward the legislature" (Gingrich and Gingrich 1981: 32).

And what about realignment? Months before the 1980 election, Gingrich spoke with considerable foresight:

> So the first stage of political realignment may happen in 1980. Domination by one party ends, and the other party gains the edge. But this may or may not mean real realignment. Many Republicans are giddy enough just thinking of a one-shot election sweep, but the first step is useless unless we take the next step. We should be thinking of how to turn a temporary rejection of Democratic stewardship into support for genuine Republican government. . . . It's not easy, but it's far from impossible. A combination of the other party's mistakes and defaults and intense creativity

on the part of Republicans everywhere can cause the transformation (*Congressional Record* 1980: 18663–18664).

NOTES

1. If this figure seems high, remember that 42 percent of adults acknowledge having a firearm in the home or garage (U.S. Department of Commerce 1994: 260).

2. The 1993 tax increase was the largest in current dollars but not in inflation-adjusted constant dollars.

4

Court and Country in American Politics: The Democratic Party and the 1994 Election

PHILIP A. KLINKNER

By any measure, the elections of 1994 were a significant reversal for the Democratic party; losing 52 House seats, 8 Senate seats[1], and majority control of both houses of Congress for the first time in 42 years[2] is no small achievement. In comparison, the average midterm loss of House seats for the president's party in the post-war era is 25.5 seats, but the average for the first midterm in an administration is only 13.3 seats (Abramson, Aldrich, and Rohde 1995: 288).

Most analysts have attributed these losses to the unpopularity of Bill Clinton and the political gaffes of his administration, but this is too simplistic. In previous midterm elections since World War II, presidents with unfavorable poll ratings and overseeing less prosperous economies have escaped the kind of drubbing suffered by Clinton and the Democrats in 1994.[3] Instead, the weaknesses of the Clinton administration and the results of the 1994 elections are both symptomatic of larger changes in the political and economic environment. In this chapter, I argue that the results of the 1994 elections stemmed from three interrelated factors—the rise of a "Court-versus-Country" dynamic in contemporary American politics, the decline of the Democratic party, and the political and policy failures of the Clinton administration—that combined together in 1994 to hand the Democratic party its worst defeat since the New Deal and to raise serious questions about its future prospects.

COURT-VERSUS-COUNTRY IN AMERICAN POLITICS

As recently as November 1992, the position of the Democratic party appeared to be uncommonly healthy. Clinton's victory ended the party's long absence from the White House, and saw the Democrats win several states in the South and the West that had long eluded them. Furthermore, the Democrats' continued control of Congress, particularly in the House of Representatives, seemed assured.

Still, the results of the 1992 election portended difficulties for the Democrats. Clinton's 43 percent of the popular vote succeeded only in the context of a three-man race and failed to improve on the party's anemic performance in recent presidential elections. Clinton's result edged out Hubert Humphrey's 42.7 percent in 1968, George McGovern's 37.5 percent in 1972, Jimmy Carter's 41 percent in 1980, and Walter Mondale's 40.6 percent in 1984, but he failed to best Jimmy Carter's 50.1 percent in 1976 or even Michael Dukakis's 45.6 percent in 1988. Additionally, Clinton provided no coattails for his fellow Democrats, who gained no seats in the Senate and lost 10 seats in the House. Among recent presidents, only John Kennedy had shorter coattails, losing 20 House and 2 Senate seats when he was elected in 1960. But Kennedy's lack of coattails seems understandable given the Democratic sweep of 49 House and 17 Senate seats in the 1958 election. In comparison, preceding Clinton's victory in 1992, the Democrats had managed to gain only 9 House seats and 1 Senate seat in 1990 (Stanley and Niemi 1994: 114–15, 124–25).

Most importantly, the circumstances surrounding the 1992 election provided ample evidence of a radically changed political environment. Several observers have commented on the growing volatility of the electorate since the late 1980s (Greider 1992; Phillips 1990, 1993, and 1994; Germond and Witcover 1993; Greenberg 1995). By most accounts, this phenomenon reached a new high in 1992, as voters expressed growing disgust with the federal government, elected officials, special interests, and politics in general, and showed a greater willingness to support the candidacies of outsiders, even those of such diverse figures as Jerry Brown, Pat Buchanan, and Ross Perot.

While many observers have attempted to label this recent political ferment as "populist," this seems inaccurate on two counts. First, the term populist is extremely broad and ill defined and is often used to describe any passion or sentiment, no matter what its ideological substance, that attracts significant popular support. Second, the more specific use of the term populist to refer to the anti–big business, anti–free market, progovernment ideology of the People's Party in the 1890s does not accurately describe the current pro–free market, antigovernment sentiment of current politics.

Others have suggested that these new political trends mark a conservative groundswell. But, this description also seems ill fitting. American conservatism has taken almost as many forms as populism. At various times in the past, conservatives stood for a powerful federal government, an activist program of national economic development, and strong support for law and order, all of which fail to describe the libertarian dimensions of the current electoral discontent (Lind 1995). Moreover, if conservatism is usually defined as the maintenance and preservation of existing institutions, then current popular sentiments are anything but.

Rather than populist or conservative, current American politics is best understood in light of the Court-versus-Country dynamic that has been a recurring theme in Anglo-American politics over the last 300 years. The label was first used to describe the intense political conflict in English politics from the Revolution of 1688 until the mid-eighteenth century.[4] Historians have also used the Court-versus-Country framework to describe the politics of America's early national period, roughly from the Articles of Confederation to the election of Thomas Jefferson.[5]

Politics in both of these periods revolved around the scope and legitimacy of governmental power. On the one side was a Court persuasion, which firmly believed in the necessity of a powerful central government to ensure prosperity, domestic order, and international prestige. "Court apologists were intensely statist. . . . They tried to endow the government with the resources and vigor necessary to command great respect abroad and maintain order at home" (Murrin 1980: 379). To achieve these ends, Court proponents advocated increased taxation, expanded government expenditures, a funded public debt, government guidance of the nation's economic and financial systems, and a bureaucracy large and powerful enough to ensure the attainment of the government's objectives.

In opposition stood the Country advocates who saw the Court proponents as a corrupt elite, antagonistic to the economic interests and cultural values of the nation and striving to increase the power of government to serve their own evil ends. Moreover, Country supporters believed that the Court faction, through its links with financial elite and through political manipulation, had managed to entrench itself in office, upsetting the political system's natural equilibrium. Once free from the usual checks and balances, they claimed that the Court elite would then set out to further aggrandize power and debase the natural rights and liberties of the people. In response, the Country supporters advocated limited government, reduction of government debt and spending, reduction and/or reform of taxes, and structural and procedural reforms of the political system as a means of restoring accountability and popular control to the government.

These Court-versus-Country themes are readily discernible in contemporary American politics. To a large extent, with its emphasis on a powerful federal government to provide direction and leadership on a range of issues, from macroeconomic management to civil rights to environmental protection, modern liberal ideology reflects the Court tradition of earlier times. In addition, the tools of increased expenditures and government debt used by liberals, were also used by the English Court supporters and their American descendants, the Federalists.

The Country attitude, with its "plain distrust of government as such, and a considerable sense of apprehension at its ever spreading tentacles" (Holmes 1987: 121), is readily apparent in current popular attitudes. Like their Country predecessors, critics of the current political system oppose excessive government, as reflected in debt, high taxes, increased spending, and extensive regulation. In particular, they share the traditional Country concern for governmental corruption, especially the ways in which elected officials, bureaucrats, and special interests combine to create an entrenched governmental elite, unresponsive and unaccountable to the public interest. In the words of Ross Perot, "The British aristocracy we drove out in our Revolution has been replaced by our own version: a political nobility that is immune to the people's will. They have created through our campaign and lobbying laws a series of incentives that corrupt the intent of the Constitution" (Perot 1992: 24). Criticisms of entrenched congressional incumbents echo the attacks of English Country advocates on the corrupt placemen and courtiers whom they believed were destroying the House of Commons. In fact, proposals for congressional term limits closely resemble the Place Acts advocated by English Country members for "purging the House of Commons from the dead weight of court officers and dependents" (Holmes 1987: 130). In addition, James Madison's concern in 1791 that, "The stock-jobbers will become the pretorian band of the Government, at once its tool & its tyrant; bribed by its largesses, & overawing it by clamours & combinations" sounds very similar to contemporary concerns regarding special interests and their role in government policy making (Elkins and McKitrick 1993: 244).

The general tone and conduct of politics in these eras has also been reflected in that of modern America. In a statement that accurately sums up current popular attitudes regarding American politics, one historian described the politics of eighteenth century England in the following way: "Deceit and double dealing on the part of kings, ministers, and politicians, and cynicism on the part of the people, produced an appalling debasement of politics. Nothing was taken on trust or at its state face-value. Self-interest, hypocrisy and corruption were taken for granted. Politicians, like revelers in a carnival, were assumed to be wearing masks in order to conceal their true features, and to aid them in the seduction of their victims" (Jones 1978: 2–3). The conflict between the Hamiltonians and Jeffersonians was also marked by the high levels of cynicism and distrust found today. One can easily imagine Rush Limbaugh as a latter-day version of Philip Freneau, the Jeffersonian editor whose gifts at calumny bedeviled his Federalists opponents as much as they delighted his fellow partisans (Elkins and McKitrick 1993: 282–92; Banning 1978: 167–78).

The rise of these Country attitudes in contemporary America seems to have resulted from a number of forces, one of which was the civil rights movement of the 1960s and the ensuing white backlash. As many commentators have noted, the federal government's support for racial liberalism in the 1960s profoundly alienated large numbers of white Americans. In addition, to the extent that they identified racial liberalism with the federal government, many whites began to question the scope and legitimacy of the governmental power on a range of issues from taxes to welfare to the criminal justice system (Edsall and Edsall 1991; Dionne 1991; Horowitz 1986).

Along with white alienation over civil rights, the lackluster performance of the U.S. economy over the last 20 years has contributed to popular distrust of government. From the New Deal until the early 1970s, economic prosperity and the identification of that prosperity with governmental activity contributed to popular support for the political system. With the end of the post–World War II economic boom, that identification has reversed itself as many Americans have increasingly come to identify the government with stagnant economic growth and growing class inequalities (Dionne 1991; Phillips 1990, 1993, and 1994).[6]

Vietnam and Watergate also added to public cynicism toward government. In the case of Vietnam, many liberals began to question the benevolence of a government that could carry out a savage and unpopular war in a faraway land for no clear reason, while many conservatives came to question the competence of a government that could lose the nation's first war, and to a small and technologically backward country at that. With Watergate, the spectacle of Richard Nixon's abuse of power, law-breaking, and bold-faced lies to the American people profoundly shook public confidence in the political system.

Finally, the end of the Cold War also undermined support for the federal government. So long as Americans believed in the existence of the Soviet threat, then they were willing to support the necessity of a powerful federal government to meet that threat. Moreover, each day that Americans awoke to find that the Soviets had not launched their missiles or invaded Western Europe provided evidence of the federal government's effectiveness. The fall of the Soviet Union undermined much of the necessity for a strong federal government and made its accomplishments less visible.

As a result of these events and developments, by the early 1990s, Country sentiments were evident among much of the public. In 1964, over 70 percent of the public said that they could trust Washington to do what was right most or all of the time; by early 1994, only 19 percent expressed similar confidence (Phillips 1994: 7). In 1964, when asked, "Would you say the government is run by a few big interests looking out for themselves or that it is run for the benefit of all people," nearly 40 percent more people agreed with the latter than with the former. In 1992 that sentiment had reversed itself, with 60 percent more people believing that the government was run for the benefit of special interests than those who believed it was run for the benefit of all (Stanley and Niemi 1994: 169). As a consequence of this marked increase in public cynicism toward government, politics increasingly revolved around such Country-oriented themes as tax revolts, anti-incumbent movements, term limits, support for independent and third-party candidates, concern over the role of special interests and corruption, attacks on congressional pay raises, political reform, and anger at policy gridlock, among others.

COURT-VERSUS-COUNTRY POLITICS AND THE DECLINE OF THE DEMOCRATIC PARTY

Though highly developed by the early 1990s, the Court-versus-Country divisions did not neatly overlay the partisan division between Democrats and Republicans until after the election of Clinton in 1992. Prior to this, Watergate, divided control of government, and the distinctly Court background and outlook (despite his Texas affectations) of George Bush prevented the Republicans from capitalizing on this divide by clearly labeling themselves as the Country party and the Democrats as the Court party. During the 1992 campaign, Democrats Paul

Tsongas and Jerry Brown, Republican Pat Buchanan, and independent Ross Perot also sought to highlight these Court-versus-Country distinctions, further obscuring its partisan aspects. In fact, Bill Clinton successfully played to Country sentiments through a variety of gestures in his election campaign: traveling by bus through small-town America, denouncing Washington corruption, attacking Bush's aristocratic bearing and disdain for domestic policy, extolling the virtues of ordinary Americans who "do the work, pay the taxes, raise the kids, and play by the rules," and distancing himself from traditional liberalism by labeling himself a "New Democrat"(Clinton and Gore 1992: 217, Germond and Witcover 1993).

Still, the emergence of Court-and-Country politics spelled trouble for the Democrats. As the party of governmental activism, the Democrats were bound to suffer from the rise of popular cynicism toward government. At the same time that Clinton won the White House, voters preferred having "government cost less in taxes but provide fewer services" to having "government provide more services but cost more in taxes" by 54 to 38 percent (Milkis and Nelson 1994: 395).[7]

Compounding the problem of the Democrats' ideological identification with Court politics was their party's organizational decline over the last three decades. During this period, the Democrats' once robust party organizations atrophied to the point of nonexistence or irrelevance. The national party organizations, represented by the Democratic National Committee (DNC) and the two congressional campaign committees, have devolved into fund-raising machines and campaign service providers, mainly for congressional incumbents, and lack any meaningful grassroots organization. The state and local parties are but a shadow of their former selves; their ability to influence the party's presidential nominations eroded by procedural reforms, and many now serve as little more than conduits for the flow of soft money from Political Action Committees (PACs) and wealthy contributors into the coffers of the national party. In the words of journalist William Greider, "The Democratic party, as a political organization, is no longer quite real itself. The various strands of personal communication and loyalty that once made it representative and responsive to the people are gone" (Greider 1992: 247).

Among extra-party organizations, the situation is little better. The Democratic Leadership Council, which once aspired (at least rhetorically) to offer a new base and a new vision for the party, never advanced far beyond its origins as a factional grouping propped up by PAC donations. Labor unions, which once provided the backbone of Democratic party organization and resources, have declined precipitously and now organize little over 10 percent of American workers and exert a diminishing influence on their remaining members.

The Democrats' organizational demise severed almost all their links with the grass roots. Consequently, by the early 1990s, most voters had little direct association with the Democratic party. Instead of the being an important part of the civic life of many ordinary Americans as it was in earlier days, the party had become an abstract entity, easily distorted by Republican attacks and visible only in the distant and often unpopular national-level politicians covered by the media.

Without party organizations to link them to Democratic politicians, it became even easier for voters to see the Democrats as a Court element comprised of a distant and unresponsive elite.

The image of the Democrats as the Court party was grounded in reality as well as perception. As voters lost touch with the party, the party lost touch with them. Where once they had been able to listen to the needs and concerns of real people voiced in party clubhouses and union halls, Democratic politicians increasingly relied upon the social and financial elites whom they resembled and with whom they increasingly associated. As a result, the Democratic party proved either unable or unwilling to respond to the growing Country anger at government in general and the Democratic party in particular.[8]

The organizational demise of the Democratic party also damaged its capacity to serve as a mobilizing institution. Such a capacity is vital to the party since the core of its support comes from those people who lack the educational and economic resources necessary to mobilize themselves. Without organizations like parties and unions to inform and encourage them regarding politics and elections, ordinary voters in general and likely Democratic voters in particular are far more inclined to stay at home (Rosenstone and Hansen 1993).

Finally, the decline of the institutions composing the Democratic party also created difficulties regarding campaign finance. Strong party organizations and powerful unions that persuaded and mobilized voters made the Democrats less dependent upon money for their political operations. What money the party did need came largely from these same sources that generally reflected the same interests as rank-and-file Democratic voters. As party organizations and unions waned, the Democrats were forced to rely on more expensive forms of campaigning: media appeals, high-priced consultants, public opinion polls, and paid campaign workers. To obtain the money that they needed, the Democrats turned to donations from special interests. These special interests, however, were less compatible with the interests of Democratic voters and were inclined to give money only in return for the access and favors granted by Democratic incumbents in Congress. Consequently, the Democratic party's actions and interests were increasingly centered around its congressional incumbents and their special-interest allies, a dangerous burden in the Court-versus-Country division of American politics.

In contrast to the demise of the Democrats, the Republican party in this period underwent an organizational renaissance, vastly expanding the capabilities of its national party institutions and increasing its ability to reach and mobilize grassroots voters through conservative interests groups like the Christian Coalition and the National Rifle Association (Green 1995). By developing a sophisticated direct-mail fund-raising operation, the Republicans abandoned their fat-cat image and relied on small donations from numerous individual donors, thereby avoiding the conflict between money and votes that has bedeviled the Democrats in recent years. Finally, the advent of satellite broadcasting and conservative talk radio gave the Republican party an important means by which party leaders could contact and listen to grassroots conservatives (Klinkner 1994: 139–41, 193–96).

As a result of its organizational decline, by the early 1990s, the Democratic party's institutional base consisted of little more than congressional incumbents. This development was both sad and ironic for the Democrats. In the 1820s and 1830s, the rise of the Jacksonian Democratic party marked the emergence of the first mass-based party organizations, and throughout their history, the Democrats have been able to rely upon an array of party and nonparty organizations to link it to the grassroots and to sustain it through good times and bad. With the decline of these organizations, one could argue that by the early 1990s the Democratic party reverted back to its pre-Jacksonian form—an elite clique centered around the party's elected officials in Congress.

COURT-VERSUS-COUNTRY POLITICS AND THE CLINTON ADMINISTRATION

Following the election of Bill Clinton, the Democratic party found itself in a high-risk position. The party now controlled the White House for the first time in over a decade, and this, along with its control of Congress, provided Democrats with the opportunity to implement policies which could help to revitalize the party and its constituent elements. More importantly, by enacting legislation that would restore prosperity and reduce economic uncertainty for average Americans, they could help rebuild confidence in the federal government and minimize the Court-versus-Country divisions that worked increasingly to their disadvantage.

Still, the election made the Democrats extremely vulnerable. As mentioned previously, unified control of the White House and Congress by the Democrats removed the partisan ambiguity regarding Court-and-Country divisions; from now on the Democrats could clearly be labeled as the party of government. Furthermore, the Democrats knew that if they were unable to enact the proposals mentioned earlier, they would fail to arrest their party's decline and deepen public cynicism toward government and themselves. Whatever the risks it was confronting, the Clinton administration appeared blissfully ignorant of them and in its first two years in office committed a series of political and policy errors that weakened the Democratic party and exacerbated Country antagonisms toward it.

The first of these errors was the abandonment of political reform, a central focus of Country sentiments, as an integral part of its agenda. In 1992 Clinton campaigned on a number of Country themes, denouncing a Congress that "raised its pay and guarded its perks while most Americans worked harder for less money" and claiming that "the last 12 years were nothing less than an extended hunting season for high-priced lobbyists and Washington influence peddlers" (Greenberg 1995: 213; Phillips 1994: 43). On election night, in his victory speech to the nation, he said:

I think perhaps the most important thing that we understand here in the heartland of Arkansas is the need to reform the political system, to reduce the influence of special interests and give more influence back to the kind of people that are in this crowd tonight by the tens of thousands. And I will work . . . to do that (Rauch 1994: 4).

This promise was soon forgotten. Clinton quickly realized that continuing his attack on special interests meant taking on some of the most important elements in his own party—congressional Democrats and the Democratic elements of the Washington lobbying community—thereby jeopardizing his other policy proposals. And this was something that Bill Clinton was unwilling to do. According to journalist Elizabeth Drew:

> Needing as he did congressional allies, Clinton talked a lot less about political reform legislation, and made less effort to achieve it, than had been suggested in the campaign. In fact, he hardly talked about it at all. He had concluded that if he wanted to get a lot done quickly, more quickly than perhaps Congress wanted, he had to work with it, push it, be a partner to it. . . . Despite Clinton's campaign pledge to bring "change" to Washington, its lobbyist/money culture remained undisturbed (Drew 1994: 375).

In addition to abandoning his political reform proposals, the President reinforced his administration's Court image by relying heavily on the Washington Democratic political establishment to staff his administration. Among those initially tapped to serve were Senator Lloyd Bentsen as Secretary of the Treasury, Congressman Les Aspin as Secretary of Defense, Democratic National Committee (DNC) Chairman and Washington lobbyist Ron Brown as Secretary of Commerce, Congressman Mike Espy as Secretary of Agriculture, and Congressman Leon Panetta as Director of the Office of Management and Budget.

Perhaps no appointment reflected the Clinton administration's cozying up the Washington Democratic establishment as much as that of Tony Coelho, who coordinated the efforts of the White House and the DNC during the 1994 campaign. Coelho served as a veritable poster boy for Country antagonism toward Washington. As a former House member, head of the Democratic Congressional Campaign Committee (DCCC), and majority whip, he was instrumental in helping incumbent Democrats shake down PACs for contributions during the 1980s. In 1989, he resigned his seat after the discovery that he had committed various ethics violations and became a managing director in the investment banking firm of Wertheim Schroeder—hardly the type of figure likely allay popular suspicions about Washington (Shalit 1995).

Clinton's decision to ally himself with congressional Democrats and the Washington Democratic establishment appears to have been a Faustian bargain. While gaining support for his economic program, the President tied his fortunes to perhaps the most unpopular elements in government and further increased the identification of the Democrats as the Court party. While many observers have noted that too close of an identification with Bill Clinton spelled political trouble for many Democrats in Congress, it also seems likely that the Clinton administration was hurt by its identification with Congress.

A series of ethical scandals further validated the perception of the Clinton administration as part and parcel of a corrupt Washington Court elite. Agriculture Secretary Espy resigned in 1994 after accepting gifts from a firm that had an interest in the regulations set by his department, and the Justice Department appointed special prosecutors to look into possible ethical misdeeds by Commerce Secretary Ron Brown and Housing Secretary Henry Cisneros. Federal prosecutors also indicted House Way and Means Committee Chairman, Dan Rostenkowski, a key supporter of the president's budget and health plans, for misusing office expenses. On top of all of this was the president and the first lady's involvement in the Whitewater affair. The accusations of cozy real estate deals, politically motivated loans, too-good-to-be-true winnings in the cattle futures market, and campaign finance irregularities composed exactly the sort of corrupt dealings that modern Country advocates have come to associate with governing elites.

Along with the abandonment of political reform and increasing identification in the minds of the public with Court corruption, the Clinton administration failed to develop economic proposals which would ease the growing economic insecurity that had done much to generate Country antagonisms toward Washington and that needed to be allayed in order to restore public support for activist government. One aspect of this failure in economic policy was the administration's early decision to sacrifice some of its more populist economic proposals at the altar of deficit reduction. This strategy met with the approval of Federal Reserve Chairman Alan Greenspan and the bond market, but despite Clinton advisor James Carville's comment that if he were reincarnated, he would want to come back as the bond market since then "you can intimidate everybody," the bond market has little ability to provide the types of tangible and lasting economic benefits necessary to build and sustain a majority coalition for the Democratic party or to allay Country fears that the government is not acting in the interest of ordinary citizens (Phillips 1994: 77; Woodward 1993: 125–26). The focus on deficit reduction also forced the administration to propose a set of regressive energy and gasoline taxes (the latter of which was finally enacted), which promised to further pinch the pocketbooks of ordinary Americans. Moreover, by so quickly and cavalierly jettisoning some of his central campaign promises, Clinton created more doubts about his promise to end "politics as usual" and increased country cynicism towards his administration.

The Clinton administration also erred in its staunch support for the North American Free Trade Agreement (NAFTA). Not only does the agreement put further downward pressure on U.S. wages, thereby increasing the income inequality at the heart of the country's anger at government, but in aggressively pursuing passage of the agreement, the Clinton administration put itself in conflict with organized labor. By attacking one of the Democratic party's most important constituencies, the administration succeeded in further weakening the Democratic coalition and exacerbating the party's organizational decline. Also, the time and resources spent by the White House and labor lobbying for and against the agreement would have been better spent on measures of benefit to both groups, such as lobbying for health care reform, an overhaul of campaign finance, or upgrading the organizational capacity of the Democratic party.

Finally, the Clinton administration failed to deliver on the central component of its economic agenda, health care reform. Health care reform represented the type of a broad-based government benefit program that had engendered popular support for activist government in the past and provided the glue which held together the Democratic party since the New Deal. Passage of health care reform would have helped to ameliorate Court-and-Country divisions by providing evidence that the government can work to resolve complex issues in a way that benefits average Americans. Alas, with the demise of health care reform, the Democrats failed to use the power of government to revitalize their coalition and in the process furthered the public's impression that government is incapable of acting in the national interest.

Despite Clinton's 1992 campaign promises, his administration proved unwilling or unable to alleviate the economic dislocation underlying the Country cynicism against government. Despite a robust economy, 59 percent of those polled in October 1994 believed that the economy was still in a recession (Abramson, Aldrich, and Rohde 1995: 324). Exit polls in 1994 showed that only 21 percent of voters thought that their standard of living was getting better, while 55 percent though it was unchanged and 23 percent thought it was worse (Wilcox 1995: 9, 19).

To the Clinton administration, these were mistaken perceptions, the result of Republican propaganda and its own failure to "get its message out." In fact, a closer look at the economic data shows that while the economy as a whole was growing, the benefits of that growth were concentrated among the wealthy, and most Americans saw their economic situation decline. According to Isaac Shapiro of the Center on Budget and Policy Priorities, "The trend appears to be that the only people who fared well during the recent recovery were upper income."[9] Other data indicate that while corporate profits and the stock market might have been booming in 1994, the real wages and compensation of workers from March 1994 to March 1995 fell by 2.3 percent (Bureau of Labor Statistics 1995). Finally, during the first two years of the Clinton administration, the number of people without health insurance increased as did the number of people in poverty (Pear 1994). One could argue that if the essence of politics is to reward your friends and punish your enemies, the Clinton administration in its first two years in office managed to do exactly the opposite.

COURT AND COUNTRY POLITICS IN THE 1994 ELECTION

The mistakes and failures of the Clinton administration provided an opportunity for the Republicans to paint themselves as the Country party and the Democrats as the Court party, and this they did with a vengeance. The centerpiece of the Republican campaign, the Contract with America, was replete with Country themes. According to it, the Republicans sought to "restore the bonds of trust between the people and their elected representatives . . . To restore accountability to Congress. To end its cycle of scandal and disgrace. To make us all proud again of the way free people govern themselves" (Gillespie and Schellhas 1994: 7–8). The Contract's specific provisions also stressed such typical Country issues as political reform, including reform of Congressional procedures and term limits; tax reduction; and limited government.

In the face of this attack, the Democrats were unable to respond effectively. Many Democratic incumbents, facing the prospect of their first difficult campaign in years, chose to retire, further diminishing Democratic chances. For those who chose to run again, the usual tactic of turning popular resentment of Washington to their advantage by stressing their local roots and local accomplishments no longer worked. Their identification with the Clinton administration, congressional scandals, and the legislative failures of the 103rd Congress, left them with little place to hide as the full force of Country sentiments fell upon them.

The impact of Country sentiments on the defeat of the Democrats can be seen from the behavior of the 1992 Perot voters, the group that seems to best symbolize modern Country sentiments. For example, polls taken after the 1994 election indicate that these voters were intensely antiestablishment[10] and were primarily concerned with the types of political reform associated with Country ideology, with 59 percent saying that their first priority for changing the political system was that "the government should be given back to the people by reducing the influence of special interests and lobbyists" (Greenberg 1995: 256).

The shift of Perot voters away from the Democrats in 1994 was staggering. In 1992, 54 percent of these voters supported Democratic House candidates. In 1994, however, they abandoned the Democrats and supported the Republicans by a margin of two to one, 67 to 33 percent (Abramson, Aldrich, and Rohde: 312, 331.) The movement of Perot voters was so decisive that only white, born-again Christians, self-identified Republicans, and self-identified conservatives supported Republican candidates more strongly (Wilcox 1995: 18–19).

A closer examination of the Perot voters indicates the influence they had on Democratic losses. As Table 4.1 shows, in seats that switched from the Democrats to the Republicans in 1994, the average 1992 Perot vote was 20.5 percent; in seats that remained Democratic, however, the average Perot vote was only 16.0 percent. This difference is found in all regions, but it is most striking in the North, where the difference between seats switching to Republicans and those held by Democrats was 5.4 percent.

Another way of looking at the impact of the Perot vote is by looking at Democratic performance in seats that had an above-average Perot vote in 1992 and in those that had a below-average Perot vote. As Table 4.2 indicates, Democratic losses were significantly greater in those seats with an above-average Perot vote (19 percent or greater). For example, although the Democrats lost just 14.6 percent of their seats in districts with a below-average Perot vote; they lost

TABLE 4.1 Average 1992 Perot Vote in Democratic Seats

	Total	Vote in Seats Switching to Republicans (%)	N	Vote in Seats Held by Democrats (%)	N	Difference (%)
All seats	256	20.5	56	16.0	200	4.5
North	173	22.6	37	17.2	136	5.4
South	83	16.3	19	15.0	64	1.3
Northeast	57	20.0	6	15.0	51	5.0
Midwest	51	21.6	16	18.6	45	3.0
West	55	24.9	15	18.0	40	6.9

SOURCE: Data compiled by the author from Duncan and Lawrence (1995).

30.3 percent of the seats in districts with an above-average Perot vote. This pattern is found in both open and incumbent-held seats and in each region.

Strategic Democratic incumbents also seemed to have picked up on the Perot voters' dissatisfaction with the Democratic party. As Jacobsen and Kernell (1983) point out, electoral difficulties are often a prod for incumbents to retire. In Table 4.3, the average Perot vote is looked at in terms of open seats and seats with incumbent candidates running. The table indicates a significantly higher average Perot vote in Democratic open seats than in those with incumbents running, particularly in the North where the Perot vote was the strongest. This suggests that discontent among Perot voters may have hastened the strategic retirements of some Democratic incumbents. In contrast to the Democratic seats, no similar pattern emerges in the vote in Republican seats, suggesting that strategic politicians' concerns about angry Perot voters were limited to the Democrats.

The decline of the Democratic party organization and the failure of the Clinton administration's economic policies also meant that the party had little with which to mobilize its core constituencies. This is evident in a class skew in the 1994 election that was even more pronounced than usual, as described in Table 4.1. Between 1990 and 1994, voter turnout among those making $50,000 a year or more rose from 59.2 percent to 60.1 percent, but turnout among those making under $5,000 fell from 32.2 percent to 19.9 percent and among those making between $5,000 and $10,000 from 30.9 percent to 23.3 percent. In addition, while white turnout rose slightly, from 46.7 percent in 1990 to 46.9 percent in 1994, black turnout fell from 39.2 percent to 37 percent, and Hispanic turnout fell from 23.1 percent to 19.1 percent.

CONCLUSION

The impact of the 1994 elections on the Democratic party goes beyond just the number of seats lost or even the loss of control of Congress. As mentioned previously, by the early 1990s the Democratic party consisted of little more than its congressional party, and with the loss of Congress, the institutional base of the party becomes hard to identify. Not only have the Democrats lost their stronghold in

TABLE 4.2 1994 Democratic Performance and the 1992 Perot Vote

Seat Type	1992 Perot Vote	Total Seats	Seats Held by Democrats	Percentage Held (%)	Seats Switching to Republicans	Percentage Switching (%)
All	Above average	119	83	69.7	36	30.3
	Below average	137	117	85.4	20	14.6
Incumbents	Above average	99	78	78.8	21	21.2
	Below average	125	112	89.6	13	10.4
Open	Above average	20	5	25.0	15	75.0
	Below average	12	5	41.7	7	58.3
North	Above average	98	68	69.4	30	30.6
	Below average	75	68	90.7	7	9.3
South	Above average	21	15	71.4	6	28.6
	Below average	62	49	79.0	13	21.0
Northeast	Above average	25	21	84.0	4	16.0
	Below average	32	30	93.8	2	6.3
Midwest	Above average	38	26	68.4	12	31.6
	Below average	23	19	82.6	4	17.4
West	Above average	35	21	60.0	14	40.0
	Below average	20	19	95.0	1	5.0

NOTE: Above average Perot vote is 19 percent or greater. Below average Perot vote is less than 19 percent.
SOURCE: Compiled by the author from Duncan and Lawrence (1995).

TABLE 4.3 Average Perot Vote in Open Seats and Seats with Incumbents Running

	Vote in Seats with Incumbents Running (%)	N	Vote in Open Seats (%)	N	Difference (%)
Democrats					
All	16.9	224	19.4	32	2.5
North	18.0	156	22.1	17	4.1
South	14.6	68	16.4	15	1.8
Northeast	15.3	53	18.5	4	3.2
Midwest	18.9	53	22.9	8	4.0
West	19.8	50	23.6	5	3.8
Republicans					
All	20.3	156	21.0	22	0.7
North	21.8	108	21.7	16	−.1
South	16.9	48	19.2	6	2.3
Northeast	19.7	34	19.6	8	−.1
Midwest	21.7	41	21.0	3	−.7
West	24.2	33	25.4	5	1.2

SOURCE: Compiled by the author from Duncan and Lawrence (1995).

TABLE 4.4 Reported Voter Turnout by Family Income and Race, 1990–1994

Family Category	Turnout 1990 (%)	Turnout 1994 (%)	Change (%)
Total	46.3%	44.6%	−1.7
Under $5,000	32.2%	19.9	−12.3
$5,000–$9,999	30.9	23.3	−7.6
$10,000–$14,999	37.7	32.7	−5.0
$15,000–$24,999	40.2	39.9	−1.3
$25,000–$34,999	46.4	44.4	−2.0
$35,000–$49,999	51.0	49.8	−1.2
$50,000 and above	59.2	60.1	0.9
Whites	46.7	46.9	0.2
Blacks	39.2	37.0	−2.2
Hispanics	23.1	19.1	−4.0

SOURCES: "Voter Turnout Falls Sharply Among the Less Affluent," *New York Times*, June 11, 1995: A16; U.S. Bureau of the Census, "Characteristics of the Voting-Age Population Reported Having Voted: November 1994," Available on World Wide Web, http://www.census.gov/ftp/pub/population/socdemo/voting; and U.S. Bureau of the Census, "Voting and Registration in the Election of November 1990," *Current Population Reports, Population Characteristics Series,* P-20, Number 453.

Congress, but they seem unlikely to return in the foreseeable future. Many of the seats lost in 1994 were in districts which had been trending toward the Republican party for years, and the remaining Democratic incumbents face an even-more-hostile electoral environment of diminished fund raising prospects and better-financed Republican challengers. Both of the factors are reflected in the number of Democrats who have chosen to either switch parties or announce their retirements since the election, developments which have further diminished Democratic chances in 1996. In addition, the opportunity to revitalize the party offered by Clinton's control of the White House is extremely limited now that he faces a Republican Congress.

Even more dismal for the Democrats is the fact that they do not have an organizational base to fall back on. After previous election losses, the Democrats could rely on their bases of support in unions and political machines to sustain and rejuvenate them and their links with ordinary voters. But no such option exists today. In this new environment, the Democrats will likely suffer through a period of intense difficulty, as they face dismal election prospects and their factions fight over what remains of the party.

Still, not all is grim for the Democrats. While regaining control of Congress seems out of reach in the near term, retaining the White House and thereby retaining some control over their own destiny is certainly within the realm of possibility for the Democrats. Bill Clinton is a remarkably protean political character, shifting back and forth from liberal to conservative, from Arkansas populist to Yale Law School and Rhodes Scholar policy wonk whenever conditions demand. His ability to resurrect his reelection chances should not be dismissed.

One should also keep in mind that despite all the talk of the 1994 election making Clinton's defeat all but certain, major losses in past midterm elections have not been clear harbingers of party switches in the next presidential elections. As Table 4.5 indicates, in 6 elections since World War II (those in 1946, 1950, 1958, 1966, 1974, and 1982), the president's party has posted midterm seat losses larger than the average loss of 25.5 seats across all elections in the period. In 2 of these elections (1946 and 1982), the president's party went on retain control of the White House, while in the other 4 (in 1950, 1958, 1966, and 1974), it lost in the next presidential elections. But, in 3 of the 4 elections when the president's party lost the White House following big midterm losses (in 1960, 1968, and 1976), it did so only by the narrowest of margins, suggesting that big midterm losses do not preordain defeat in the next presidential election. One should also remember that the last 2 switches in control of the White House (in 1992 and 1980) followed relatively strong midterm performances by the president's party.

Nor is their any guarantee that the Republicans will be any more successful than the Democrats at alleviating the concerns of Country voters. In fact, many of the current realities of Republican politics and governance contradict the Country rhetoric that the Republicans used so successfully in 1994. Despite their desire in the 1994 elections for "wresting power from the special interest groups

TABLE 4.5 Relationship Between Midterm Seat Losses and Control of the White House

Midterm	House Seats Lost by President's Party	Change in Control in Next Election?	Winner's Margin in Next Election (%)
1946	55	No	4.4
1950	29	Yes	10.7
1954	18	No	15.4
1958	47	Yes	0.2
1962	4	No	22.6
1966	47	Yes	0.7
1970	12	No	23.2
1974	43	Yes	2.1
1978	11	Yes	9.7
1982	26	No	17.2
1986	5	No	7.8
1990	9	Yes	5.6
Average	25.5		

SOURCE: Stanley and Niemi (1994): 114–15, 124–25.

and returning it to the people," now that they are in office, the Republicans are proving even more willing and adept than the Democrats at developing their own links with organized interests (Gillespie and Schellhas 1994: 14). Since the election, the Republicans have begun a brazen and aggressive effort to shake down PACs for contributions to their incumbents (Berke 1995b). Congressional Republicans have also increased the policy making influence of corporate lobbyists by allowing them to actually draft bills on issues in which their firms have large financial interests (Cloud 1995). Given their association with corporate special interests and newly increased access to PAC money, it is doubtful that the Republicans will seriously attempt the political reforms sought by Country advocates. Finally, Republican economic policies seem unlikely to reverse the growing income inequality that underlies much of the current Country sentiment.

Ironically, the bad news for the Democratic party in the 1994 may also be the good news. While losing control of Congress will cause the party immense difficulties in the short term, in the long term the loss may finally force the Democratic party to undertake the rethinking and rebuilding that it has so long needed but avoided. As long as the party controlled Congress, it remained mired in the status quo. Restoring the party's links to the grass roots was unnecessary so long as PAC money assured the near invincibility of Democratic congressional incumbents, and rethinking the party's purpose and program was inconceivable when doing so would have meant alienating its congressional incumbents and their special interest benefactors. Freed from these constraints, the Democratic party can finally begin the difficult but essential task of rebuilding its organization, restoring its links with the grass roots, and developing policies that better represent its core constituencies. If it fails in this task, it can look forward to more elections like that in 1994.

NOTES

1. The loss in Senate seats rose to 9 the day after the election when Alabama Democrat Richard Shelby announced that he was switching parties and to 10 a few months later when Colorado Democrat Ben Nighthorse Campbell also decided to cross the aisle.

2. While it has been only 40 years (1954) since the Republicans last controlled Congress, it has been 42 years (1952) since the Republicans had been able to win a majority of seats in the elections for the House and Senate.

3. For example, in 1982 the Republicans had lost only 26 seats, despite the fact that the economy had been in the worst recession since the Great Depression. Also, the inability of political science models to come even reasonably close to predicting the outcome of the election provides evidence for this assertion (Wilcox 1995: 9; Abramson, Aldrich, and Rohde 1995: 323)

4. Court-and-Country divisions both preceded and carried on past this period, but it was during this time when the conflict was at its height. In addition, while the Whigs were generally associated in this era with Court persuasion and the Tories with the Country, the partisan orientation of the Court-and-Country divide was highly fluid, and thus, party labels provide only a very rough guide to the often-shifting nature of English politics in decades after 1688.

5. The best sources on Court-and-Country politics in England in this period are Webb (1980), Jones (1978), Owen (1974), and Holmes (1987). Analyses of Court-and-Country politics in America's early national period and their connections to earlier Court-and-Country divisions in English history are found in Elkins and McKitrick (1993), Banning (1978), Murrin (1980), and Pocock (1975).

Though the connection is not explicitly made by historians, there are also elements of Court-and-Country politics in America during the Progressive Era. Once again, public opinion became deeply concerned over the corruption of politics. Progressive reformers, in their desire to institute the direct election of U.S. Senators, anticorruption laws, civil service, and limits on the power of political parties, bore more than a passing resemblance to the Country politicians in England 200 years previously who advocated Place Acts to make government more responsive to the public. Much like the Anti-Federalists and Jeffersonians of the previous century, they sought lower tariffs and reform of the system of taxation, and they feared the corrosive effect that industrialization and urbanization would have on the health of both political and civil society. While there are also important dissimilarities, the connections between these periods deserve closer scrutiny.

6. Periods of Court-versus-Country politics seem to have overlapped important economic transformations. In eighteenth century England and in America's early national period, Court-and-Country divisions arose out of the development of a commercial economy in the cities and the movement away from a political and economic system based upon agriculture and landed wealth. If one extends the Court-and-Country description to the Progressive Era, it would seem to correspond to the nation's shift toward urbanization and industrialization. In contemporary America, the rise of Court-and-Country politics has come in conjunction with the shift away from a domestic industrial economy to an information and service economy increasingly tied to global markets.

7. One can further add that previous settlements of Court-and-Country disputes in American history favored the Country side. The Jeffersonians triumphed while the

Federalists disappeared. A century later, Progressive reformers won out over the party bosses. In eighteenth century England, however, the settlement favored the Court side (Elkins and McKitrick 1993: 21).

8. For the best description of the modern Democratic party, see Greider (1992). On a more personal note, research on an earlier project required me to interview people who had worked in the Democratic and Republican parties from the late 1950s to the present. In the course of these interviews, I found that the Republicans were scattered about the country. The Democrats, in contrast, were almost exclusively found on Capitol Hill or in Washington, D.C., K Street lobbying firms.

9. See "Number of People Living in Poverty Edged Up in '93." *The Wall Street Journal*. October 7, 1994: A2.

10. Defined as "a belief that the system rewards those who get around the rules and that public officials and corporations are indifferent to the public interest" (Greenburg 1995: 251).

5

Money in the 1994 Elections and Beyond

THEODORE J. EISMEIER
PHILIP H. POLLOCK III

After nearly a decade of sluggish growth, the economy of campaign finance surged again in the 1994 congressional elections. The $616 million spent by House and Senate candidates in the general elections was 16 percent above 1992 levels, and another $108 million was spent by candidates in special elections and by losers in primaries. As usual, it was extravagance—the more than $28 million Michael Huffington contributed in California to his own campaign for Senate and the almost $21 million raised by Virginia's Oliver North in his campaign for Senate—that gained the most attention. By some accounts, however, such celebrated cases were emblematic of a broader Republican advantage in campaign finance, which helped produce a political cataclysm. Comparing the destruction of the Democratic Congress in 1994 to the destruction of Pompeii and Herculaneum by the eruption of Mount Vesuvius, an observer noted in the aftermath of the election that "sudden, violent changes in an ocean of money are less visually dramatic than shifts in the Bay of Naples. But long before the Federal Election Commission unveils its final report on the financing of the 1994 midterm elections, it is already clear that in the weeks before the explosion that buried alive the Democratic Party, changes in financial flows occurred that were as remarkable as anything Pliny and his terrified cohorts witnessed 2,000 years ago: A sea of money that had been flowing reliably to Congressional Democrats and the party that controlled the White House abruptly reversed direction and began gushing in torrents to Republican challengers"(Ferguson 1994: 792).

However, now that the Federal Election Commission (FEC) has closed the books on the 1994 midterm elections, the evidence shows that there was no tidal wave of Republican money, at least not a wave large enough to explain the extraordinary results of the election. The fact that money continued to flow into congressional campaigns in much the same way in 1994 that it had for the last several election cycles—despite significant signs of a political upheaval in the months before the election—is powerful testimony to the inertia of the campaign economy. Still, there were interesting ripples of change in this election, and Republican control of Congress is certain to roil the waters of campaign finance.

We begin our assessment of the role of money in the 1994 election and beyond with a brief overview of the flows of money into general election races for the House and Senate. The numbers are then placed in the broader context of developments in campaign finances in the 20 years since the 1974 amendments to the Federal Election Campaign Act. Finally, we turn to a consideration of change, both the small signs of change that were discernible in the campaign and the prospects for a critical realignment of money in the wake of the election.

CONTOURS OF MONEY IN THE ELECTION

The biggest infusion of money in 1994 came in Senate elections, where spending soared from $195 million in 1992 to $271 million in 1994. Because there was the usual idiosyncrasy in Senate contests, Table 5.1 displays the spending in all of the races. The table shows how aggregate figures about spending are skewed by the lavish campaigns of two Republican losers, Huffington and North. In fact, these two races account for most of the difference between the parties in total spending for Senate races. The almost $50 million raised by the two came from different places—Huffington's from his personal fortune and North's from an unprecedented success in soliciting contributions from individuals. Elsewhere there was not a decisive Republican advantage in money. Political Action Committee (PAC) contributions, which declined from $45 million in 1992 to $43 million in 1994, were split almost evenly between Democrats and Republicans. PACs contributed $26.4 million to incumbents and only $5 million to challengers. Most incumbents comfortably outspent their opponents, and the long odds facing most Democratic challengers attracted meager investments. Many more Republican challengers raised enough money to wage credible campaigns, and the 2 who won—Rick Santorum in Pennsylvania and Bill Frist in Tennessee—outspent their opponents.

The real story, of course, was not that 2 of 26 incumbents lost, but that Republicans captured all 9 open Senate seats. In these races Republicans spent $30 million, $7.5 million of which came from PACs, and Democrats $24 million, including $4.2 million from PACs. Yet in contests that were thought before the election to be the most competitive—those in Michigan, Minnesota, Ohio, Oklahoma, and Tennessee—there was substantial parity between the parties. At the margin, money may have made a difference in some races for open seats, but it hardly explains the Republican sweep.

Spending in House races increased only slightly between 1992 and 1994, from $333 million to $343 million. In the aggregate, Table 5.2 shows, the pattern of campaign finances for the House followed a familiar pattern. Incumbents spent three times as much as challengers, and Democrats $30 million more than Republicans. The $126.8 million in PAC contributions to candidates for the House—up only $8 million from 1992—went overwhelmingly to incumbents. Incumbents raised nearly ten times as much from PACs as challengers; contributions from PACs accounted for about a third of total receipts of all candidates and half of the receipts of Democratic incumbents. Open seats continued to attract

TABLE 5.1 Spending in Senate Races

State	Candidates	Spending ($ Millions)
Open Seats		
Arizona	Kyl	4.1
	Coppersmith	1.6
Maine	Snow	2.0
	Andrews	1.5
Michigan	Abraham	4.4
	Carr	3.0
Minnesota	Grams	2.4
	Wynia	2.7
Missouri	Ashcroft	4.1
	Wheat	3.5
Ohio	Dewine	6.1
	Hyatt	4.8
Oklahoma	Inhofe	1.9
	McCurdy	1.9
Tennessee	Thompson	3.8
	Cooper	4.0
Wyoming	Thomas	1.1
	Sullivan	.7
Democratic Incumbents		
California	Feinstein	14.4
	Huffington	30.0
Connecticut	Lieberman	3.2
	Labriola	.2
Hawaii	Akaka	.4
	Hustace	.002
Maryland	Sarbanes	2.7
	Brock	3.2
Massachusetts	Kennedy	10.5
	Romney	7.6
Nebraska	Kerrey	4.5
	Stoney	1.8
Nevada	Bryan	3.0
	Furman	.8
New Jersey	Lautenberg	7.1
	Haytaian	5.1
New Mexico	Bingaman	3.2
	McMillan	1.5
New York	Moynihan	5.8
	Castro	1.6
North Dakota	Conrad	1.9
	Clayburgh	.9

(continues)

TABLE 5.1 (Continued)

State	Candidates	Spending ($ Millions)
Democratic Incumbents		
Pennsylvania	Wofford	6.3
	Santorum	6.7
Tennessee	Sasser	4.7
	Frist	7.0
Virginia	Robb	5.5
	North	20.6
West Virginia	Byrd	1.6
	Klos	.3
Wisconsin	Kohl	7.4
	Welch	1.2
Republican Incumbents		
Delaware	Roth	2.2
	Oberly	1.6
Florida	Mack	3.8
	Rodham	.6
Indiana	Lugar	4.1
	Jontz	.5
Mississippi	Lott	2.1
	Harper	.3
Montana	Burns	3.1
	Mudd	1.1
Rhode Island	Chafee	1.9
	Kushner	.8
Texas	Hutchison	6.1
	Fisher	3.4
Utah	Hatch	3.5
	Shea	.3
Vermont	Jeffords	1.0
	Backus	.3
Washington	Gorton	4.8
	Sims	1.3

SOURCE: Compiled by the author based on data published by the Federal Election Commission.

money, as Democratic candidates spent $27 million in these 47 races, and Republicans $30 million. PACs contributed $14.5 million to these races. Republican party committees provided $2 million in direct contributions to all House candidates and another $8.9 million in coordinated expenditures, and Democratic committees matched the support with $1.5 million in direct contributions and $8.5 million in coordinated expenditures.

TABLE 5.2 Finances of House Candidates

House Candidates	Spending ($ million)	Individual Contributions ($ million)	PAC Contributions ($ million)
Democrats			
Incumbents	$137.0	$60.0	$70.7
Challengers	21.0	10.7	5.5
Open seats	27.3	14.3	8.3
Republicans			
Incumbents	72.3	48.3	29.7
Challengers	52.8	33.1	6.2
Open seats	30.1	16.7	6.2

SOURCE: Compiled by the author based on data published by the Federal Election Commission.

TABLE 5.3 Median Spending of Various House Candidates

House Candidates	Median Spending
Incumbent-held seats	
Losing Democratic incumbents	$896,985
Winning Republican challengers	611,156
Winning Democratic incumbents	
with less than 55 percent of vote	643,947
Losing Republican challengers	320,520
Republican incumbents	
with less than 55 percent of vote	768,072
Losing Democratic challengers	497,570
Open seats	
Winning Republican open seats	595,576
Losing Democratic open seats	495,975
Winning Democratic open seats	601,394
Losing Republican open seats	374,406

SOURCE: Compiled by the author based on data published by the Federal Election Commission.

Neither in open-seat races nor in the races in which Democratic incumbents lost did Republican money "buy" victory. Open-seat races were split almost evenly in terms of which party spent more. As we see in Table 5.3, on average losing Democratic incumbents spent almost half again as much as their challengers did, including almost $500,000 in contributions from PACs. Only 6 winning Republican challengers outspent their opponents, and only 20 raised $100,000 or more in PAC contributions. The spending gap was even wider for the 41 Democratic incumbents reelected with less than 55 percent of the vote; their median spending was twice that of their challengers. If more Republican money had flowed into these marginal races instead of into the coffers of safe incumbents, the damage to Democrats could have been worse.

Of course, the campaign economy has little in the way of centralized planning to direct or even nudge dollars to the best partisan advantage, and Republicans did well to increase spending by their challengers by $12 million between 1992 and 1994. As a result, the number of Republican challengers with the wherewithal to wage credible campaigns increased significantly. Between 1992 and 1994 the proportion of Republican challengers who raised at least $200,000 increased from 31 percent to 42 percent, and the proportion with $400,000 or more in receipts increased from 12 percent to 24 percent. Democratic challengers fared worse. Only 30 percent raised at least $200,000, and only 16 percent raised $400,000 or more. Whether this underfunding of Democratic challengers was a cause or a symptom of the party's problems, the fact is that in retrospect there were very few good bets for such venture capital. Only 4 percent of Republican incumbents secured less than 55 percent of the votes as compared to 32 percent of Democratic incumbents. Only 13 percent of Republican incumbents had less than 60 percent of the vote as compared to half of the Democrats.

Since spending by individuals and PACs that is made without the cooperation or knowledge of the candidate it is intended to help was constitutionally protected by the Supreme Court in its 1976 *Buckley v. Valeo* decision, the specter of "independent" expenditures has haunted reformers. Yet even at its peak of $9.4 million in 1986, independent spending in congressional elections was only 2 percent of the amount of direct expenditures (Sorauf 1992: 181). In 1994, as Table 5.4 shows, such spending was only $4.5 million, less than one-half of one percent of total spending. With the notable exception of independent spending in the race against North, most of this money was spent to benefit Republicans. Yet even in the races with the largest amounts of independent spending, this support was insignificant.

Far more interesting than independent expenditures is the increase in the investments of candidates that were made through contributions and loans in their own campaigns, which began in the 1992 election and continued in 1994. Between 1990 and 1994 such candidate contributions increased from $38 million to $123 million. Even excluding the Huffington anomaly, such contributions tripled in Senate races, and they more than doubled in House races. In primaries and the general elections for the House in 1994 some 163 candidates contributed $50,000 or more to their own campaigns. Thirty-nine supported their own campaigns with more than $200,000, including 6 who contributed or loaned more than $1 million. The list of the biggest self-contributors reveals, not surprisingly, that incumbents were the least likely to draw heavily on their own resources, and candidates for open seats, the most likely. Republicans turn up more than do Democrats as bankrollers of their own campaigns, but for candidates of both parties, these substantial investments did not guarantee results. Of the top 50 self-contributors 43 were unsuccessful, including Eugene Fontenot in the 25th district of Texas, who contributed $2.4 million to the campaign that spent $4.7 million in a losing race for the open seat.

Even at a time of low public esteem for Congress, seats in the institution apparently remained valuable enough commodities for many to invest substantial sums of their own money in campaigns with long odds. Many of these financial self-starters did not fit the image of the new American politician—careerists working their way up the occupational ladder of politics. Like the well-publicized Senate candidacy of Frist in Tennessee, many of these self-financed races were conducted by amateurs coming to politics from other walks of life. One observer, (Ehrenhalt 1991), argued that professionalism has been a natural advantage for Democrats in congressional elections. Whether it has been the product of poignantly felt grievances against government or hints of realignment (Canon and Sousa 1992), the continued rise of self-financed amateurs would constitute an important new pathway to power for Republicans. It might also make future freshmen classes more like the class of 1994, which one new member described as "an ideological class that really believes we were sent here to make a difference" (Calmes 1995).

THE REVOLUTION THAT WASN'T: PACS IN THE 1994 ELECTION

The last election that inspired talk of realignment was in 1980, when Ronald Reagan defeated Jimmy Carter and Republicans took control of the Senate and gained 33 seats in the House. Ominously, the Democratic debacle was accompanied by the appearance of aggressive antagonism on the part of corporate and trade PACs. For the first time since their legitimization by the Federal Election Campaign Act (FECA) amendments of 1974, these groups showed not only a strong Republican tilt but also a willingness to risk their contributions on nonincumbents. In certain respects the same dynamics that helped make these PACs a financial arm of the Republican Party in 1980 were also present in 1994. In both elections relatively unpopular Democratic presidents incurred the wrath of important segments of the business community, and in both cases there was ample evidence that these were auspicious years for Republicans.

Yet the success of Republicans in 1994 had little to do with PACs. PAC contributions continued on a flattened trajectory, and a small proportion of PAC money went to challengers. Only 45 House challengers, for example, raised $100,000 or more in PAC contributions, and half of those were Democrats. Table 5.5 presents the behavior of PACs in 1994 in finer detail and shows data about the contributions of the four major PAC types: corporate, labor, trade/membership, and nonconnected. Labor PACs, which account for a declining share of all PAC money, were the most important allies in national Democratic strategy. Although more than 70 percent of the contributions of labor PACs went to anxious Democratic incumbents, the $11 million labor invested in Democratic challengers and candidates for open seats in the House and Senate accounted for most

TABLE 5.4 Independent Expenditures in 1993–1994

	Expenditures For	Expenditures Against
Senate		
Democrats	$ 204,212	$433,947
Republicans	1,309,572	537,531
House		
Democrats	502,621	488,479
Republicans	1,088,356	50,815
Campaigns with the largest independent expenditures in support		
Frist (Tennessee)	189,141	
Thompson (Tennessee)	187,989	
Stoney (Nebraska)	137,892	
Furman (Nevada)	114,571	
McMillan (New Mexico)	100,477	
Campaigns with the largest independent expenditures against		
North (Virginia)		404,956
Foley (Washington)		168,845
Kennedy (Massachusetts)		128,596
Gorton (Washington)		98,019
Bingaman (New Mexico)		66,518

SOURCE: Compiled by the author based on data published by the Federal Election Commission.

of the PAC money raised by Democratic nonincumbents. Nonconnected PACs, those once-feared ideological outfits without organizational homes, were relatively small players in this election and actually gave more to Democrats than Republicans. What is most interesting is the cautious behavior of corporate and trade PACs, which have come to dominate the PAC economy. Of the $47.9 million contributed by trade PACs in House and Senate races, almost half went to Democratic incumbents; only $3.1 million went to Republican challengers. Although corporate PACs were once more venturesome on behalf of Republicans, there is scant evidence of that behavior in 1994. Corporate PACs contributed $27.9 million to Democratic incumbents, $19.8 million to Republican incumbents, and only $4.1 million to Republican challengers.

Why were PACs such bystanders? The story of this timidity began well before 1994. Indeed, 1994 marked the 20th anniversary of the most sweeping campaign finance reforms in history. Our reading of developments since those reforms suggests three main themes. First, PACs are best understood not as catalytic agents for the transformation of American politics but as derivatives of larger changes in the political system. Second, there was less substance to the "PAC explosion" in the

TABLE 5.5 PAC Contributions

	Corporate ($ thousands)	Labor ($ thousands)	Trade ($ thousands)	Non-Connected ($ thousands)
Senate				
Democrats				
Incumbents	$ 6,100	$ 3,500	$ 3,600	$ 2,000
Challengers	100	1,400	200	200
Open seats	1,000	1,500	800	700
Republicans				
Incumbents	5,600	200	3,200	1,100
Challengers	1,700	20	800	500
Open seats	4,400	40	2,200	700
House				
Democrats				
Incumbents	21,800	22,100	18,600	5,400
Challengers	300	3,700	800	600
Open seats	1,000	4,300	1,900	1,000
Republicans				
Incumbents	14,200	1,200	11,100	2,000
Challengers	2,400	40	2,300	1,200
Open seats	2,500	80	2,400	900
Total	61,100	38,000	47,900	16,300

NOTES: Not included in this table are the PACs of cooperatives and corporations without stock, which together made contributions of $6.3 million in 1994; dollar amounts are rounded to nearest thousand.
SOURCE: Compiled by the author based on data published by the Federal Election Commission.

1980s than meets the eye. The main players in the PAC economy were born either before, in the case of many labor PACs, or within a few years of the FECA amendments of 1974. The comings and goings of thousands of peripheral PACs amounted to little more than noise in a system dominated by the early PAC giants. Finally, the American system of campaign finance tends toward a high degree of entropy. The disruption of this financial equilibrium in 1980, when business interests had the motive and opportunity to forsake pragmatism for partisanship and were joined by a host of conservative nonconnected PACs, led some observers to predict a permanent PAC-induced tilt toward Republicans. Almost immediately, however, Democrats began to blunt this potential threat, and by the end of the decade, campaign finance was driven by the imperatives of incumbency and legislative pragmatism. This history helps explain why the PAC dog did not bark in the 1994 election and offers some clues to the future of campaign finance.

The 1971 FECA and the important 1974 amendments were followed in the next two years by key administrative and judicial actions and that profoundly altered the public face of political money. Of several developments subsequent to the reforms, the sudden emergence of PACs was the most visible. These financial intermediaries, most of which were adjuncts to preexisting organizations, demonstrated an efficiency in gathering and dispersing money to candidates that alarmed many.

Given the timing of the legal changes and the impressive arrival of PACs, it is natural to view the FECA as a beginning, a fresh blueprint institutions could use to build vehicles for mobilizing untapped political reserves. By this logic, the reforms dramatically reduced the threshold for political giving and thus induced dormant but predisposed organizations into the political arena. This new wave of entrants sharply increased the number of organized participants and perhaps disrupted existing political alignments. For example, the FEC's 1975 SunPAC decision, which allowed the overhead expenses of PACs to be absorbed by committee sponsors, is seen by some as granting enduring privilege to corporations (Clawson, Neustadtl, and Scott 1992). And some worried the sweeping away of statutory limits on independent expenditures in *Buckley v. Valeo* a year later would produce an explosion of activity by ideological groups.

Yet the rise of PACs is properly placed at the end of more than two decades of upheaval in the larger system of interest groups. The post–World War II battle between traditional membership groups was joined in the 1960s by a multitude of citizen groups, new breeds of organization with weak occupational bases, strong commitments by outside benefactors, and broad social agendas (Walker 1991). This "invasion of externality groups" as (Salisbury 1990) calls it was followed by yet another change—the heightened activity of business. Spawned by a deterioration in the economic climate and the perceived costs of social regulation, the mobilization of business was well under way by the early 1970s (Vogel 1989). Important structural change was also taking place. Institutions, once accustomed to mediating demands through associations, assumed direct political roles, which led to a fragmentation of interest representation. Many of these actors opened Washington offices or hired Washington agents—a nationalization of the advocacy explosion that was very much in evidence by the end of the 1960s. Viewed against the backdrop of this history, the founding of PACs signaled not so much an organizational revolution as the rapid adaptation of a new strategic form by established political interests.

In fact, an examination of the population dynamics of PACs shows that the most widely publicized numbers about the history of PACs—the growth in their numbers and the growth of their spending in the 1980s—presents a misleading picture. Laying these data alongside one another suggests that the 1980s were a period of unbridled mobilization of new PACs and new money. Yet the thousands of PACs that came and very often went after those founded in 1978 account for a relatively small share of the spending of these organizations. Of all the spending by PACs in the 1992 elections, for example, two-thirds was accounted for by the PACs that had been formed in the 1978 election cycle. After a few years of explosive growth, the spending of this first generation of PACs slowed considerably, and new

TABLE 5.6 The Distribution of PAC Contributions in House Races, 1978–94

Distribution by PAC	House Races								
	1978	1980	1982	1984	1986	1988	1990	1992	1994
Corporate PACs									
Percent to Democratic incumbents	34%	35%	32%	42%	44%	48%	49%	48%	51%
Percent to Republican challengers	16	20	9	11	3	3	3	4	6
Trade PACs									
Percent to Democratic incumbents	35	36	33	44	42	48	50	44	50
Percent to Republican challengers	14	16	8	7	3	2	2	3	6
Labor PACs									
Percent to Democratic incumbents	60	66	51	69	59	61	66	62	70
Percent to Democratic challengers	17	16	28	17	19	19	12	14	12
Nonconnected PACs									
Percent to Democratic incumbents	12	19	24	37	28	38	41	38	49
Percent to Republican challengers	37	38	15	22	7	6	6	7	18

SOURCE: Compiled by the author based on data published by the Federal Election Commission.

entrants did not pick up the slack. Thus, between 1986 and 1994 the contributions of PACs to all congressional candidates actually declined in constant dollars.

Both the early and later entrants to the PAC economy also became increasingly cautious during the 1980s. At the beginning of the decade, corporate and trade PACs showed signs of becoming important new resources for electing Republican challengers and keeping them in office (Eismeier and Pollock 1986). By the end of the decade, "the pipers had begun to call their own tunes. In terms of the system of campaign finance, incumbents seized the initiative from PACs, probably contributed to the end of PAC proliferation, and certainly ended PAC plans to make an unprecedented impact on American electoral politics" (Sorauf 1992: 96). Table 5.6 shows the magnitude of this change. Throughout their history, labor PACs have invested in Democratic incumbents and, when conditions are ripe, in Democratic challengers. Democrats also benefited from the fact that conservatives clearly lost their corner on the market of nonconnected PACs. The most important change, however, is the one that occurred among corporate and trade PACs. By the middle of the decade, the numbers show, these groups had apparently decided that it was better to join House Democrats than to fight them.

Although there was a slight uptick in PAC giving to Republican challengers in 1994—as a group corporate and trade PACs gave only $2 million more to Republican challengers for the House than they did in 1992—the financing of these remarkable elections fit the pattern of the last several years. Apparently, few players in campaign finance took seriously Newt Gingrich's prediction of a Republican House majority. Thus, the economy of campaign money turned once again on the power of governing, which worked to the advantage of Democrats since Tony Coehlo, then Chairman of the Democratic Congressional Campaign Committee, warned business PACs in the early 1980s that, "we are going to be in the majority in the House for many, many years, and I don't think it makes good business sense for you to try to destroy us." Moreover, while the disarray of congressional Democrats no doubt fed public hostility to Congress, it created many investment opportunities for PACs among Democratic incumbents. Groups that were opposed to President Clinton's health care plan, for example, were almost as likely to find allies and potential beneficiaries of PAC largesse among Democrats as Republicans. To borrow a phrase from Ross Perot, that "giant sucking sound" that was heard again in 1994 was the sound of incumbents, particularly vulnerable Democratic incumbents, extracting money from PACs.

STIRRINGS OF CHANGE

All was not business as usual, however. Although there was no torrent of money to Republican challengers, even before the election trickles sprang from the first cracks in the dike of Democratic incumbency and although the great bulk of business money was channeled in the usual direction, anecdotal evidence suggests that there were some actors whose contributions reflected a more partisan stance. Soft money contributions to Republicans before and after the election were boosted by "a different money crowd—younger, less of the establishment, more ideological, and more willing to attempt revolutionary change in government than denizens of the the *Fortune 500* Business Roundtable. These newcomers prided themselves on not being old-line GOP defenders of the status quo. Some of them were engaged in high-risk, high-return businesses. Others represented companies that saw the government as a threat to their very existence. What they shared was a strong libertarian, antigovernment streak that set them apart from traditional business donors, who have often tended to give to politicians of both parties, depending on who was in power (Abramson and Rogers 1995). For these newcomers, for whom the regulatory thrust and the health care plan of the Clinton administration were symbols of government intrusion, the 1994 election had many of the same elements of a crusade as the 1980 election did for an earlier generation.

As we have seen, there is little evidence that antigovernment, anti-Democrat antagonism affected the aggregate spending of PACs. But it may have turned up in individual contributions, which surged for Republicans. Between 1992 and

TABLE 5.7 Individual Contributions by Size

	Contributions Less than $200 ($ millions)	Contributions From $200–$499 ($ millions)	Contributions From $500–$749 ($ millions)	Contributions Greater than $749 ($ millions)
Senate				
Democrats				
Incumbents	$14.1	$3.4	$ 7.7	$21.7
Challengers	2.0	1.0	1.4	4.1
Open seats	5.9	3.2	4.4	11.4
Republicans				
Incumbents	7.8	2.6	3.3	7.4
Challengers	25.7	4.6	5.8	13.4
Open seats	10.1	3.8	5.4	14.7
House				
Democrats				
Incumbents	18.7	9.2	12.5	21.0
Challengers	6.5	2.4	2.4	4.4
Open seats	7.9	3.6	4.0	7.8
Republicans				
Incumbents	20.4	7.3	8.5	12.4
Challengers	14.5	5.6	6.4	12.2
Open seats	9.3	3.9	4.6	9.3

NOTE: The data in this table include both primary and general elections. Since individuals may contribute to multiple candidates up to a maximum of $25,000, no inferences can be made from the data about the number of different people contributing.
SOURCE: Compiled by author based on data published by the Federal Election Commission.

1994 there were increases of 25 percent in individual contributions for House Republicans and 50 percent for Senate Republicans as compared to 8 percent for House Democrats and 5 percent for Senate Democrats. If the case of North was any indication, Republicans succeeded in tailoring traditional fund-raising techniques to exploit the grievances potential contributors felt about government in general and the Clinton administration in particular. That there was such a grassroots financial mobilization dovetails with evidence that antipathy toward President Clinton and those in Congress who supported his domestic program mobilized a significant part of the electorate in moderate to conservative districts and helped defeat Democratic incumbents (Brady, Cogan, and Rivers 1995).

The FEC's reporting protocols do not permit detailed analysis of the sources of this surge in individual contributions to Republicans, but Table 5.7 does present aggregated data about the contributions to candidates of both parties. If there was a Republican advantage, the data show it did not come from an ability to generate more money in large individual contributions. In fact, Democrats actually raised a smaller proportion of their funds in contributions of less than $200 and a larger proportion in contributions of $750 or more than did Republicans. The difference is especially striking in the data for Senate races, which were skewed by the North factor. Even in the House, however, Democrats relied less on small contributions and more on large contributions than did Republicans. For example, on average House Democratic incumbents received $83,000 in contributions of less than $200 and $93,000 in contributions of $750 or more; Republican incumbents received an average of $130,000 in contributions of less than $200 and $77,000 in contributions of $750 or more.

If the 1994 election showed that, in retrospect, the electoral base that kept Democrats in power in Congress for most of this century was fragile, evidence about PACs and individual contributors paints a similar portrait of the party's financial base. By the end of the 1980s Democratic incumbents seemed not only to have survived the threat of PACs but to have turned it to their own advantage. All along, however, their relationship with many of these PACs was a marriage not of love, but of convenience. At the same time the base of their individual contributions became tilted more toward large donations. Meanwhile, even with the stalwart support of labor PACs, Democratic challengers faced chronic shortages of money. The natural allies of Republicans in the PAC community were of far more help to the GOP's incumbents than to its challengers. Yet incumbents and challengers for the Republicans had the capacity to generate significant money not only in large individual contributions but in small ones as well. There is an irony here. The Republican party that gained control of Congress in 1994 did so in part because of its ability to mobilize small individual contributions in a way that fit traditional Democratic rhetoric. The Democratic party that lost its grip on power had a financial base that, except for labor, looked like what one might traditionally have expected for Republicans.

CONCLUSION

Now, the loss of governing power has jeopardized much of the Democrats' financial base. It was power that enabled Democrats to collect spectacular sums from PACs—$1,158,072 for Speaker Tom Foley, $799,199 for once–Ways and Means Chairman Dan Rostenkowski, $829,967 for his successor, Sam Gibbons. Money did not save Foley or Rostenkowski, and the $1,155,373 spent by Gibbons earned him only 52 percent of the vote against challenger Mark Sharpe, who spent less than half a million dollars, including only $47,064 from PACs. Ranking Minority Member Gibbons, one strongly suspects, will be a much less attractive donee to inhabitants of "Gucci Gulch" than was Chairman Gibbons. Groups seeking to use campaign contributions to gain access on specific issues of policy will still gravitate to power, but in the 104th Congress that power is held by Republicans.

Republicans began their efforts to redirect interested political money even before the election when Gingrich warned, "for anyone who's not on board now, it's going to be the two coldest years in Washington." And after the election, Charles

Mack, President of the Business Industry Political Action Committee, wrote of Republican leaders to his members, "I am being told that they are scrutinizing to whom companies and business associations are currently giving" (Stone 1995). In the early days of the 104th Congress Republicans held a record number of fundraisers, including a dinner that raised $11 million for the Republican National Committee. Early reports show a tilt toward Republicans. The PACs of the American Bankers Association (ABA) and RJR Nabisco, for example, were models of bipartisanship in their contributions. In the 1994 election the ABA gave $640,050 to Democrats and $703,100 to Republicans, and RJR Nabisco gave $366,500 to Democrats and $417,650 to Republicans. In the first month of the 104th Congress, however, the ABA gave $2,500 to Democrats and $63,250 to Republicans; RJR Nabisco gave $1000 to Democrats and $42,500 to Republicans (Stone 1995).

In addition to parochial interests, classwide interests may also drive money to Republicans. The Reagan Revolution, such as it was, barely put a dent in the American welfare/regulatory state, and when the limits of that revolution became clear, business quickly abandoned the pursuit of its collective interest in favor of firm-specific interests (Vogel 1989). On matters ranging from taxes to regulation to liability reform, a Republican Congress could be the vehicle for a real revolution. For tactical and strategic reasons, therefore, money is likely to pour into Republican coffers for 1996. There will be more than enough money to defend Republican seats in the House and Senate and go after open seats. There will also be a substantial pool of venture capital available to credible Republican challengers taking on the large number of Democrats in the House who lost the aura of invincibility in 1994.

The financial stakes are indeed high in 1996. If Democrats regain control of the House, the hemorrhaging of campaign money could be stanched. With fewer of them vying for funds, Democratic survivors will probably be able to fund adequately their 1996 campaigns. But it will require more hustling, an unappealing prospect that may nudge some into retirement. Between defending incumbents and attempting to win back seats lost in 1994, the resources of labor PACs will be stretched very thin. Even with the support of labor PACs, Democrats have lagged far behind Republicans in money for challengers. Between 1986 and 1994, for example, the receipts of Republican House challengers tripled, while receipts for Democratic challengers remained flat. To be sure, there will be many targets of opportunity for Democrats. The keys to success will be not only in recruiting strong candidates but in mobilizing individual contributors to support them in the way that Republicans did in 1994. If Democrats fail to do so, Republican incumbents may become entrenched, and money to defeat them, or for that matter to defend Democratic incumbents, more and more scarce.

As the ups and downs of the Contract with America testify, the fate of the Republican revolution in policy remains uncertain. So too is the fate of the nascent realignment in political money. In the short term, as we have seen, the new realities of power in Washington will be a financial boon for Republicans. In the longer term, however, this wealth may be a mixed blessing. Contributions from special interests, Democrats learned the hard way, can be debilitating for a governing party. Thus far, House Republicans have demonstrated an impressive cohesiveness on their agenda. For example, on the matter of reducing punitive damages and limiting product-liability suits, an item of great importance to small business, Republicans stood firm against the rich and politically powerful groups representing trial lawyers. In the absence of a unifying passion, such as the one they have for small business, Republicans may become more fractious, and campaign funds flooding in from all shades of interest on difficult issues may only exacerbate such intraparty squabbling.

The larger problem for Republicans is to fashion a program of governance that knits together durable coalitions of voters and contributors. What has emerged thus far is an amalgam of fiscal austerity, social control, and laissez-faire. How well these themes play with the American electorate remains to be seen. In practice, as opposed to rhetoric, few Americans like their capitalism unleavened, and opposition to unfettered markets springs not only from the left, but from the populist right (Phillips 1994). On the face of it, the new laissez-faire would seem the right ideological glue to hold together a financial coalition that, if not instrumental in putting Republicans in power, could be invaluable in keeping them there. Less government is what many business interests claimed they really wanted in the years that they were forced into accommodation with Democrats. Yet for all its annoyances, the vast web of regulation and subvention that has been woven around American business in this century might be difficult to live without, and the Clinton administration's international boosterism of business would make a Republican administration blush. If it means eliminating the Commerce Department and all of its promotional programs, as well as other forms of corporate welfare, "less government" may be more appealing to the relatively small number of cowboy capitalists who joined the Republican crusade in 1994 than to the much larger number of business pragmatists, who may begin to worry that they have been punished by having their wish granted.

Public discourse about campaign finance "relies too often on a monistic explanatory system, one unified and consolidated by the driving force of money" (Sorauf 1992: 24). Such an account of the role of money in the 1994 midterm elections misses the mark. The hundreds of millions of dollars that flowed into congressional campaigns in 1994 are properly placed in the broader context of recent American political developments. Some of these developments—the proliferation of interest and ideological groups, the financial power of incumbency, the rise of candidate-centered politics increasingly populated by self-starting entrepreneurs, the arms race between national party committees to provide an edge to their candidates—were well under way before 1994. What was different about 1994 was the nationalization of the campaign and, of course, the electoral surge toward Republicans. To the extent that money either reflected or played a role in these developments, it was not the organized money of PACs but instead that of candidates and individual contributors.

If the 1994 election warrants revived scholarly attention to partisan realignment, political scientists would do well to remember the admonition that realignments are matters not only of election returns but also of policy (McCormick 1982). Indeed, the Republican victory in 1994 has encouraged far-reaching national debate about issues ranging from a balanced budget to a flat tax, from regulation to federalism, and from school prayer to term limits. As much as anything else, it will be the outcome of this free-for-all over ideas that shapes future electoral coalitions and the finances that undergird them.

6

The 1994 Electoral Aftershock: Dealignment or Realignment in the South

PAUL FRYMER[1]

Waiting for the next realignment to occur in American politics has been likened to "waiting for Godot" (Ladd 1991). Despite a rather dramatic shift in national political discourse over domestic spending, regulation, welfare, and race, analysts remain hesitant to label the post–New Deal electoral transformations an actual "realignment." This reluctance stems primarily from two nonevents: the lack of sustained Republican majorities in Congress and the relative lack of national voters identifying with the Republican party. Instead, analysts interpret these nonevents as products of a widespread "dealignment," stemming from a decline in the influence of party organizations and involving significant portions of the voting-aged population who have either detached themselves from partisan politics (Wattenberg 1990) or opted to drop out of the electoral process altogether (Burnham 1987).

At first glance, the Republican victories of 1994 do not appear to be indicative of the long-awaited realignment. No dramatically divisive issue like the Civil War or the Great Depression emerged during the campaign, nor did early exit polls detect a notable shift in voter partisan identification. Instead, voters have once again chosen to divide the government between the two major parties, an act which has been perhaps the most defining characteristic of the dealignment era. Since many voters have been ambivalent towards the policies and ideologies of both parties, they are thought to be deliberately splitting their tickets in order to provide some kind of balance and moderation (Alesina and Rosenthal 1989, Fiorina 1992b, Jacobson 1990a). Given this "cognitive Madisonian" assessment (as termed by Ladd 1995b: 18) of the modern-day electorate, it is less than surprising that the Republicans' ultimate takeover of Congress would more or less coincide with the Democrats' takeover of the presidency.

Explanations of the 1994 election results seen through the lens of dealignment theory, however, become problematic when the focus centers on possession of 60 House seats that turned over from Democratic to Republican representatives.[2] For instance, balancing theories assume that moderate, independent, and ambivalent voters are most responsible for dividing the government. Yet, in 1994 the districts that switched to Republican House candidates consisted of quite conservative voters. According to national election data (see Table 6.1), the voters from these districts were significantly more conservative than voters from districts that chose Democratic representatives in 1992 and 1994 and no less conservative than voters from districts that elected Republicans in 1992. Scores regarding both individual ideological identification and specific issue-realms adhere to this pattern, as only on the issue of defense spending were the respondents undistinguished from their counterparts who voted Democratic in 1992 and 1994 (as well as from their counterparts who voted Republican in 1992 and 1994). Since these were conservative Democratic districts, we might also expect higher levels of ticket splitting in national elections prior to 1994 (Frymer 1994). Indeed, only 6 of the 60 districts supported Democratic presidential candidate Michael Dukakis in 1988, and only 1 gave Bill Clinton more than 50 percent of the vote in 1992.

A second reason to view dealignment explanations for the results of the 1994 elections with some suspicion is that a disproportionate number of the Republican House victories came from the South.[3] This is significant not only

TABLE 6.1 Ideological Features of the 1994 House Vote by National and Southern Voters

	District Vote			
	Democratic 1992 and 1994	Republican 1992 and 1994	Democratic / Republican 1992/1994	Split Ticket 1992[a]
National voters				
Overall ideology	3.98	4.42	4.45	4.93
Spending/government services	3.67	4.02	4.09	4.42
Government aid for standard of living:	4.04	4.51	4.54	5.22
Defense spending	3.42	3.53	3.53	3.68
Southern voters				
Overall ideology	4.06	4.35	4.67	b
Spending/government services	3.61	3.92	4.42	b
Government aid for standard of living	3.73	4.37	4.91	b
Defense spending	3.64	3.82	3.86	b

[a] Split refers specifically to those voters who (a) split their ticket between George Bush and a Democratic House member in 1992, and (b) are from districts that elected Democrats in 1992 and Republicans in 1994.
[b] The sample is too small for comparison in split-ticket cases.
NOTE: Ideological features are indicated by mean identification placements; all ANES scores are based on a 1–7 scale, with 1 being most liberal.
SOURCE: Scores are derived from the 1992 American National Election Study, variables 3509, 3701, 3707, 3718, and 3724.

because these districts tend to be quite conservative (as shown in Table 6.1) but also because electoral scholars have long expected the next realignment would revolve around white southern voters. Southern whites have rather consistently voted Republican in national elections, a fact that has led scholars to assume that the voters would and should desire the same party to champion their interests in Congress as well. However, when election after election failed to reflect a southern realignment at the congressional level, many of these theorists turned out of frustration from realignment theory to theories of dealignment and divided government to explain the widespread phenomenon of split-ticket voters in the region and ultimately in the nation (see, for instance, the progression of Sundquist 1983: 269–97; 1988).

With the huge Republican gains in 1994, that denied the Democrats a majority of the region's House seats for the first time since Reconstruction, it seems clear that realignment theory deserves at least a second look. Although certainly not the entire explanation, nor as tidy and predictable an explanation as scholars once assumed, realignment theory offers some important insights as to why these voters first waited to vote and then in 1994 voted for Republican House members. In one of the last expositions of realignment theory, James Sundquist (1983) argued that in some regions of the United States, realignments can take many years to culminate, and even as the region consistently votes for a new party at the national level, the lack of the new party's organizational strength and the peculiar characteristics of the old party's members enable the old party to remain popular in elections that are not national elections. Realignment, then, takes place in these regions, not all at once, but through a series of "aftershocks."

Two factors, I argue, have been critical in delaying realignment in the South: the lack of Republican party challengers in southern Democratic districts and the ability of southern Democrats to differentiate themselves from the national party image. The 1994 election offered the opportunity for a significant realignment aftershock because, for the first time, both of these factors were simultaneously diminished; the Republican party forcefully challenged Democratic incumbents in House districts; and the party had a unique opportunity to link southern Democrats with their more liberal national party image.

The aftershock, in turn, has consequences for dealignment theory. It suggests that voter intentions may not be the primary reason for the continual occurrence of divided government. Voters who have been splitting their tickets between Republican presidential candidates and Democratic House candidates have in fact been quite consistently making conservative choices. Focusing on candidate behavior, then, offers an alternative way to understanding why people have been splitting their votes in the past and why many turned to the Republican party in 1994.

THE SOUTH'S REFUSAL TO REALIGN

As previously mentioned, analysts have expected the South to realign itself with the Republican party for many decades, especially because of the region's voting behavior in presidential elections. Southern voters have not supported a non-southern Democratic presidential candidate since John Kennedy in 1960, and the combination of economic conservativism and white racial prejudice has made it acceptable for many southern whites to begin to vote for Republican party candidates after almost a century of Democratic party dominance. Some southern states first bolted from the Democratic party in the 1948 presidential election, supporting Dixiecrat candidate Strom Thurmond over either of the major party candidates. In the 1950s southerners supported a Republican for the first time, giving Dwight Eisenhower a majority of their votes in the 1956 election. Republican Barry Goldwater's opposition to the Civil Rights Act attracted votes from southern whites in 1964 as the rest of the country voted in a landslide for Lyndon Johnson. Although southern Democratic presidential candidates have had some success since 1964 in the region, only Jimmy Carter in 1976 received a majority of the southern vote, no party candidate has received a majority of the white vote, and no non-southern presidential candidate has received as much as 35 percent of the white vote (Black and Black 1992: chapter 12).

The hesitancy to identify the South as having actually realigned is due to the continued success of Democratic congressional candidates in the region, as well as to the enduring identification among southern whites with the Democratic party. In 1972, although every southern state supported Richard Nixon in overwhelming numbers over George McGovern, American National Election Study (ANES) data reflect that less than one-third of southern white voters labeled themselves Republicans and that southern voters elected 85 Democrats to their 121 House seats. In 1984, as southern states took part in the Reagan landslide, southern Democratic House members won 2 out of every 3 seats, and the number of southern white Democrats continued to outnumber southern white Republicans. Although, again according to ANES data, voting a straight Democratic party ticket dropped from 60 percent in 1964 to less than 35 percent in 1988 and 1992, voting a straight Republican party ticket in national elections has remained at less than 30 percent, with the other third of the electorate splitting their tickets between the parties. In accordance with balance theories, then, many southern voters have seemed content to be somewhat supportive of Republican presidential candidates in national elections and to prefer Democratic candidates in House and (to a lesser degree) Senate elections.

This interpretation, however, overlooks some important characteristics of and trends in the voting patterns of those southern voters who split their tickets. First of all, although the move towards identification with the Republican party has been quite slow, it is nevertheless notable when viewed over a four-decade period (see Figure 6.1). By 1992, the percentage of southern whites identifying with the Republican party was almost equal to those identifying with the Democratic party, and in 1994 Republicans for the first time became the majority party among this group.[4]

This phenomenon is not the result of southern voters becoming more conservative. Split-ticket voters in the South, for instance, by most measures have been equally

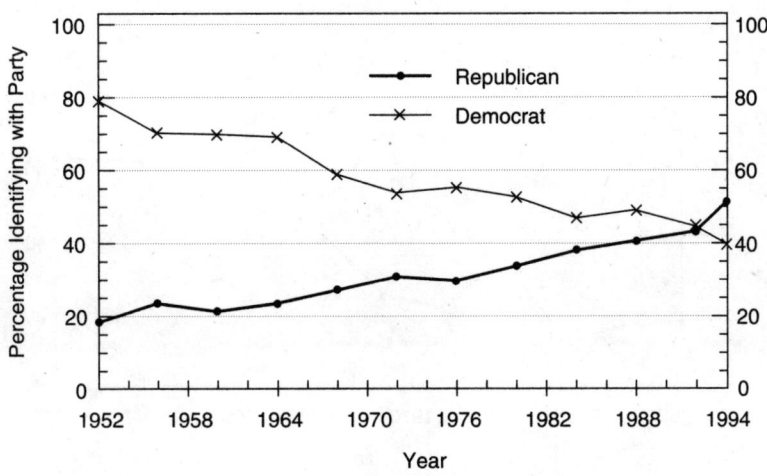

FIGURE 6.1
Party Identification of Southern Whites, 1952–1994

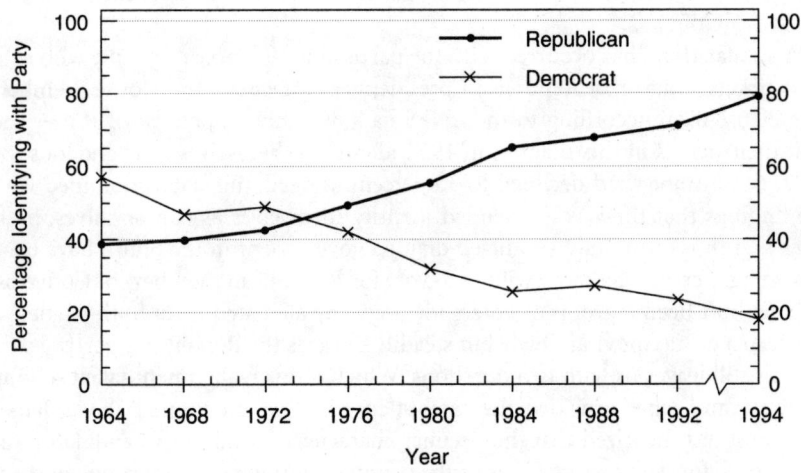

FIGURE 6.2
Party Identification of Conservative Respondents, 1964–1994

as conservative as Republican voters in the region and more conservative than Republican voters outside of the South (Frymer, Kim, and Bimes 1995). Instead, the trend toward realignment has been the result of already conservative voters slowly aligning themselves with the Republican party. Self-proclaimed ideological conservatives recently have been much more likely to identify themselves as Republicans

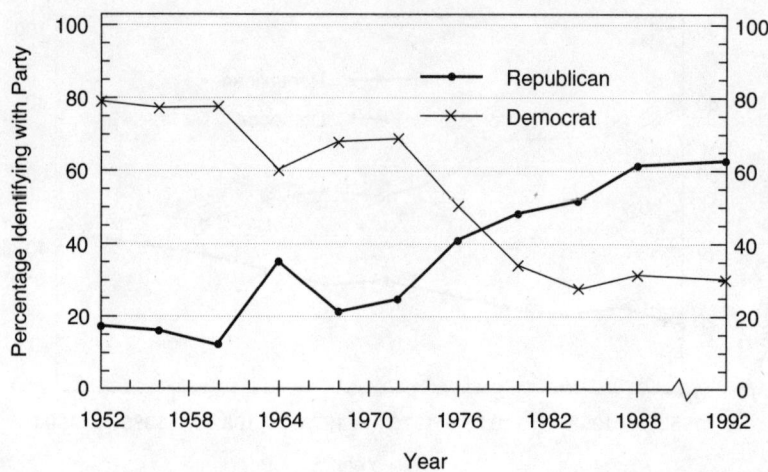

FIGURE 6.3
Party Identification of Split-Ticket Voters, 1952–1992

than they were three decades ago (see Figure 6.2). In 1964, more than half of those who considered themselves conservative also identified with the Democratic party. By 1994, less than one-quarter of conservative respondents identified themselves as Democrats.

A similar trend has occurred with the partisan preferences of people who split their tickets in favor of Republican presidents and Democratic House members (see Figure 6.3). According to the ANES data, roughly 80 percent of those who split their tickets in this manner in 1952 identified themselves as Democrats. By 1992, this number had declined to 30 percent. Indeed, this data, combined with the findings that these voters tended identify themselves as conservatives, indicates that those who have produced divided government in the South have been becoming increasingly more willing to vote for Republican members of Congress. This has not been a group of voters ideologically alienated from both parties; it has been a group moving slowly but steadily towards the Republican party.

This still leaves us with two questions: Why has this realignment taken so long to occur, and what provided the catalyst in 1994? As mentioned above, James Sundquist has theorized that the peculiar character of local party candidates was responsible for why some regions of the country continue to support one party at the local level and at the same time shift quite dramatically to the other party at the national level. Candidates representing voters' old party loyalties were able in the short term to differentiate themselves from their national party leaders. Furthermore, candidates representing the voters' new national party loyalties were at first tentative about running and lacked the necessary organizational skills to compete successfully (Sundquist 1983: 284–87). A closer look at southern House districts over time supports this theory quite well. Southern Republican candidates have been slow to challenge incumbent Democrats, although, at the same time, these southern Democratic House members have quite successfully distanced themselves ideologically from the national Democratic party candidates.

REPUBLICAN OPPOSITION IN SOUTHERN HOUSE ELECTIONS

A well-known reason for the dominance of House incumbents across the nation in congressional elections during the 1970s and 1980s was the lack of quality opposition (Jacobson and Kernell 1983). To explain the success of the Democratic party in maintaining a majority of southern districts until 1994, one need not look at the level of quality of challengers since in many races there has simply been no Republican opposition at all. Between 1966 and 1990, there were between 25 to 45 Democrats running unopposed in House elections (see Figure 6.4).

Southern Democrats have gone unchallenged despite the fact that their districts have consistently voted for Republicans in national party elections. In 1988, for instance, George Bush won a majority of the votes in 21 of the 30 uncontested Democratic House seats. The lack of challengers has been especially prominent in states deep in the South and in Texas. In 1966, 17 of the 21 Democratic districts in Texas were won without opposition. While the state has become more competitive since then, a number of races in its districts have remained unopposed despite support in the district for Republican presidential candidates. Even though 62 percent supported Reagan in 1984, Democrat Jim Chapman ran unopposed in the Texas 1st district in 1986. Marvin Leath ran unopposed in the conservative 11th district 5 times straight in the 1980s, and Omar Burleson and Chuck Stenholm combined to run unopposed in Texas' 17th district in 11 out of 12 races between 1968 and 1990. Only in 1976 did their district support a Democratic presidential candidate.

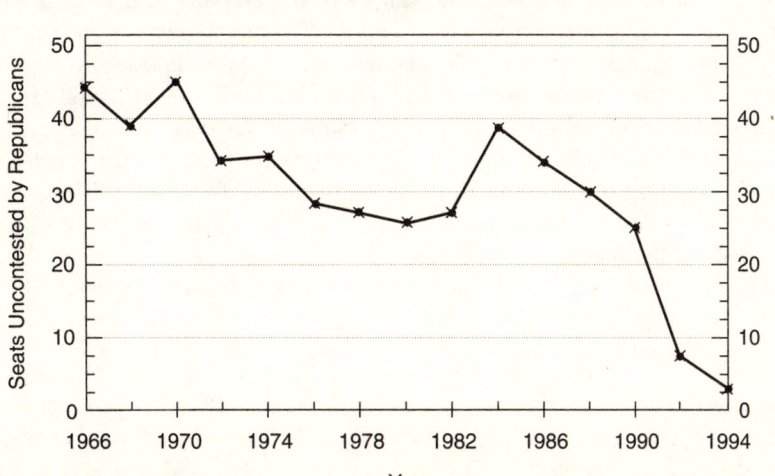

FIGURE 6.4
House Seats Uncontested by Republican Challengers, 1966–1994

This trend has not been confined to Texas. As Reagan swept Alabama's 3rd, 4th, and 5th congressional districts with 60 percent of the vote in 1984, the three Democratic incumbents, Bill Nichols, Tom Bevill, and Ronnie Flippo, all ran unopposed. Bevill has run unopposed 7 times since 1968, and only in 1994 did a Republican candidate receive as much as 25 percent of the vote in his district. Between 1970 and 1990, Arkansas Democrat Bill Alexander ran unopposed 6 times, and in another race, his Republican opponent received less than 10 percent of the vote. Mississippi's Sonny Montgomery ran unchallenged in 11 consecutive races between 1970 and 1990, and no Republican opposed either Dawson Mathis or Charles Hatcher in Georgia's 2nd district in 8 of 9 elections between 1970 and 1986, despite McGovern receiving only 20 percent of the vote in 1972 and Walter Mondale receiving 42 percent of the vote in 1984.

Notice in Figure 6.4 the significant drop-off in the number of unopposed Democratic House races since 1990. A number of Democrats to lose their seats recently have come from districts that have continually supported Republicans in presidential campaigns but have failed to offer Republican opposition at the House level. Before losing Georgia's first district to a Republican in 1992, the two Democratic representatives (Bo Ginn—who ran unopposed in his first attempt at the open seat in 1972—and Lindsey Thomas) ran unopposed 6 times and were not threatened in other races. Earl Hutto of Florida, who was replaced by a Republican in 1994, did not face substantial competition until 1990 and ran unopposed in 1984 despite Reagan receiving 76 percent of the vote in his district. Bill Nelson consistently represented the Florida district that Jim Bacchus would subsequently lose in 1994 without substantial opposition, and before Tom Barlow lost Kentucky's first district, Carroll Hubbard ran unopposed 7 consecutive times. Finally, Jamie Whitten, who retired in 1994, did not receive serious opposition in Mississippi's first district until 1992. When Reagan gained 63 percent of the vote in 1984 and when Richard Nixon gained 80 percent of the vote in 1972, Whitten ran unopposed.

In fact, only 4 of the 22 southern Democrats who lost in 1994 (Buddy Darden of Georgia, David Price and Stephen Neal of North Carolina, and Mike Synar of Oklahoma) faced consistent opposition in past elections. The significance of this is only further emphasized by ANES data. Between 1980 and 1988, more than one-third of the southern voters sampled who split their tickets between Republican presidents and a Democratic House members did so in districts without Republican House candidates to choose from. In open seats, by contrast, less than 5 percent of the voters during this period split their tickets in a similar manner. These voters, then, have not dealigned by choice: Republican party candidates (or the lack thereof) have decided this for them. As the next section will show, the actions of Democratic party candidates have also played an important role in this phenomenon.

CONTINUED PROMINENCE OF THE CONSERVATIVE COALITION

The conservatism of southern Democratic House and Senate members is well known. That they were able to block civil rights legislation until the 1960s and to provide the crucial votes in favor of Reagan's economic agenda in the early 1980s has prompted national attention to their role in a conservative coalition with Republicans. Yet two events are assumed to have brought conservative Democrats more in line with the rest of the Democratic party: the necessity of southern Democrats to appeal to growing numbers of comparatively liberal African-American voters after 1965 and reform of the Democratic party caucus in the House that provided the leadership more power to persuade rank-and-file members to vote along party and ideological lines, as well as the increased capability to punish those who disobeyed (Rohde 1991).

Nonetheless, southern Democratic House members have invariably been able to distinguish themselves to their constituents as separate from their national party image. A study of the 1988 election found that southern voters perceived their Democratic representatives to be much more akin ideologically to the Republican party and Bush than to the Democratic party and Dukakis (Frymer, Kim, and Bimes 1995). In part, this ability of southern Democratic House members to differentiate themselves from their national party's image has been due to "home-style" campaign methods, as representatives such as Bill Alexander have continually stressed that they are not "national" Democrats but "state" (in his case "Arkansas") Democrats.

This ability to differentiate themselves, however, has not been due solely to their successfully avoiding national issues in district election campaigns (i.e., Jacobson 1990a, Petrocik 1991). Confronted with districts that have been consistently conservative on a wide range of issues, Democrats in the South have distinguished themselves from their national counterparts by quite explicitly aligning themselves with the national Republican party image. This has been done quite frequently through criticism of Democratic presidential nominees and their policies or even more directly, as in the case of Arkansas Democrat Tommy Robinson, who ran newspaper ads welcoming Reagan to Little Rock or the case of North Carolina Democrat Martin Lancaster, who ran campaign ads with pictures of his Republican opponent shaking hands with Clinton.

Just as important as public pronouncements of difference on the campaign trail, Democratic representatives from conservative districts have maintained quite conservative voting records in Congress. The Americans for Democratic Action (ADA) calculate scores indicating how liberal or conservative representatives' voting records are. Although the number of southern Democrats who compile ADA

TABLE 6.2   Southern Democratic House Members with ADA Ratings of 50 or Less, 1972–1992

Year	Number
1972	85
1976	78
1980	75
1984	62
1988	34
1992	53

SOURCE: American National Election Study.

ratings of 50 or less (100 being most liberal, 0 representing most conservative) has declined since the early 1970s, a significant number of those with conservative ratings have remained into the 1990s (see Table 6.2). In fact, most of the Democrats to lose in the last two House elections compiled, at least until very recently, consistently low ADA scores (see Table 6.3).

Did voters in 1994 suddenly change their perceptions of their Democratic House members? Did these Democratic House members suddenly become more liberal? Having a Democratic president in the White House certainly placed new pressures on these southern Democrats and made it increasingly difficult for them to distance themselves from the national party in the eyes of their constituents. Whereas in the past, southern members could dodge the party leadership on issues which caused trouble in their districts, out of necessity President Clinton targeted many of these members to get a number of crucial pieces of legislation passed. Both the 1993 budget vote (which included a well-publicized tax hike) and the 1994 crime bill (with its antifirearm measures) came very close to being defeated in the House. Clinton was compelled to lean heavily on moderate to conservative Democrats in order to ultimately provide the margin of victory. The fact that Clinton himself is not only from the South but was formerly chair of the Democratic Leadership Council, a party strategy organization with a significant number of conservative southern Democrats, only added further pressure on these members to try to help the president's faltering legislative agenda gain momentum. Under this pressure a number of conservative Democrats went along with the President, allowing him two of the most significant victories of his struggling presidency.

These two votes came back to haunt many of these members. Buddy Darden and Don Johnson of Georgia and Jack Brooks of Texas, all strong opponents of gun control, were this time targeted by the National Rifle Association for their votes on behalf of the crime bill. Johnson was dubbed "Judas Johnson" after his crime-bill vote and was similarly maligned for his vote in favor of Clinton's budget plan in 1993. Bill Sarpalius of Texas, meanwhile, was hurt by the claim that he had been successfully strong-armed by fellow Texan and Clinton-cabinet-member Lloyd Bensten to support the budget plan. A number of members cited their support of Clinton's tax increase as the chief mobilizing issue leading to their electoral defeat. After initially having put their hopes in Clinton's ability to steer the Democratic party in a more conservative direction, southern Democrats were suddenly faced with angry voters who for the first time linked their Democratic House members with party leadership.

Although, at the time of writing this chapter, the 1994 national election data were only beginning to materialize, there is already some evidence that many Democratic representatives appeared considerably more liberal to their conservative constituents than they had in the past. A post-election survey conducted by Greenberg Research, for instance, found that health care and other Clinton programs have changed the perception that conservative voters had about their Democratic members of congress. An initial glance at the 1994 ANES data indicates that the data reflects a similar trend. In a 1990 post-election survey, 44 percent of southern voters sampled from the districts where there was party turnover

TABLE 6.3 ADA Scores from Districts Electing Republicans in 1994 and 1992

Democrat House Members	Year					
	1972	1976	1980	1984	1988	1992
1994						
Sikes-Hutto (Fla.)	13	5	22	20	20	15
Nelson-Bacchus (Fla.)	—	—	33	20	45	70
Davis-McDonald-Darden (Ga.)	6	0	6	30	45	55
Stuckey-Evans-Rowland (Ga.)	0	10	6	45	55	42
Stephens-Barnard-Johnson (Ga.)	6	10	11	15	25	15
Landrum-Jenkins-Deal (Ga.)	0	5	6	35	45	25
Stubblefield-Hubbard-Barlow (Ky.)	13	25	22	30	50	50
Natcher (Ky.)	31	45	50	60	75	85
Whitten (Miss.)	6	15	28	50	65	50
Fountain-Valentine (N.C.)	6	0	17	20	33	45
Henderson-Whitley-Lancaster (N.C.)	13	10	28	25	39	45
Andrews-Price (N.C.)	—	35	28	45	75	85
Neal (N.C.)	—	45	44	65	70	60
Riesenhoover-Synar (Okla.)	—	32	61	80	100	95
Steed-McCurdy (Okla.)	19	37	56	35	60	50
English (Okla.)	—	25	6	15	40	45
Dorn-Derrick (S.C.)	19	36	56	50	70	80
Lloyd (Tenn.)	—	10	22	35	45	37
Evins-Gore-Cooper (Tenn.)	19	20	50	65	70	50
Brooks (Tex.)	25	38	28	55	75	75
Hightower-Sarpalius (Tex.)	—	15	17	10	—	35
1992						
Erdeich (Ala.)	—	—	—	25	50	45
Pryor-Thornton-Anthony (Alaska)	25	20	22	50	80	65
Bennett (Fla.)	13	25	22	30	65	60
Lehman (Fla.)	—	80	89	85	100	55
Hagan-Ginn-Thomas (Ga.)	0	15	33	45	50	35
Brinkley-Ray (Ga.)	19	11	11	20	20	25
Levitas-Jones (Ga.)	—	40	28	—	—	65
Perkins-Perkins (Ky.)	38	60	56	63	85	75
Passman-Huckaby (La.)	6	0	11	25	40	10
Mann-Patterson (S.C.)	0	20	—	45	45	45
Kazen-Bustamante (Tex.)	13	15	22	70	70	60
Olin (Va.)	—	—	—	55	70	45

NOTE: Democrats lost 11 seats, but gained 10 new seats in 1992; the names of House members in districts that were represented by more than one member during the period are separated by hyphens.

in 1994 categorized their Democratic House candidates as conservative.[5] This dropped among respondents from these districts in 1994 to just 18 percent. This change is quite notable given past research showing that voters are significantly more likely to split their tickets when they perceived little to no difference between their Democratic House candidate and the Republican opponent (Frymer, Kim, and Bimes 1995). It is also telling that in the 15 southern districts that voted for Bush in 1988 and 1992 but reelected Democratic House members in 1994, the perception of their House members has remained considerably more conservative, (of these voters 45 percent perceived their House members as conservative).

CONCLUSION

One of the ironies of the Democratic party's losses in 1994 is that even with fewer southern Democratic House members than ever before, there are now more liberal Democratic House members from the region than at any time prior to 1992. The implementation since the 1990 Census of minority-majority House districts, districts created to include a majority of racial minority voters in order to comply with the Voting Rights Act, is largely responsible, and the representative styles of those serving African-American and Latino majorities have changed dramatically (Grofman, Griffin, and Glazer 1994; Bullock 1994). The impact of these districts has extended beyond a collective change in voting scores among southern House members; the increased number of African-American representatives has significantly bolstered the influence of the Congressional Black Caucus as a legislative organization. After years of watching its legislative efforts from the margins of the Democratic party, the 38 members of the Caucus wielded considerable influence in the 103rd Congress on highly visible matters, such as the 1994 crime bill, President Clinton's Haitian policy, and important budget and deficit-reducing proposals.

Nonetheless, racially based redistricting is currently a popular explanation for the Democratic party's electoral losses in the South. It is argued that moderate white Democrats were defeated by Republican challengers in 1992 and 1994 because a sizeable number of their constituents were moved into newly created districts designed to provide safe majorities for African-American candidates (Hill 1995). This has effectively divided the two parties in the region along quite stark racial lines. In Georgia, for example, Nathan Deal's switch to the Republican party after the 1994 election left the state with 8 Republican representatives, all of whom are white, and 3 Democratic representatives, all of whom are black.

To blame Democratic electoral defeats solely on minority-majority districts, however, is to neglect the ongoing transformation in southern white voting behavior. As the research in this chapter suggests, more and more white voters have been moving towards the Republican party for the last three decades. The significance of minority-majority districts on the electoral outcome of the 1994 elections is not just that the loss of black constituents left white Democratic incumbents vulnerable but that an influential Congressional Black Caucus inadvertently helped speed up the realigning process by aiding the passage of liberal policies unpopular with moderate and conservative white voters. That so many white voters, not only in the South but across the nation, reacted negatively to the Caucus' increased influence should alert scholars to focus not so much on the specific ramifications of the Voting Rights Act but instead on the broader difficulty that a majority-based legislative system has in accommodating the substantive voice of its African-American representatives. More attention should be paid to electoral structures, such as cumulative voting supported by Lani Guinier and Clarence Thomas, that deemphasize the strategic incentives for white candidates to make appeals along racial lines.

Meanwhile, the recent preference shown by a majority on the Supreme Court to overturn congressional districts drawn specifically to aid descriptive representation on behalf of African-Americans will in all likelihood fail to lead to the resurgence of the Democratic party in the region. Of the conservative Democrats left in the South, a few members have since switched their party affiliation, others have openly discussed the possibility of switching to the Republican party, while still others have announced plans to retire as of 1996. Democrats will likely lose more conservative districts, then, as a strengthened Republican party in the region continues to appeal to those voters who have long been voting Republican in national elections. The realignment among southern white voters and the changes in candidate behavior, then, make it unlikely that the results of 1996 will be similar to those in 1954 when the Republicans last lost the majority in the House of Representatives after only two years.

As for the other 38 seats nationwide to turnover in 1994, it is certainly a bit foolhardy to link them together under realignment theory. However, although the South's distinctive history with the Democratic party makes comparisons with other regions difficult, some of the factors leading to a realignment aftershock in the South are evident in the nation as a whole. Changing voter perceptions of Democratic House members and preexisting conservative ideology played important roles in explaining which voters switched to the Republican party in 1994 and which voters did not. Even when measured against other potentially important indicators of voting behavior, these two variables show significant strength. In the analysis of Table 6.4, I show the effect of both of these variables and with other potentially important signifiers of whether people who voted for Democratic House members in 1992 switched their votes in the 1994 elections. Both the voters' preexisting ideology and its interaction with their perception of the Democratic House members have important effects. Voter approval ratings of Clinton, the crime bill, and the health care bill are not significant, even when isolated to avoid collinearity problems.

The evidence presented in this chapter illustrates that the supposed trend among voters to balance parties out of dislike or ambivalence is overstated. In the South, voters have been splitting their tickets in part out of lack of choice and in part because southern Democrats have been compatible ideologically with Republican presidents. Now that the Republican party is more competitive in southern elections, it will be difficult for the Democrats to gain many of these voters back. White southern voters have been electing conservatives to the House for a

TABLE 6.4 Determinants of Choice for House in 1994 among Those Voting Democratic in 1992

Variable	Logit Estimate[a]	Standard Error
Intercept	−1.31	0.86
Democratic incumbent	1.69	0.67
Republican incumbent	−1.17	0.92
Party identification	−1.29	0.38
Respondent ideology in 1992[b]	−0.67	0.27
(Perception of Democratic House member in 1994 × respondent ideology 1992)	0.13	0.06
Approval of Clinton in 1994	0.04	.16
Support of Health Care Bill in 1994	.03	.18
Support of Crime Bill in 1994	.06	.19

[a]Since the dependent variable, the House vote in 1994 (0 = R, 1 = D), is a dichotomous measure logit, rather than ordinary least squares, was used.
[b]Ideology of 1992 respondents was taken from the 1994 ANES panel study, 1 = liberal, 3 = conservative.
NOTE: Number of cases equals 157; estimates were obtained by maximum likelihood.
SOURCE: American National Election Study.

long time. Only now has the Republican party truly replaced the Democratic party as the dominant conservative party of the South.

Evidence of a delayed realignment in the South does not mean, however, that political scholars need to recharge old theories of critical elections. Although proclamations of the "end of realignment" (Shafer 1991) are perhaps premature, the evidence in this chapter raises as many questions about realignment theory as it answers. While it provides some coherence to a long-term trend of southern ticket splitting, it leaves unanswered questions such as: When did the realignment first actually begin? Is the 1994 aftershock a final culmination of a realignment first started in the 1930s? If so, what does realignment theory offer political scholars when realignment can take six or more decades to accomplish?

To some degree, however, these questions are misdirected. Because conservatives have dominated the political agenda, as they have over the last few decades, it seems somewhat less relevant whether voters have actually changed their party identification or not. More important is the meaning of their votes in terms of ideology and the implications it has for political life. Once scholars focus more closely on ideological identification, they will find a rather consistent political order that is dramatically different from that of 40 years ago when Republicans last lost the majority.

NOTES

1. I would like to thank Terri Bimes, Jake Bowers, Jon Cowden, Peter Gold, Tom Kim, Phil Klinkner, David Mayhew, Jon Oberlander, and Eric Schickler for their help and suggestions.

2. This analysis includes the districts of Democratic incumbents William Natcher of Kentucky, who passed away shortly before the 1994 November elections, and Nathan Deal of Georgia, who switched to the Republican party shortly after the election.

3. By southern states I am referring to all 11 ex-Confederate states as well as Kentucky and Oklahoma.

4. Note, however, that this movement has occurred only among southern whites. According to the 1994 ANES, 82 percent of southern blacks identified themselves with the Democratic party.

5. This question was not asked in the 1992 ANES. As a result, the survey did not take into account redistricting which could have biased the comparison.

7

The Politics of Pragmatism: The Christian Right and the 1994 Elections

J. CHRISTOPHER SOPER

The Republican party's stunning gains in the 1994 midterm elections left analysts wondering who or what to credit for the party's success. Chief among the groups claiming and receiving responsibility for the election results has been the Christian right. According to a national exit poll, white evangelical or born-again Christians represented 20 percent of the votes cast on election day, and they voted by a margin of over three to one for Republican House candidates. The Christian Coalition, the largest organization in the Christian right with an estimated 1.5 million members, endorsed 60 of the 73 House Republican freshman in 1994. Several candidates closely identified with the Christian right including Senators Michael DeWine (Ohio), Rick Santorum (Pennsylvania), and John Ashcroft (Missouri); Representatives Ron Lewis (Kentucky), Steve Largent, and J. C. Watts (Oklahoma); and Governor David Beasley (South Caraliona) won office. In addition, evangelical Christians were active in Republican party politics in the previous two years and provided the GOP with key resources for electoral success: grassroots organizations, financing, and well-organized and devoted activists. It is hard to dismiss Ralph Reed, Executive Director of the Christian Coalition, who contends that conservative Christian voters were instrumental in over half of the Republicans 52-seat gain in the House and their 9-seat pickup in the Senate.

Despite the clear signs of the influence of the Christian right, in 1994, there were also some setbacks for the movement. Republican party leaders did not include the moral issues of abortion, gay rights, and school prayer in their ten-point Contract with America; Oliver North, who openly identified with the Christian right, was defeated in Virginia's Senate race, as were anti–gay rights initiatives in Oregon and Idaho; and Republicans ignored social issues in their first 100 days in office.

The purpose of this chapter is to examine the influence of the Christian right in the 1994 midterm elections. I argue that the Christian right was an important faction within the Republican party in 1994 and a growing force in American politics. The election, however, also demonstrated the limits to the movement's political power. The family and moral issues around which conservative Christians have mobilized were not decisive in these elections. The Christian right contributed to the GOP victory, but it was part of a broader conservative coalition that propelled the Republicans to power. Second, I evaluate the future prospects of the Christian right in the Republican party. The leadership of the Christian right pursued a pragmatic strategy that helped solidify evangelical ties with the GOP; white evangelicals are now among the most stable sources of support for the Republican party. There are, however, tensions between socially moderate and conservative factions within the party that will likely intensify as the euphoria of the Republican victory in 1994 subsides and the party begins the process of selecting a candidate for the presidential election of 1996. The evangelical-GOP alliance is strong, but it remains open to fracture.

THE BACKGROUND: THE GOP-EVANGELICAL ALLIANCE EMERGES

The Christian right has grown steadily in political influence and sophistication since it burst onto the national scene with the founding of Jerry Falwell's Moral Majority in 1979. Fueled by an antipathy to the liberalizing and secularizing social norms and practices of the 1960s and 1970s, evangelical and fundamentalist Christians formed a number of organizations to defend deeply held values (Wilcox 1992; Soper 1994). The religious convictions of conservative Christians provided them with clear priorities and policy stances, while a well-integrated network of churches, radio and television stations, and schools made them relatively easy to mobilize (Wuthnow 1983). The formation of the Christian right coincided with Ronald Reagan's first presidential campaign. Reagan appealed to evangelicals on the issues of abortion, pornography, and school prayer and won their votes away from the Democratic party whose liberal positions on these issues alienated many believers (Wald 1992). The Republican party platforms throughout the 1980s reflected Reagan's commitment to conservative social and political values, and by 1992 evangelicals were a core voting bloc within the GOP coalition (Kellstedt et al. 1994).

The 1992 platform, with its positions on abortion, gay rights, and family values, showed evangelical strength in the party. When George Bush lost the 1992 presidential election, the national news media and GOP moderates concluded that the party's moral conservatism and religious extremism were responsible and dismissed evangelicals as a political liability. Ironically, the media, which has never understood the complexity and attraction of the movement, rediscovered the Christian right in the aftermath of the 1994 elections (Green 1995).

Evangelical groups, led by the Christian Coalition—the largest and most important organization of the Christian right—responded to Bush's defeat in two ways. First, it mobilized support within state Republican parties to wrest control from party regulars. This type of political activism played to the strengths of the Christian Coalition. With a $20 million annual budget, a membership of 1.5 million that was spread out in over 1,100 local chapters, and a well-developed network of institutions linking group members, in 1994 the coalition used its resources to gain influence within state Republican party organizations. Members of the coalition and socially conservative allies committed time, energy, and resources and turned out for party leadership positions to which few party members have paid attention. While there has been much variation among state political parties (Mayhew 1986), as a rule American parties have been weak and thereby open to the mobilization of active, dedicated voters and organizations. This influx of newcomers caused considerable tension within a number of state Republican parties (Hertzke 1993), but the porousness of state party structures provided the ideal context for Christian right activism. Party moderates could not stop this influx of enthusiastic activists, and because turnout in party elections has been low, conservative Christians were able to win important posts in a number of state Republican parties. According to one estimate (Persinos 1994), social conservatives had a "dominant" influence in 18 state Republican organizations and a "substantial" influence in 13 more.

The Christian right used its newfound authority within the GOP to draft state party platforms and sponsor candidates for elective office, particularly those in the suburbs—the Christian right's power base (Green et al. 1993). Demonstrating an impressive political sophistication, the Christian right shaped its political strategy to take full advantage of the opportunities provided by each state's political institutions. In Virginia, evangelicals packed the party convention and secured the 1994 GOP Senate nomination for North (Wilcox, Rozell, and Coker 1995); Christian right delegates to Minnesota's state party convention won the pre-primary endorsement for fellow evangelical Allen Quist over the Republican incumbent Governor Arne Carlson (Gilbert 1995); and evangelicals in states as disparate as California, Oklahoma, and South Carolina sponsored candidates in political primary elections (Bendar and Hertzke 1995; Guth 1995).

Second, the leadership of the Christian right, particularly Reed and others in the Christian Coalition, pursued a more pragmatic strategy in an attempt to maximize evangelical political influence and minimize divisions within the Republican party. Between the presidential election of 1992 and the midterm elections of 1994, the coalition gave a lower priority to divisive moral issues, such as abortion, gay rights, and family values. Calling it a "tactical shift" to broaden the coalition's appeal, Reed focused on issues that united Republicans: crime, taxes, government waste, and health care (Reed 1993). The coalition openly supported such Republican supporters of abortion rights as Senators Kay Bailey Hutchison (Texas) and Paul Coverdell (Georgia) and demonstrated a new willingness to work with the party to elect moderate candidates to office.

California is a particularly good example of this pragmatism at work. The two Republican candidates for statewide office, Mike Huffington for Senate and Pete Wilson for Governor, were pro-choice and social moderates. Wilson had to overcome a historically testy relationship with Christian conservatives in the party who had vigorously opposed him in previous campaigns. Huffington defeated William Danneymeyer—a candidate with close ties to the Christian right—in the

Republican party primary. Under the guidance of the Christian Coalition of California, however, evangelicals worked hard for Wilson and Huffington. The coalition distributed hundreds of thousands of voter guides throughout the state in sympathetic churches the Sunday before the election. Though ostensibly nonpartisan, the voter guides made it clear whom the organization favored in the 1994 elections. The scorecard carefully avoided moral issues that would have exposed the Republican candidates' moderate social views. It also highlighted positions where Wilsons and Huffington's policies coincided with those of the coalition and it contained questions worded in such a way as to differentiate the Democratic and Republican politicians as much as possible. On abortion, for example, the voter guide focused on taxpayer funding for abortion, which Wilson and Huffington opposed and both Democrats supported, rather than on a repeal of abortion, which all four candidates opposed.

There are a number of reasons why the Christian right adopted this policy pragmatism. Moderation was in part a natural response to a party culture that stressed accommodation and unity for the good of the party (Freeman 1986) and a national party organization that limited factional conflicts (Klinkner 1994). The Christian right also discovered, as have numerous social movements before it, that time and involvement in the political process lead almost invariably to political compromise (Moen 1994). Finally, pragmatism was a tactic born of political necessity. The Christian right is not large enough to win political primaries or general elections on a consistent basis, particularly in states outside of the Bible Belt where evangelicals have been a significant, but not controlling, faction within the party. This pragmatism marked a new stage in the political maturation of the Christian right. Instead of abandoning party candidates who were less than ideal from a conservative Christian standpoint, as they had done in previous elections, leaders of the Christian right embraced Republican moderates and urged fellow evangelicals to support GOP candidates for the goal of partisan victory in 1994.

THE 1994 MIDTERM ELECTIONS: THE PARTISAN ALLIANCE SOLIDIFIES

The data from the 1994 midterm elections shows that evangelicals were an important group within the electorate and a significant voting bloc in the Republican party. A national exit poll by Mitofsky International on the 1994 elections indicated that 27 percent of all voters identified themselves as a born-again or evangelical Christians, up from an estimated 18 percent in 1988 and 24 percent in 1992. When controlled for race, a still impressive 20 percent of the 1994 electorate emerged.

Evangelicals supported the GOP by a large majority. Republican House candidates outpolled Democrats among white evangelicals by 76 to 24 percent. In an election where the parties split the national vote evenly, this 52-percentage-point margin among this large group of voters was significant. The political impact of evangelical voters varied from state to state. The Christian right provided valuable resources to Republican party candidates, and in close races they helped provide the winning margin for the GOP. The Christian Coalition distributed over 30 mil-

TABLE 7.1 Sources of House Vote by Issue

Issues	Total Mentions	Percentage Voting	
		Democrat	Republican
Crime	35	53%	47%
Campaign finance reform	4	62	38
Abortion	13	42	58
Health care	22	67	33
Family values	21	27	73
Foreign trade/NAFTA[a]	3	39	61
Education	18	64	36
Economy/jobs	26	55	45
Taxes	23	30	70

[a]North American Free Trade Agreement.
NOTE: Since more than one response was permitted, the resulting figures for total mentions do not add up to 100.
SOURCE: Mitofsky International.

lion voter guides for the election. It is impossible to measure the impact of such an effort, but the Republican party clearly benefited from the grassroots, mobilizing efforts of the Christian Coalition. Evangelicals voted for Republican candidates across the board. In California, for example, 78 percent of white evangelicals voted for the pro-choice, socially moderate Wilson and 70 percent for Huffington.

Moral issues were not, however, decisive in most races as is shown in Table 7.1. Nationwide, voters mentioned crime, the economy, and taxes most frequently when asked which two issues mattered most to them in deciding how they voted for candidates for the U.S. House. Fewer voters cited the social issues of abortion and family values, but those who did voted by large majorities for Republican House candidates.

In theory, the Democratic party had an opportunity in 1994 to appeal to evangelical voters. Republican moderates might have been vulnerable to centrist Democratic candidates who made appeals on those parts of the Christian right agenda that were popular: government support for traditional moral values, the teaching of virtue, and the importance of individual responsibility. In practice, however, the party did nothing to attract conservative Christian voters. Led by Vic Fazio, Chairman of the Democratic Congressional Campaign Committee, the Democratic party criticized the Republicans for being willing to turn over their party to the "intolerant religious right." This approach failed on two fronts: It intensified evangelical opposition to the Democratic party, and it did not make the election a referendum on the Christian right.

Fazio's reproach did not even mobilize Democratic partisans. Voters who called themselves Democrats were much less likely than Republican partisans to mention the issues of abortion and family values as reasons for their House vote (see Table 7.2). White evangelicals, by comparison, were more likely than any

TABLE 7.2 Issue Preference by Party and White Evangelical

	Mentioned Issue		
Issues	Percentage of Democrats	Percentage of Republicans	Percentage of Evangelicals
Crime	38%	32%	22%
Campaign finance reform	6	3	4
Abortion	11	15	26
Health care	28	14	16
Family values	12	31	45
Foreign trade	2	3	3
Education	24	13	10
Economy/jobs	29	23	17
Taxes	13	31	22

NOTE: Since more than one response was permitted, the resulting figures for total mentions does not add up to 100.
SOURCE: Mitofsky International.

TABLE 7.3 Party Vote by Selected Religious Groups

Religion	Percentage of House Vote	House Votes		Proportion of House Vote	
		Democrat	Republican	Democrat	Republican
White evangelical	30%	24%	76%	9%	30%
Highly religious[a]	21	44	56	19	24
Secular	10	58	42	12	7
Jewish	4	71	29	5	2

[a]The highly religious are those voters who claimed to have attended church once a week but were not evangelical.
SOURCE: Mitofsky International.

other group in the electorate to base their voting decisions on those two issues. The Republican party benefited electorally from the issues of abortion and family values because social-issue conservatives cared more deeply about those issues than social liberals did.

The 1994 elections solidified a deepening religious and cultural cleavage between the parties. As Table 7.3 shows, Republican House candidates did particularly well among evangelical Christians and nonevangelical, but highly religious mainline Protestants and Roman Catholics. Combined, these two groups provided over one half (54 percent) of all Republican House votes in 1994. The Democratic party, by

TABLE 7.4 Party Identification and Ideology by Selected Religious Groups

Religion	Party Identification		Political Ideology		
	Democrats	Republicans	Liberal	Moderate	Conservative
White evangelical	20%	54%	6%	33%	61%
Highly religious	34	39	15	48	37
Secular	44	27	31	47	22
Jewish	57	13	36	50	14
All voters	41	35	18	47	35

SOURCE: Mitofsky International.

contrast, won significant support among Jewish voters and nonbelievers. These two groups combined to give the Democratic party 17 percent of its House votes.

There was a similar pattern in the partisan identification and political ideology of religious voters (see Table 7.4). Of white evangelicals 54 percent described themselves as Republicans and only 20 percent as Democrats; highly religious voters were also more likely to be Republicans by a margin of 39 to 34 percent. In terms of political ideology, these religionists tended to be more conservative than did the electorate as a whole. Jewish and secular voters were more likely than the average voter to be politcally liberal and identify with the Democratic party. Like the findings of Kellstedt et al. (1994) for the 1992 presidential election, the 1994 data suggest that evangelicals and secularists have, respectively, become the cultural cores of the Republican and Democratic parties.

Religion has always been an important factor in American party alignments, but historically denomination was the key religious variable that divided voters into the Democratic and Republican camps. The emerging party alignment is based less on denomination and more on the salience, or importance of religious belief to voters (Guth and Green 1991). The Republican party has increasingly attracted religionists who organize their lives around their faith, while the Democrats have appealed to nonbelievers, who are a growing percentage of the electorate, and to those voters for whom religion is not very important (Green and Guth 1991). The Christian right and the "secular left," both of which have impressive political resources, have helped to shape their respective partys' policies. The Democratic party has been socially liberal, "tolerant," and progressive because a growing percentage of its party activists have not been religious and have not perceived a cost in religious and social accommodation. The Republican party has been socially conservative, less "tolerant," and traditionalist because party activists have cared more about sacred matters and have believed that there is a high cost to accommodating their religious norms to secular or liberal values. Religious alignments have solidified as each party has responded to its religious core. Evangelical support for the GOP has increased as the Republican party has become more culturally conservative and the Democratic party culturally liberal.

CONCLUSION

Conservative Christian leaders did not make abortion or gay rights a litmus test for the elections and there were no major rifts in the evangelical-GOP alliance. As a result, the Christian right contributed to the Republican surge in 1994. Since the midterm elections, the Christian right has strengthened its ties to the GOP and moved to the center of political power. The party infighting that marked relations between social conservatives and moderates after Bush's presidential defeat in 1992 was largely absent in first few months of euphoria for the party's victories in 1994. Reed of the Christian Coalition is widely credited with helping to deliver the evangelical vote to the GOP, and he has become a key player among Republican lawmakers and candidates for President. He attended strategy sessions at the office of House Speaker Newt Gingrich, and he agreed to push for passage of the Republican Contract with America before moving to a consideration of social issues. The coalition financed a $1 million lobbying campaign on behalf of passage of the contract. It was clear that the Christian right had arrived as a powerful political faction when dozens of prominent Republican lawmakers and party presidential hopefuls joined Reed when he announced the Christian Coalition's ten-point Contract with the American Family (Berke 1995a).

While integration into the Republican party has provided political opportunities for the Christian right, there have also been costs for evangelical interest groups that are nonpartisan in name only. Reed and the Christian Coalition have helped to persuade evangelicals to care about issues other than abortion and gay rights, and increasingly the economic and foreign policy views of conservative Christians have coincided with the Republican party (Guth et al. 1993). The evangelical identification with the GOP was particularly apparent when 70 percent of evangelicals in California voted for Huffington, who was pro-choice and supported gays serving in the military. Reed's strategy succeeded, but it threatens to undermine evangelical electoral independence. With evangelicals closely attached to the GOP and the Democratic party firmly committed to social-policy liberalism, it is unlikely that the Christian Coalition could mobilize conservative Christians to abandon the Republican party on social issues alone. This is not to suggest that the coalition should have pursued a "purer" ideological strategy in which it openly challenged moderate GOP candidates. The group's pragmatic strategy increased the political relevance of conservative Christian voters, but there were costs associated with its political accommodation.

Like any social movement, the Christian right faces the challenge of finding a political strategy that broadens the movement's appeal without risking the support of activists. Tensions between purists and pragmatists are common for a social movement, but they seem particularly strong in the Christian right. Under Reed's leadership, the Christian Coalition has played very well to the pragmatists. He has broadened the Christian right's agenda and toned down its harsh rhetoric that had frustrated the movement's effort to move beyond its sectarian core following.

The danger of Reed's pragmatic strategy is that it risks alienating Christian activists for whom the issues of abortion and gay rights are the reasons they originally became politically involved. These Christian activists will wonder what it profits them to gain access within a political party if they must lose their souls in the process. How long will they be content to put party unity ahead of religious principles? Fred Barnes, an evangelical Christian and a political writer for the *New Republic*, is one of the first people within the conservative Christian camp to question if Reed has gone too far at minimizing social issues for the sake of influence within the GOP (Barnes 1995). He will not be the last. It will not go unnoticed among activists in the Christian right that the coalition's Contract with the American Family did not mention an issue that has mobilized religious conservatives in the past: opposing civil rights protections for homosexuals.

Because of tensions within the Christian right, party leaders cannot take for granted that the evangelical-GOP alliance will continue to hold. Reed has recently pushed harder on social issues, but in doing so he has highlighted real divisions between socially conservative and moderate Republicans that will continue to produce intraparty friction. While there is considerable public support for traditional family values, opposition to the Christian right within the party will intensify as it defines what these values imply for public policy. The coalition's Contract With the American Family, for example, includes controversial proposals for allowing voluntary prayer in public schools and the use of religious symbols in public places, for restricting abortion and pornography, and for sending block grants to states to be used for private school vouchers (Niebuhr 1995). The Christian Coalition has also turned up the rhetoric on the always-divisive abortion issue. It released a survey of 1,000 likely voters in the GOP primaries that found that 62 percent of those polled favored retaining the pro-life plank in the GOP platform (*Hotline Weekly Report* 1995). Christian broadcaster and founder of the Christian Coalition, Pat Robertson, has warned that the nomination in 1996 of a Republican presidential or vice presidential candidate who favors abortion rights could "bring the ticket down" by alienating social conservatives (Brownstein 1995). Activists at state and local levels have continued to mobilize for control of state party organizations. In Washington, Ken Eikenberry, who is chairman of the GOP in the state, faced a challenge to his leadership position from Christian Coalition member Ron Taber less than a month after the midterm elections ended.

The presence of factions within the Republican party is not unusual, nor is it necessarily a sign of party weakness. Factional disputes are endemic to political parties which must by necessity form coalitions with different political agendas (Baer 1993). The issue is how well the Republican party manages the division between the Christian right and party moderates. Given their political power in state party organizations, it is naive to think that moderates can or should rid the GOP of the Christian right. The Republican party cannot win without evangelicals who have become as important to the GOP as labor unions have traditionally been for the Democratic party. Christian conservatives represented over 30 percent of the GOP

House vote in 1994, and they are among the most sophisticated and active groups within the party. While evangelicals are not likely to abandon the GOP on social issues alone, the Christian right can threaten to withhold its formidable resources from the Republican party in 1996. The Christian Coalition might do this if its members do not enthusiastically support the party's 1996 presidential candidate.

In an era of candidate-centered elections, Republican party hopefuls need the resources and enthusiasm which the Christian right provides. Few groups within the GOP can organize voters as effectively as the Christian Coalition can. Even well-known party moderates, such as California's Wilson, have recognized the political power of the Christian right and have shifted their views accordingly. Wilson actively courted the evangelical vote in 1994 and moved to the right on selected moral issues that concerned the leadership of the Christian right. While he did not abandon his pro-choice views, Wilson did not advertise them, and he spoke more than he has in the past about the importance of traditional family values (Lesher 1995). The Republican party can no more ignore the concerns of evangelical voters and the Christian right than can the Democrats reject black voters or labor unions.

Despite lingering tensions in the evangelical-GOP alliance, both sides have powerful incentives to negotiate a settlement. The Christian right provides the party with political resources and enthusiastic activists; identification with the GOP has given the Christian right new opportunities to exercise political influence. The Republican party gives the movement a conduit into a political system that discourages third party candidates and rewards politically active groups with influence over party policy. As evangelicals have become more involved in Republican party politics, they have helped shape party policy, have exercised leadership on candidate selection, and, most importantly, have been better able to build coalitions with like-minded factions in the party. The Republican party and evangelical Christians are growing in political strength, and neither has a long-term interest in disrupting a coalition that has brought increased political power and influence to each of them.

8

In Search of the Angry White Male: Gender, Race, and Issues in the 1994 Elections

GRANT REEHER
JOSEPH CAMMARANO[1]

Aside from the change in the party control of Congress, the aspect of the 1994 elections that has probably received the most attention from media analysts is the supposed phenomenon of the "revenge of the angry white males." Looking at the voting data, we see the analysts have good reason to posit such a phenomenon: Although there have been for some time both gender and race gaps in American voting behavior, in which women and blacks have been more supportive of Democratic candidates than men and whites, in 1994 these gaps were particularly large. The gender gap in the support for Democratic House candidates, for example, went from 3 percent in the mid-term House elections of 1986 and 1990 to 8 percent in 1994.[2] More important for the angry-white-male thesis, however, is the fact that statistically, the increase in this gap was caused entirely by defections of men from the Democratic to the Republican candidates. In 1986, 1990, and 1994 women's support for Democratic House candidates remained constant at 54 percent, an 8 percent margin over that for Republicans. In contrast, in 1986 and 1990 men supported Democratic candidates by a 4 percent margin, while in 1994 they supported Republican candidates by an 8 percent margin. But most important for the thesis and perhaps most startling was the magnitude of the decrease in support for Democratic candidates among white men. White men supported Republican candidates by a 6 percent margin in 1986 and a 4 percent margin in 1990; in 1994 this margin was 24 percent.

Of course, media analysts had described American voters as angry well before the 1994 elections. In 1992, they held that voters were disenchanted with their futures, particularly their economic futures, and that this disenchantment in turn led them to reject an incumbent president whom they had overwhelmingly supported just 16 months earlier. But despite the media attention given to the angry voter (for example, *Time* magazine's devotion of its cover story to this theme in the spring of 1992), more systematic analyses of voters in 1992 found few departures from past patterns (Frankovic 1993).

Enter 1994 and the large drop-off in support for Democratic candidates among white men. Qualifying past descriptions with race and gender distinctions, media analysts accounted for this phenomenon by positing that several related factors—that together constituted the angry-white-male thesis—have been occurring in the lives and in the minds of white male voters. These factors are similar in many respects to those described by Thomas and Mary Edsall (1991) in an earlier work primarily directed at white voting in Presidential elections. They include declining real incomes for the working classes and decreased job security more generally, rising overall tax burdens, increased fear of crime with an accompanying subjective association of crime with race and poverty, a subjective association of poverty and welfare with race and with the Democratic Party, and apparently race-specific redistributional initiatives on the part of government, in particular affirmative action in education, employment, and contract awards, that have in turn been associated with the Democratic Party.[3] According to analysis done by the Edsalls, these factors combined in a "chain reaction" resulting in anger and resentment among whites, and subsequent defections from the Democratic Party. These nationally based factors were certainly part of Ronald Reagan's populist appeal (despite the upwardly redistributional reality of his policy proposals), but until 1994 they apparently did not have much of an impact on what were considered to be mostly locally oriented House elections. In the aftermath of 1994, national politicians have once again responded to them; President Clinton has appeared to make further rhetorical adjustments to appeal to voters motivated by these factors (at least prior to the Oklahoma City bombing), while Republican presidential aspirants have apparently attempted to cash in on their support.

According to post-election media analysts, there were at least two other important factors contributing to the outcome in 1994 that were more specific to the two years prior to the elections: the effects of the growth of (mostly conservative) talk radio shows, which were thought to make the white male not only angrier but also more likely to vote, and the failure of health care reform and its contribution to a general perception of failure on the part of both the Clinton Presidency and the Democratic Congress.

Excerpts from an autobiographical paper written in April 1995 by one of our white male students, who voted for the first time in the 1994 elections, provide an intriguing glimpse into some aspects of this frame of mind.[4]

> Is it fair to force taxpayers to pay for able-bodied people that refuse to find a job? Welfare is ... unjust to both the people in it, and especially to the taxpayers supporting it. ... [E]xcept for the truly disabled, why do we need programs such as welfare? ... Taxpayers are sick and tired of paying for able-bodied people to do nothing with their lives. ...
>
> In our current system, mothers are encouraged to have more children because each child that they have increases the money that they receive. Each child is also guaranteed, at the expense of taxpayers, free health care and food stamps. It would make sense to cut off these benefits to welfare mothers who continue to have children, because they should know that they have no right to abuse the system by having lots of children if the American taxpayers are supporting them. ...

[Recently,] I went into [an urban grocery store] because I had to buy a few things. While waiting on the check out line, I noticed a man in front of me with two filled shopping carts. In it were the best and most expensive brands available in the supermarket.... Instead of taking out cash, or a check, the man ripped out $250 worth of food stamps.... How can the government and its taxpayers allow people like this to milk the system?... It angers me to see people like this buy all the best and most expensive brands, and show no remorse for taking extra taxpayer dollars....

Although I am strongly pro-choice, I have sided with the Republicans on most major issues and I recently became a registered Republican.... The night of the elections was quite exciting. To see practically everyone that I voted for win was a great feeling of accomplishment.

But what does more systematic data on voters in the 1994 elections reveal about the notion of the angry white male? Was there indeed an angry-white-male revenge at the polls? Our investigation of these questions was based on the recently available data from the 1994 American National Election Studies (ANES). Our findings indicate that while there is support for a continued, and in some instances, increasing gap between men and women, the drop-off in Democratic support among white males does not appear to be the product of a changed and significantly different set of views about affirmative action, welfare, and other related issues. White males may have been angry at the polls, but they were angry in ways different from those posited by media analysts. There is evidence for some kind of angry-white-male phenomenon regarding turnout, however, in which white males, and apparently dissatisfied (if not angry) white males, turned out at a comparatively higher rate. Furthermore, when we examine a broader combination of both attitudes and mobilization, a picture of the "ambivalent female" emerges in addition to the angry white male. This ambivalence on the part of women was expressed in skepticism toward both political parties and helps to explain why women voted at lower rates than men did in 1994.

A third finding also reinforces a mobilization-based explanation of the outcome in 1994. A key piece in the Democrats' winning coalition in 1992 was young voters. Although voters under 30 years of age continued to support the Democratic Party in 1994, their turnout declined dramatically in comparison to other age groups. This decline in turnout deeply wounded Democratic candidates, as these younger voters were more loyal to Democrats than any other age group.

The other significant finding from the 1994 elections is an old tale: the wide political gap between the races, regardless of gender (see Huckfeldt and Kohfeld 1989; Carmines and Stimson 1990; Bennett et al. 1995). A glance at the voting data alone tells this story. While support for Democratic candidates among white men took a huge dive in 1994, the movement appears to have been associated with race as much as gender. Consider the fact that the differences in support for Democratic candidates between white men and women were 3 percent in 1986, 4 percent in 1990, and 7 percent in 1994, while the differences among white and black men were 37 percent in 1986, 31 percent in 1990, and 47 percent in 1994. Between whites and blacks of both genders, these differences were 37 percent in 1986, 29 percent in 1990, and 46 percent in 1994.

LOOKING FOR THE ANGRY WHITE MALE

A recent effort by Bennett et al. (1995) to locate the emergence of the angry white male, using ANES data from 1972 to 1992, as well as other data, turned up little evidence of the phenomenon. Looking at responses to questions concerning racial issues and affirmative action, the researchers found that "sex has little impact on opinions about racial preferences" and that although race did matter on these views, "there is no evidence of recent changes in whites' opinions about racial preference policies" (Bennett et al. 1995: 1). Regarding gender, these findings are consistent with other ANES-based studies on basic values which indicate that women and men have equally strong commitments to individualistic and egalitarian values (Conover 1988; Cook and Wilcox 1991; Fine 1993).

In a recent analysis of the 1994 elections, based on pre- and post-election surveys conducted in Ohio, Tuchfarber et al. (1995) also found little evidence to support the angry-white-male thesis. Instead of an angry-white-male phenomenon, their data support "the hypotheses that the election was a referendum on President Clinton, the Democratic party and liberalism, and that the election reflected concerns about America's economic future" (Tuchfarber et al. 1995: 1). Although the researchers found that white males were more supportive of the Republican party and conservatism than other race and gender groups, the characterizations that fit white males also fit white females, only to a lesser degree (Tuchfarber et al. 1995: 9). "The data show that white males and white females voted for conservatives and the Republican party, and against liberals, the Democratic party, and President Clinton" (9).[5]

Does the ANES data from the 1994 elections, in which support by white males for Democratic candidates took a large dive, indicate a change from the patterns found by Bennett et al. (1995) and the emergence in 1994 of an angry white male who apparently did not materialize in Ohio? In short, no.

TABLE 8.1 Views on Government Aid to Minorities by Race and Sex, 1992 and 1994

	1992				1994			
	Whites		Blacks		Whites		Blacks	
	Women	Men	Women	Men	Women	Men	Women	Men
Government should help minorities	39.9%	36.6%	16.9%	16.1%	43.1%	31.7%	17.8%	15.9%
Neutral	22.9	22.0	27.6	23.0	26.7	28.0	26.6	21.7
Minorities should help themselves	26.1	32.6	45.3	54.7	22.4	28.0	49.6	56.8
No opinion	11.2	8.9	10.3	6.2	7.8	12.2	6.1	5.7
Number of cases	188	123	985	903	116	82	787	706

SOURCE: American National Election Study.

Bennett et al. used responses to three questions from the ANES to look for distinctive views about affirmative action among white males. The first question concerned support for government efforts to help minorities, the second concerned preferential treatment for blacks in the job market, and the third concerned preferential treatment for blacks in college and university admissions (Bennett et al. 1995: 2). We examined responses to the first two questions in 1994; the third did not appear in the 1994 ANES. Like Bennett et al., we found that the responses of white men and women were comparable and that there were no significant changes from previous years. Table 8.1 presents our findings for the first question from the 1992 and 1994 ANES. On the second question, regarding preferential treatment in the job market, however, there were some changes among blacks. From 1992 to 1994 blacks became somewhat more polarized on this issue. Table 8.2 presents these findings. But note that the largest differences were between blacks and whites.

When we examine responses to several other questions from the 1994 ANES that tap into views about affirmative action, such as whether blacks have "gotten less than they deserve;" whether, if blacks "would only try harder, they could be just as well off as whites;" or whether "society should do whatever is necessary to make sure that everyone has an equal opportunity to succeed," we found again that there were no large differences between men and women of the same race; rather, the gulf that separates the responses was racial, not gendered.

Bennett et al. also examined the relationship between an index of "opinions about blacks" and opinions about affirmative action (Bennett et al. 1995: 5). They concluded from this analysis that "whites' opinions about blacks may play at least some role in their views of racial preference programs" (5). We made a similar investigation of the relation between that index and responses to the question concerning preferential treatment in the marketplace. Like Bennett et al., our findings from the 1994 ANES indicated a relation between views about blacks and support for affirmative action. But also note regarding the angry-white-male thesis that there was no significant change from 1992. Table 8.3 presents these findings. When we broke down

TABLE 8.2 Position on Preferential Hiring, by Race and Sex, 1992 and 1994

	1992				1994			
	Whites		Blacks		Whites		Blacks	
	Women	Men	Women	Men	Women	Men	Women	Men
Favor strongly	51.2%	35.8%	5.6%	5.1%	33.9%	34.5%	4.3%	2.8%
Favor not strongly	6.4	16.0	7.4	6.4	11.9	8.3	5.0	6.3
Oppose not strongly	11.0	19.8	19.5	15.5	21.2	15.5	20.7	20.4
Oppose strongly	25.0	23.6	63.1	70.7	27.1	26.2	64.1	65.6
No opinion	11.2	8.9	10.3	6.2	5.9	15.5	6.0	4.9
Number of cases	188	123	985	903	118	84	754	684

SOURCE: American National Election Study.

the data by gender (which Bennett et al. did not do), there were no large differences, although support by white women for affirmative action appears to have been somewhat less related to their views about blacks. Table 8.4 presents these findings.

Bennett et al. also examined possible relations between whites' views about affirmative action and views about economic insecurities, an important link in the angry-white-male thesis. But they found "virtually no relationships between whites' economic concerns and recent experiences in the job market and their views about affirmative action" (Bennett et al. 1995: 6). Using similar measures, we also found no such relations in 1994. Furthermore, when we broke down the data by gender, there was no significant relation. Also note, regarding another facet of the angry-white-male thesis, that there was no difference between men and women on their approval or disapproval for Congress regarding health care; both groups expressed disapproval by a three-to-one margin.

In short, then, there did not seem to be much attitudinal data from the ANES that support the angry-white-male thesis as an explanation for the outcome of the 1994 elections, at least as that thesis has been commonly understood. But the fact of a large drop-off in white male support for Democratic candidates in 1994 remains, and is reflected in the attitudinal data by the fact that 7 percent more white men than white women said that they had been angry with President Clinton. This phenomenon still needs to be explained. Perhaps the ANES data on mobilization to vote yields some clues. For example, 4 percent more men than women reported that they had voted in 1994.

GENDER, AGE, AND MOBILIZATION

In addition to its standard election-year survey in 1994, the ANES also conducted a panel study of a smaller number of citizens who were surveyed in 1992. In comparing turnout between 1992 and 1994 by gender for this set of respondents, we found that women who had voted in 1992 were less likely than men to vote in 1994; of the women who reported voting in 1992, 28 percent said they did not vote in 1994, as opposed to 20 percent for men (we did not break down the data by both gender and race because of the small numbers of cases). By the same token, 19 percent of the men who reported not voting in 1992 said they voted in 1994; for women, this figure was only 4 percent. So there does seem to have been a gender-based mobilization factor at work in 1994.

Regarding age, note that there was a comparatively large drop-off in turnout among those aged 18–29, a group that supported Clinton in 1992; among those aged 18–29 who reported voting in 1992, 48 percent said they did not vote in 1994. This percentage was 24 points higher than that of any other age group.

What does more specific data on turnout in 1994 from the general ANES and the 1992–1994 panel study reveal? The clearest patterns were those we have come to expect: Persons with strong partisan attachments and higher levels of education and socioeconomic status were more likely to vote. More relevant to our concerns here is the finding that those who either disapproved of or had a negative view (as revealed

TABLE 8.3 Whites' Attitudes about Affirmative Action in Hiring, by Racial Attitudes Index, 1992 and 1994

	1992					1994			
	Very Pro-Black	Pro-Black	Neutral	Anti-Black	Very Anti-Black	Very Pro-Black	Pro-Black	Neutral	Anti-Black	Very Anti-Black
Number of cases	100	306	528	583	192	53	219	601	449	90
Favor	50.0%	18.9%	10.4%	7.4%	2.6%	40.5%	18.3%	8.7%	2.6%	3.9%
Oppose	47.0	78.7	86.0	90.1	95.9	57.4	79.2	87.7	96.3	95.4
No Opinion	3.0	2.3	3.6	2.6	1.6	2.1	2.5	3.4	1.1	1.7

SOURCE: American National Election Study.

TABLE 8.4 Whites' Attitudes about Affirmative Action in Hiring, by Racial Attitudes Index and Sex, 1994

	Women					Men				
	Very Pro-Black	Pro-Black	Neutral	Anti-Black	Very Anti-Black	Very Pro-Black	Pro-Black	Neutral	Anti-Black	Very Anti-Black
Number of cases	38	112	317	223	48	15	107	284	226	42
Favor	39.5%	15.2%	10.1%	2.7%	6.3%	46.7%	24.3%	8.1%	3.1%	2.4%
Oppose	60.5	84.8	89.9	97.3	93.8	53.3	75.7	91.9	96.9	97.6

SOURCE: American National Election Study.

by a feeling thermometer) toward Clinton, his handling of health care, and the Democratic party were somewhat more likely to vote, and these relations were more pronounced among men than women. In addition, those with only weak attachments to the Republican party were more likely to vote than those with weak attachments to the Democratic party, and these differences were greater among women than men. These findings indicate that there might have been an ambivalent-female phenomenon among independents leaning toward the Democratic party in the 1994 elections, as well as a more general angry-white-male phenomenon.

Our findings are consistent with the fact that independents supported Republican House candidates by a 12 percent margin ("Portrait of the Electorate," *New York Times*, November 13, 1994). They are also consistent with the findings from the study by Tuchfarber et al. of Ohio voters, which suggested that "[s]wing voters tended to vote for conservatism, the 'religious right' and the Republican party and against liberalism, Bill Clinton, the Democratic party, and Washington D.C. politicians" (Tuchfarber et al. 1995: 7). As a corollary, our findings suggest that such-minded persons were also more likely to vote than other swing voters with different attitudes.

But we still have not made much headway finding an explanation for the drop-off in Democratic support by white males or the difference in mobilization indicated by the data. Are they related to the angry-white-male thesis? One possible tack would be to create a multivariate equation to predict turnout that includes a measure of the angry white male and the ambivalent female.

TURNOUT, VOTE CHOICE, AND THE ANGRY WHITE MALE AND AMBIVALENT FEMALE

In order to test the importance of various factors on voter turnout, we conducted a multivariate analysis of several potentially significant measures. Past research on voter turnout has found that among other influences, the following are particularly strong: age, education, strength of partisan attachment, employment status, external political efficacy, and contact made by the parties (Rosenstone and Hansen 1993). We included these measures in our analysis, but in order to evaluate the supposedly unique characteristics of the 1994 elections, we added two attitudinal measures. The first measure was designed to tap into the angry voter and was a compilation of anger toward President Clinton, the Democratic Party, and interest groups clearly associated with the Democratic Party. The second measure tapped into ambivalence about the capacity of either party to solve important political, economic, and social issues. The results from this analysis support the indications from our earlier analyses and are presented in Table 8.5.

As in past elections, age and education were important predictors of turnout, as were partisanship and political efficacy. But we also found support for attitudinal influences on turnout in 1994. The more angry persons were with the Democrats, the more likely they were to vote; conversely, persons who were ambivalent toward either party's ability to solve problems were less likely to vote than those who thought one or the other party was better able to solve problems.

TABLE 8.5 Probit Estimates of Voter Turnout (Whites Only), 1994

	Coefficient	Standard Error
Intercept	−1.817	.285
Independent variables		
Age	.023	.003
Education	.998	.199
Income	.009	.005
External political efficacy	.427	.142
Strength of party identification	.314	.153
Sex	−.121	.095
Race	−.174	.160
Index of anger with Democrats[a]	.520	.172
Index of ambivalence with parties[a]	−.480	.095

[a]The scales were created as follows:
Anger with Democrats—Respondents were asked if they disliked something about the Democratic Party; about their approval of President Clinton on health care and the economy; and whether Clinton ever made them feel angry; and respondents were asked to rank their feelings on a feelings thermometer for President Clinton, Hillary Clinton, the Democratic party, liberals, the women's movement, environmentalists, and gays/lesbians.
Ambivalence with parties—If respondents answered "neither" or "same" to questions asking which party would raise taxes and which would best handle the economy, pollution, crime, foreign affairs, health care, and welfare reform, they were coded as ambivalent.
Each response was standardized (0 = no anger or ambivalence; 1 = anger or ambivalence) and added into the respective index, which was again standardized from a scale of 0 to 1. The reliability alpha for the anger-with-Democrats scale was .81 and for the ambivalence-with-parties scale, .83.
NOTE: Any coefficient larger than twice its standard error is statistically significant at $p < .05$.
SOURCE: American National Election Study.

In order to test the notions of the angry white male and the ambivalent female, we conducted separate analyses of white male and white female respondents. As reported in Table 8.6, there was support, in terms of turnout, for both notions. For white men, age, education, external political efficacy, and anger toward Democrats led to higher levels of turnout. For white women, age and education increased turnout, while ambivalence lowered it.

We have thus found much evidence to support the argument that the 1994 elections can be largely explained by the mobilization of voters. Factors that influence turnout across elections—such as age and education—appeared to work in favor of the Republican Party. Factors specific to 1994—anger toward Democrats from white males and ambivalence from women—mobilized those more likely to vote for Republican candidates and demobilized those more likely to vote for Democratic candidates.

Is there similar evidence concerning the effects of anger and ambivalence on vote choice as well as turnout? From election-day exit polls, we already know many of the

TABLE 8.6 Probit Estimates of Voter Turnout, by Sex (Whites Only), 1994

	Women		Men	
	Coefficient	Standard Error	Coefficient	Standard Error
Intercept	−1.810	.393	1.962	.410
Independent variables				
Age	.022	.004	.026	.005
Education	1.030	.283	.928	.288
Income	.012	.007	.007	.007
External political efficacy	.331	.196	.556	.210
Strength of party identification	.326	.218	.270	.218
Index of anger with Democrats	.465	.465	.595	.254
Index of ambivalence with parties	−.587	.200	−.368	.223

NOTE: Any coefficient larger than twice its standard error is statistically significant at $p < .05$.
SOURCE: American National Election Study.

important factors associated with vote choice in 1994: Whites, the middle-aged, married persons, men, and Christians were more likely to vote for Republicans; African-Americans, the young, single persons, women, and Jews were more likely to vote for Democrats. As we did with turnout, we now turn to a multivariate analysis of ANES data to investigate vote choice in terms of anger and ambivalence.

We used several measures to test the various explanations for voting decisions in 1994. The first measure was the approval rating of President Clinton, to test for an anti-Clinton effect. The second measure was the approval rating of Congress as an institution, to measure an anti-Congress and anti-Washington effect. To control for incumbency effects, we included a variable that indicated whether there was a Democratic incumbent in the election. We used two measures to test the effects of economics: the respondent's personal financial situation and the respondent's assessment of the U.S. economy. We also included our measures of anger toward the Democrats and ambivalence toward either party and the traditional control variables of age, education, employment status, and party identification. This analysis is presented in Table 8.7.

The results presented in Table 8.7 indicate that the only significant, independent influences on vote choice were party identification and the presence of a Democratic incumbent in the race (which had a positive effect on Democratic support). Both effects are well-known factors in mid-term congressional races. Our analysis did not support the direct, independent influence of an anti-Congress or anti-Clinton sentiment, economic factors, age, education, or employment status. When we broke down the data by gender, however, the results changed slightly. This analysis is presented in Table 8.8. For men, approval of President Clinton had a significant effect; disapproval of Clinton led men to be more likely to vote for the Republican candidate. For women, no such effect emerged. This analysis lends

TABLE 8.7   Probit Estimates of Vote Choice (Whites Only), 1994

	Coefficient	Standard Error
Intercept	−1.637	.588
Independent variables		
Age	−.006	.005
Education	.319	.334
Party identification	2.496	.293
Sex	.230	.161
Employment status	.082	.493
Personal economic situation	−.132	.202
Evaluation of U.S. economy	.063	.207
Presence of Democratic incumbent	−.884	.159
Clinton approval rating	.599	.352
Congressional approval rating	−.112	.336
Index of anger with Democrats	.223	.455
Index of ambivalence with parties	−.014	.246

NOTE: Any coefficient larger than twice its standard error is statistically significant at $p < .05$.
SOURCE: American National Election Study.

TABLE 8.8   Probit Estimates of Vote Choice, by Sex (Whites Only), 1994

	Women		Men	
	Coefficient	Standard Error	Coefficient	Standard Error
Intercept	−.810	.894	−2.843	.835
Independent variables				
Age	.009	.020	−.001	.007
Education	−.363	.504	.737	.496
Party identification	3.136	.488	3.584	.430
Employment status	−.623	.821	.516	.748
Personal economic situation	−.343	.298	.109	.293
Evaluation of U.S. economy	.273	.317	−.025	.289
Presence of Democratic incumbent	−.852	.247	−.877	.221
Clinton approval rating	−.667	.626	1.410	.476
Congressional approval rating	−.032	.530	.137	.465
Index of anger with Democrats	.057	.733	.130	.618
Index of ambivalence with parties	−.531	.374	.427	.368

NOTE: Any coefficient larger than twice its standard error is statistically significant at $p < .05$.
SOURCE: American National Election Study.

further support to the notion that the elections of 1994 were marked by strong anti-Clinton and anti-Democratic party effects among white men.

Thus, for Democratic candidates the cumulative effect of mobilization and vote choice in the 1994 elections was that they were hit twice. First, important elements of their traditional coalition were less likely to vote, due in part to an apparent ambivalence toward the party. Secondly, those persons who were more mobilized to vote were, in turn, more likely to be angry toward Clinton and thus were more likely to vote for Republican candidates. Given these conditions, it is no surprise that the Congress underwent an historic change in party control in 1994.

CONCLUSION

Like the results of other studies of the 1994 elections, our findings do not bode well for President Clinton and the Democrats in 1996. Although the angry-white-male thesis, as it has been set forward by media analysts, does not appear to be real, it is clear that certain constituencies which supported Clinton and the Democrats in 1992 now appear to be more ambivalent and less mobilized than they were at that time. Those who were angry with the President, the Democrats, and the ideology associated with them—particularly white males—appear to have been more mobilized. When combined with the facts of a slow "generational replacement of older, more Democratic voters with younger, more Republican voters;" the apparently increasing conservative nature of the electorate more generally; and the advantage of incumbency for Republicans in Congress (Tuchfarber et al. 1995: 13), the future for the Democrats does indeed seem bleak. From a strategic point of view at least, Democrats need to engage in something more ambitious and expansive than rearguard actions during the next two years, and beyond.

NOTES

1. The order of names was decided by a coin toss.
2. See "Portrait of the Electorate," *New York Times,* November 13, 1994. We have chosen to concentrate on mid-term House elections, since Senate elections are incomplete from a national perspective and Presidential elections may influence voting for House seats in ways that vary from election to election.
3. Note, for example, that since 1986 male blue-collar wages have fallen more dramatically than either male white-collar or female blue-collar wages, while female white-collar wages have increased (Mishel and Bernstein 1994: 120). For data on incomes and tax burdens more generally, see Mishel and Bernstein (1994) and the Congressional Budget Office's *Green Book* (1994).
4. These excerpts are taken verbatim from a longer paper.
5. It should also be noted, however, that the magnitude of the differences between white males and females regarding these factors was large. See Tuchfarber et al. (1995: 20).

9

Re-exploring the Weak-Challenger Hypothesis: The 1994 Candidate Pools

L. SANDY MAISEL
ELIZABETH J. IVRY
BENJAMIN D. LING
STEPHANIE G. PENNIX[1]

THE END OF DEMOCRATIC HEGEMONY IN THE HOUSE OF REPRESENTATIVES

The 1994 midterm elections were so exceptional that commentator after commentator, analyst after analyst, feels compelled to repeat summary statistics with which he or she knows the audience is familiar. We cannot resist.

Of course, the key numbers are 40 and 52. The Republican party gained control of the House of Representatives for the first time in 40 years; the GOP did so by gaining 52 seats previously held by Democrats. The 52-seat gain was the largest midterm partisan swing since the Republicans picked up 55 seats in the midterm elections in 1946, after the death of Franklin Roosevelt, Harry Truman's succession to the presidency, and the end of World War II.

While this chapter examines only elections to the House of Representatives, we should note that all elections of 1994 were totally one-sided. Not only did no Republican incumbent seeking reelection lose a seat in the House, but *not one* incumbent Republican governor or U.S. senator lost either. This level of support for incumbents of one party is all but unprecedented in recent electoral history. Even in the Democratic landslide of 1974, following the Watergate revelations and the resignation of President Nixon, 4 incumbent Democrats lost. Even in the Republican landslide of 1966, when the GOP picked up 47 House seats, 1 incumbent Republican was defeated. And even in recent elections when incumbents were virtually unbeatable, like that in 1986 when only 7 incumbents lost, the losers were divided between the parties. In informal comments at the 1995 Annual Meeting of the Midwest Political Science Association, Duke University professor and defeated Congressman David Price (D.-N.C., 1986–94) summarized the election results in North Carolina with a statement that reflected the situation in many states, "In county after county throughout the state, we woke up on November 9th and not a Democrat was left standing."

Not only did Democratic incumbents lose, but Democratic candidates also lost in open-seat races. From 1954 through 1992, the period of Democratic hegemony in the House, the Democrats maintained control not only by winning as incumbents but also by controlling open-seat races. During that period, 711 seats came open through incumbent retirement or death. In 527 of those races the new member of the House of Representatives was from the same party as the member leaving Congress. In 107 of the remaining 184, Democrats took seats previously held by Republicans; but in only 77 did Republicans take Democratic seats. In only 5 of those 20 elections did Republicans take more seats from Democrats than they lost to Democrats; 3 of those 5 were the Republican presidential landslide elections of 1972, 1980, and 1984. The 1966 and 1978 midterms were the only 2 midterm elections in which Republicans made net gains among open seats; those were net gains of 1 and 2 seats, respectively.

In 1994, the Republicans gained 39 seats in open races.[2] Of the 52 seats that came open in 1994, 31 were previously held by Democrats and 21 by Republicans; Republicans won 22 of the Democratic seats and lost only 4 of those they previously held. Their net gain of 18 more than doubled what they achieved in any election since the Democrats gained control of the House in 1954.[3]

After the election the nation's newspapers trumpeted the surprising results. The *Washington Post* headline screamed out "THE ELEPHANT'S ROAR; FOR THE GOP A STAMPEDE OF VICTORY." The *Baltimore Sun* echoed, "UNHAPPY VOTERS CHOOSE RADICAL CHANGE," and the *Houston Post* chimed in, "IT'S A WHOLE NEW BALLGAME; BIG SWEEP LEAVES D.C. IN TURMOIL." When the Democrats caucused to organize for the 104th Congress, they were said to be in a state of denial. Used to calling each other "Mr. Chairman," because for years nearly all Democrats with any seniority chaired either a full committee or a subcommittee, they had to become used to thinking of themselves as ranking minority members. And as they looked around, they noticed the absence of their leader, Tom Foley (Wash.), the first Speaker of the House defeated for reelection since 1860, and such venerable Democratic institutions as Jack Brooks (Tex.), chairman of the Judiciary Committee who was defeated after 21 terms by Steve Stockman, and Dan Glickman (Nebr.), chairman of the Intelligence Committee, an 18-year veteran who lost to Todd Tiahrt.

On the Republican side the situation could not have been more different. Newt Gingrich, the new Speaker, was omnipresent. But just as important from our point of view were the 75 freshmen Republicans whose victories brought the Republicans to majority status and Gingrich to the Speakership. Gingrich recognized the importance of this group by appointing a number of them to key positions in the planning process as the GOP determined how it was to organize the House and implement its Contract with America. Among the most prominent were "Mac" Thornberry of Texas, who defeated Agriculture Subcommittee Chair Bill Sarpalius; Zach Wamp of Tennessee, an early and enthusiastic supporter of the GOP Contract with America; and Jon Fox of Pennsylvania, who defeated

Marjorie Margolies-Mezvinsky in a highly publicized race in which he castigated her for her casting the decisive vote in favor of the Clinton budget.

THEORIES OF CONGRESSIONAL ELECTIONS: A BRIEF REVIEW

Others have and will comment on the causes of the 1994 Republican success (see, as a good example, Jacobson 1995). Our purpose in this chapter is more narrow. For some time political scientists have sought to explain the Democratic party hegemony in the House of Representatives by presenting various theories to account for this long period of one-party rule. Many of the explanations have dealt with "incumbent advantages" of various descriptions—beginning with David Mayhew's seminal work on the electoral connection (Mayhew 1974a; 1974b) and continuing with studies on personal advantage due to name recognition, experience, and personality (Abramowitz 1975; Mann 1978; Maisel and Cooper 1981; Cain, Fiorina, and Ferejohn 1987); on the decline of partisanship (Burnham 1975; Fiorina 1978); on gains from the provision of district services (Fiorina 1977; Yiannakis 1981; Johannes 1984; Fiorina and Rivers 1989); on redistricting (Tufte 1973; Brady and Grofman 1991); on advantages in raising money (Jacobson 1980; 1990b; Abramowitz 1991); and on other possible causes. While all of these explanations have proved interesting, none has been sufficiently powerful to merit wide-ranging acceptance.

Rather, as a community of scholars, we have settled on the explanation that incumbents tend to win because they frequently face weak challengers, a conclusion which emerged from the 1978 American National Election Study (NES) that demonstrated most respondents had no contact from the campaign of the people challenging their incumbent representatives (Hinckley 1980; Mann and Wolfinger 1980). The most common set of explanations for weak challengers has come from the work of Gary Jacobson and Samuel Kernell (1983) which posited that the best challengers in congressional races were experienced politicians and that politicians acted strategically in deciding on potential candidacies (see also, Kazee 1983; Bond, Covington, and Fleisher 1985; Jacobson 1989b; and Canon 1990).

In earlier work Maisel et al. (1988; 1994) developed a model of candidate emergence, drawing on ambition theory (Schlesinger, 1966) and on the work of Jacobson and Kernell (1983) but modifying that theory to include many of the personal factors that have become so prevalent in recent years and institutional factors that have been the subject of recent reform efforts. That model has been tested in an exploratory study, looking at the decisions made by potential candidates for Congress in six states (Maisel and Stone 1994). The results of the exploratory study indicated that personal factors and institutional factors played minor roles at best. The decisions made by candidates for office were largely strategic; they did not run, even if they desired to hold a seat in Congress and were considering running in the future, because they did not believe that their chances of victory were at all promising.

In a further examination of one aspect of the same phenomenon, Brady, Maisel, and Warsh (1994) hypothesized about the particular problems faced by the Republican party in recruiting potential candidates for office (see also Fiorina 1992a; 1996). They developed an opportunity-cost model that posited that the likelihood a candidate would run for office should be predicted by the expected value of running (EVR) for that candidate; the EVR in turn is the sum of the expected value of winning (EVW) and the expected value of losing (EVL). The following formula describes the relationship:

$$\begin{aligned} EVR &= EVW + EVL \\ &= p_i \text{ (benefits of winning } - \text{ opportunity cost lost by winning)} \\ &= (1 - p_i) \text{ (benefits of losing } - \text{ opportunity cost lost by losing)} \end{aligned}$$

In other words, $EVR = p_i + (1 - p_i)$

An exploration of this model leads to the conclusion that for the "best" Democratic potential candidates for Congress, the benefits of winning are greater and the opportunity costs lost by winning is less than is the case for the "best" Republican candidates for office; the Democrats are more likely to meet policy goals through active service in the Congress than are Republicans, and typically they leave less-well-paying jobs to run for office (compare this analysis to the discussion in Ehrenhalt 1991). Thus, the EVW for Democrats is higher than it is for Republicans.

Similarly, in an interesting way, the EVL for Democrats is higher than it is for Republicans because the stereotypical Democrat is given more credit by his community and his peers for seeking elective office than is the stereotypical Republican, whose peers view service in elective office with a jaundiced eye.

Summing the higher EVW and the higher EVL for Democrats leads to the conclusion that the EVR for the best Democratic candidates is higher than that for the best Republican candidates; the model thus posits that more highly qualified Democrats will run for Congress than highly qualified Republicans, a prediction that explains past experience.

As Gary Jacobson has written, "Republicans have failed to advance in the House because they have fielded inferior candidates on the wrong side of issues. . . . " (1990b: 3). In fact, only twice during the period for which Jacobson has accumulated data (1966 to 1992) have the Republicans fielded more "qualified" candidates than have the Democrats; in this case "qualified" candidates are those who have successfully won elective office (Jacobson 1995: 10).

The question to which we turn in the remainder of this chapter is the extent to which the experience in the 1994 House elections confirmed or ran counter to the theories that have dominated the discussion of candidate emergence during the period of Democratic hegemony. That is, if the theories of candidate emergence and the impact of candidate emergence on the congressional electoral process were as useful in explaining the experience in 1994 as they have been in past elections, then our estimate of their power will be enhanced. On the other hand, if these theories fail to explain the 1994 experience, as for instance did virtually all of the forecasting models put forth by political scientists in this election, then these theories will need revisiting just as do the forecasting models.[4]

METHODOLOGY OF OUR STUDY

The purpose of our study then was to determine if the experience in 1994 requires modification in the theories that have been used to explain candidacies in and results of previous congressional elections. In order to do this, we began by examining the candidates who sought office in 1994.

Most of the studies of congressional candidacies have emphasized the candidates who run in general elections. Thus, for example, Jacobson (1990a; 1992; 1995) has noted the number of Democratic or Republican incumbents who have faced experienced challengers in the general election. That research strategy was appropriate for explaining the results of those particular general elections.

We believe, however, that the initial decisions of potential candidates for office to enter a race is the variable one must explore in order to ascertain whether the number of "qualified" challengers in general elections rises or declines. To examine these initial decisions, we go back to the decision to enter primary elections; for whether or not one wins a primary, the decision to contest for the office is the relevant one for our analysis. Either more "qualified" candidates are likely to emerge in the general election if more compete in the primaries or further thinking must be done about the importance of previous experience for electoral success.[5] In either case, the initial decision is the one that is relevant for exploring motivations of potential candidates; the link to the general election is clearly secondary. Thus, we began by gathering biographical information on every candidate who entered either a Republican or a Democratic primary in 1994.

Following Jacobson's lead, we noted those candidates who were previously elected officials; however, we expanded his definition to include previous winners who won recently even if they were not holding office at the time of the 1994 election. In addition, we added a separate category of those candidates who were unelected officials at the time they entered the race for Congress; in this category we included both those serving in appointive government office and those in political offices. Again, our reason was that we feel holding these types of position often gives one exposure to the same resources that holding elective office does and therefore is a good predictor of a quality candidate.[6] We maintained a separation of the candidates based on type of position throughout our data gathering and analysis in order to allow comparison with the work of others.

Previous electoral experience should allow us to construct a spectrum of strategic contexts in which potential candidates might run. The Maisel and Stone (1994) model, for instance, demonstrates that potential candidates—especially potential experienced candidates—are least likely to run if an incumbent member of Congress in their own party is seeking reelection; very few incumbents have

TABLE 9.1 Summary of Data on Primary Candidates

All Candidates	Number of Candidates	
Division a		
Incumbents seeking reelection	388	
Others running in race with incumbents running[a]	808	
Candidates running in districts with open seats[b]	366	
Division b		
Primary winners		
General election winners	435	
General election losers	383	
	818	
Primary losers	744	
Total primary candidates (either a or b)		1562
Incumbents		
Incumbents winning reelection	349	
Incumbents losing in general elections	34	
Incumbents losing in primaries	5	
Total incumbents seeking reelection		388
New members		
Open seat winners	47	
"Post-primary open seat" winners	5	
Incumbents defeated in general elections	34	
Total new members		86
Primary losers		
Losers in primaries for open seats	272	
Losers in primaries in which incumbents ran		
Loser to incumbents	169	
Loser to people who beat incumbent	8	
	177	
Losers in primaries for chances to oppose incumbents	295	
Total primary losers		744

(*continues*)

lost primaries in recent years. At the other extreme, open seats are most attractive to all potential candidates. Therefore, we next divided the 870 potential primaries (a Republican and Democratic potential primary in each of the 435 congressional districts) according to the political context—opposing an incumbent in his or her own party, seeking the nomination to run against an incumbent of the other party, running in an open seat—that potential candidates would face.

Table 9.1 summarizes the pool of primary candidates on whom we gathered biographical data. As you can see, it is possible to cut this pool in a number of ways. Of the 1,562 candidates whom we studied, 388 were incumbent members of the House seeking reelection. Only 4 of these lost primaries, 1 withdrew after entering the primary because of ill health, another 34 lost in the general election, and the remaining 349 (193 Democrats, 155 Republicans, and 1 Independent)

TABLE 9.1 (*Continued*)

All Candidates	Number of Candidates
Primary winners[c]	
Winners	
Incumbents	349
New members	86
	435
Losers	
Incumbents	34
Challengers	297
Open-seat losers	47
"Post-primary-open-seat" losers	5
	383
Uncontested seats	
No Democratic candidates	35[d]
No Republican candidates	17
	52

[a] These candidates ran against incumbents seeking reelection (in 388 districts).
[b] There were 47 seats that were open because incumbents retired, sought other office, or died.
[c] General election candidates.
[d] The Democrats failing to field a candidate in Vermont's at-large seat against incumbent Independent Bernie Sanders, who caucused with the Democrats, was not counted.

were reelected. A total of 366 candidates entered primaries for 47 seats that were open because of incumbents' retirements, seeking other office, or death—an average of nearly 8 candidates per district. By comparison, only 1,196 candidates (including the 388 incumbents) were on the ballots in the other districts—an average of just over 3 per district (or just over 2, if one excludes the incumbents). Even this cursory review of the pool demonstrates that in 1994 running for open seats was more attractive to more candidates than was running in districts with incumbents seeking reelection.

Since the original work on strategic politicians by Jacobson and Kernell (1981), analysts have noted that some years are better for one party or the other. By all indications, one would have expected that 1994 was going to be a better year for Republican candidates than for Democrats. Thus, we divided our sample by party as well as by context.

Finally, Fowler and Maisel (1991) found that many Republican victors in the elections of the 1990s did not fit the predicted mold of "quality" challengers but were rather amateurs who were able to fund large portions of their own campaigns. As many Republican candidates in the 1994 general elections campaigned as anti-politicians, outsiders, or amateurs, even though some of them had rather elaborate political résumés, we took a second look at the successful Republican candidates who did not fit our "qualified" candidate definition.[7] Our purpose here was to begin an exploration of finding a more complete definition of "qualified" candidates for further research.

ANALYSIS OF THE DATA

In all, we gathered data on 1,562 major party candidates in primary elections. Of these, 388 were incumbents.[8] Of the remaining candidates 210 held elective office at the time they ran for Congress or had recently held elective office. While the majority of these were members of state legislatures, among the others were state office holders (e.g., lieutenant governors), mayors, members of city councils and county legislators, district attorneys, and elected judges.[9] Another 82 of those for whom we found biographical data held unelected offices at the time they sought seats in Congress; these were aides to members of Congress and other elective officials, White House assistants, ambassadors (one), appointed judges, state and county party officials, and holders of many other positions.[10] The remaining candidates had an incredibly wide variety of backgrounds, probably reflecting the breadth of the American citizenry more than the members of Congress themselves ever could. In addition to the large number of lawyers that conventional wisdom would expect us to find, this group included doctors, dentists, and nurses; bankers; contractors and realtors; businessmen—in small and large businesses—engineers and scientists; union leaders and blue-collar workers; teachers and students; social workers and their clients; airline pilots and fire chiefs; ministers and football players; and those who were combinations—the variety that is America.

Our concern in analyzing these data dealt first with whether those who had made their careers in politics and who were likely to be the strongest candidates chose their races strategically.

Challenging Incumbents in Primaries

Table 9.2 presents data on those candidates who decided to take on incumbents seeking reelection in primary contests.

Traditionally such challenges are viewed as long shots at best. Despite the fact that 19 incumbents lost in primary elections in 1992, that number must be viewed as something of an aberration. If one segregates out the elections in districts that have been redistricted right after redistricting (districts in which many members run in newly drawn districts and in which often incumbents have to face each other in primaries), the average number of incumbents defeated in primaries over the last two decades has been between 3 and 4; the total number who lost primaries in the four elections following the redistricting in 1982 was 7.

Only 57 Republicans (in 157 districts) challenged incumbent Republicans in primaries in 1994; nearly two-thirds of all Republicans seeking reelection were unopposed for their party's nomination. This lack of competition reflects historical patterns (Fowler and Maisel 1991). Of those who opposed incumbent Republicans in primaries, only 7 were previously officeholders and 1 held an ap-

TABLE 9.2 Candidates Opposing Incumbents in Primaries

	Democrats		Republicans[a]	
	Percentage	Number	Percentage	Number
Level of experience of all candidates				
Previously elected officials	16.96%	19	12.28%	7
Unelected officials	3.57	4	1.75	1
Non-quality candidates	79.46	89	85.96	49
Total		112		57
Candidates who won primaries				
Previously elected officials	66.67	2	100	1
Unelected officials	0	0	0	0
Non-quality candidates	33.33	1	0	0
Total		3		1
Candidates who won general election				
Previously elected officials	100	2	100	1
Unelected officials	0	0	0	0
Non-quality candidates	0	0	0	0
Total		2		1

[a] Excluded from this table is Rodney Frelinghuysen, who won nomination after the incumbent Republican stepped down in New Jersey's 11th district.

pointive office. The only winner, Daniel Frisa, who beat David Levy in New York's fourth congressional district, was formerly a state representative whose entry into the race was triggered by intraparty warfare on Long Island; thus he had good reason to think that his was a strategically sound decision.[11]

Conventional wisdom held that Democratic representatives might be slightly more vulnerable than might their Republican colleagues; but a potential candidate would have to think that some particular circumstances existed to believe that a race against an incumbent was anything but a most-risky undertaking. Reflecting this assessment, only 112 candidates entered primaries to challenge the 230 Democratic incumbents seeking reelection; again a majority of the incumbents faced no primary opposition at all. More than 1 in 6 of the 19 challengers held elective office; another 4 held appointive office at the time they made their races. Only 3 of the challengers defeated incumbent Democrats. Of the 3 winners 2—State Senator Chaka Fattah in Pennsylvania's 2nd district and City Councilor Shiela Jackson Lee in the 18th district in Texas were experienced politicians who viewed particular incumbents as vulnerable. More typical—except for the outcome of his race—of the candidates opposing incumbents was the 71-year-old retired teacher, Virgil Cooper, who defeated Mike Synar in Oklahoma's second district before going on to lose in the general election to another amateur, physician Tom Coburn. This first cut at the data then leads one to conclude that quality potential candidates in districts in which incumbents were seeking reelection were generally making strategic decisions and not taking on seemingly hopeless races. We also have evidence that confirms that those who won these races tended to be candidates with special electoral advantages.

Seeking Nominations to Challenge Incumbents in the General Elections

Table 9.3 presents data on those candidates who sought major party nominations to oppose incumbents not in their parties. While more incumbents lose in general elections than in primaries, for more than two decades over 90 percent of the incumbents seeking reelection in all general elections have been successful. Thus, once again, potential candidates would have to view entry into such races as risky endeavors. However, in 1992 Republicans made some inroads on the Democratic majority by defeating 16 incumbents. In addition, the victory margins of many more Democratic incumbents decreased precipitously. Republicans were thought to be advantaged in the 1994 election; thus the strategic-politician model would suggest that more experienced Republican candidates would run than would be the case for the Democrats.

Over 400 Republicans sought congressional nominations in the 230 districts in which incumbent Democrats were seeking reelection.[12] However, only 11 percent of these (45 candidates) were experienced candidates; only 22 of the others had obviously relevant experience. Thus, the vast majority (83 percent or 338 candidates) were political amateurs. To look at these data another way, less than 1

TABLE 9.3 Primary Candidates for Seats with Incumbents in Opposite Party

	Democrats		Republicans	
	Percentage	Number	Percentage	Number
Level of experience of all candidates				
Previously elected officials	14.41%	33	11.11%	45
Unelected officials	6.11	14	5.43	22
Non-quality candidates	79.48	182	83.46	338
Totals		229		405
Candidates who won primary				
Previously elected officials	16.53	20	14.22	30
Unelected officials	6.61	8	6.16	13
Non-quality candidates	76.86	93	79.62	168
Totals		121		211
Candidates who won general election				
Previously elected officials	0	0	38.24	13
Unelected officials	0	0	11.76	4
Non-quality candidates	0	0	50.00	17
Totals		0		34

Democratic incumbent in 5 had any chance of facing an experienced challenger in November because no experienced challenger sought the nomination in that incumbent's district.

The data confirm that experienced challengers in the Republican party achieved the kind of success one would expect. Two-thirds (30 challengers of 45) of the experienced challengers and nearly 60 percent (13 of 22) of those who were classified as unelected officials won their primaries. Further, 13 of the 30 experienced nominees and 4 of the 13 unelected officials beat incumbent Democrats in the general elections. By contrast, despite the fact that many of them faced no opposition at all, only half of the "amateur" candidates won nominations, and only 17 of the 168 nominees in this category won general elections. Seventeen of the 34 Republicans who beat Democratic incumbents in the November general elections were among the 43 nominees who were either experienced politicians or unelected officials; the other 17 winners were spread out among the other 168 districts in which amateurs opposed incumbent Democrats.

From this data we see that the advantage experienced candidates have had in winning elections in the past was clearly reflected in 1994.[13] However, we do not see a significant increase in the number of experienced Republicans seeking their party's nomination that one would expect in a potentially strong Republican year. Furthermore, despite the success that experienced nominees enjoyed, the Republican triumph in the 1994 elections was as much a result of victories by "amateur" candidates as it was improvement in the overall quality of Republican challengers. In point of fact, one is left to wonder if the Republicans might not have done better had they been able to field more experienced candidates. We will return to this point later.

What about Democratic candidates seeking to oppose Republican incumbents? Here our data seem to confirm the expected findings. In what looked to be a poor Democratic year, only 33 experienced Democrats sought congressional nominations to oppose incumbent Republicans; only 14 unelected officials joined them. Thus, approximately two-thirds of the Republican incumbents did not have to worry about facing strong challengers, at least as defined by previous experience, before the primary elections even were held. While the more experienced candidates were more successful in winning their party's nominations (20 of the 33 experienced candidates won; 8 of the 14 unelected officials won), none of these went on to beat an incumbent Republican in the fall.

Democratic politicians were avoiding congressional challenges to incumbent Republicans all over the country. In fact, for the first time in recent electoral history, more Republicans (36) were given a "free ride" in the general election because the Democrats failed to file any nominee than was true of Democrats given a "free ride" (17) in November because of lack of a Republican competitor.[14] Nearly a quarter of the Republican incumbents seeking reelection in November of 1994 had no Democratic opposition at all; only 1 in 6 of the remaining incumbent Republicans seeking reelection faced an experienced challenger. The number of unchallenged Republican incumbents has only been approximated once in the last 40 years and is a clear indication of the Democrats conceding district after district, many of them in the once solidly Democratic South, to the Republicans. The number of Republican incumbents facing an experienced challenger represents a reduction of almost a third from the average over the last four decades. Both then are clear indications of Democratic politicians acting strategically, and each contributed at least potentially to the Republican landslide in the general election.

Contesting in Open Seats

According to the strategic-politician model, one would expect to find the most competition and the most experienced nominees in the primary races for the nominations in open seats. Forty-seven seats were open in 1994.[15] Because parties historically have been able to hold most of the open seats their representatives are vacating, one would have expected more competition in the 28 Democratic open seats than in the 19 Republican open seats. However, the expectation that 1994 would be a good year for Republicans could have led to the prediction that Republican nominations in seats being vacated by Democrats would have been highly valued.[16] Table 9.4 presents the data on candidacies in the open seats.

Nearly the same number of Republicans and Democrats entered primaries for the 47 open seats, an average of about 4 per seat. The Democrats had more experienced candidates, though the Republicans had more unelected officials. We did not see the same advantage for the Democrats here as has been shown in earlier

TABLE 9.4   Primary Candidates in Open Seats

	Democrats		Republicans	
	Percentage	Number	Percentage	Number
Level of experience of all candidates				
Previously elected officials	31.32%	57	27.17%	50
Unelected officials	10.44	19	11.96	22
Non-quality candidates	58.24	106	60.87	112
Totals		182		184
Candidates who won primary				
Previously elected officials	53.19	25	40.43	19
Unelected officials	12.77	6	17.02	8
Non-quality candidates	34.04	16	42.55	20
Totals		47		47
Candidates who won general election				
Previously elected officials	63.64	7	44.44	16
Unelected officials	27.27	3	16.67	6
Non-quality candidates	9.09	1	38.89	14
Totals		11		36

work (Fowler and Maisel 1991). Experienced candidates were more likely to win primaries than were unelected officials or amateurs; 44 percent of the experienced Democrats and 38 percent of the experienced Republicans received their parties' nominations. Once again, unelected officials were more successful than amateurs.

In terms of the general election, the results differed drastically from what one would expect. The Republicans won 36 of the 47 elections. More than 84 percent of their experienced candidates won; 75 percent of their unelected officials won, and even 70 percent of their candidates without these kinds of qualifications won. The Democrats won so few races that it is difficult to make generalizations. However, 7 of the Democratic winners were experienced candidates and 3 others were unelected officials. Thus, the fact that they did recruit some qualified candidates may have helped the Democrats avoid an even greater disaster.

The results of the analysis confirm the advantage that experienced challengers to incumbents and candidates in open seats have in general elections. However, they call into question the extent to which recruiting more such candidates helped the Republicans sweep to victory. The Republican candidate pool, by and large, did not look very different from how it looked in the past. Experienced challengers did emerge and were victorious but largely in expected numbers. To some extent a greater contribution to the Republican victory came from a lack of strong Democratic challengers.

Before we conclude about the degree to which this analysis of the 1994 primary candidates confirms or calls into question previous conclusions about how potential candidates make decisions regarding running, it seems appropriate to turn to a further analysis of why Republican amateurs contributed so heavily to the GOP victory. Specifically we are interested in determining whether these amateurs were "quality" candidates of a type not so easily recognized previously.

Republican "Amateurs" Winning Seats in the House

Earlier research has stressed that Republicans have been at a disadvantage in congressional elections because their "farm system" of experienced candidates has been less well stocked with potential quality challengers than has been the parallel Democratic pool (Ehrenhalt 1991; Jacobson 1992; 1990a) and that many of the relatively few Republican winners did not emerge from the pool of potential experienced challengers (Fowler and Maisel 1991). The 1994 pool of Republican challengers did not differ significantly from previous pools, if one relies on the traditional measure of experienced candidates or even our expanded measure of candidates with relevant unelected office experience.

However, commentator after commentator noted during the election campaigns that many of the most prominent Republican candidates were campaigning overtly as outsiders, those without previous electoral or even governmental experience. Drawing on the widespread public dissatisfaction with the Congress, they were turning the disadvantage of inexperience into an asset. However, noting campaign strategy is not the same as having the ability to identify quality candi-

TABLE 9.5 Financing of Republican Nonincumbent Winners

	Open Seats	Defeated Incumbents
Experienced candidates or unelected officials		
Number of cases	22	17
Contributed greater than 10 percent of receipts	4	2
Contributed greater than $100,000	1	1
Contributed less than $1,000	12	6
Average contribution[a]	$13,567	$18,203
"Amateur" candidates		
Number of cases	14	17
Contributed greater than 10 percent of receipts	7	6
Contributed greater than $100,000	4	6
Contributed less than $1,000	7	7
Average contribution	$65,196	$87,319

[a] These averages exclude $228,500 contributed by Sonny Bono of California (an open-seat candidate) and $1,644,809 contributed by Enid Green-Woldholtz of Utah (a defeated incumbent) as each was so out of line as to make averages meaningless.

dates in advance, for surely not everyone without experience turned into a quality candidate.

Nevertheless it should have been possible objectively to identify some of these amateurs as quality challengers in advance of the election. One way to do so would have been to examine filings with the Federal Elections Commission (FEC). Table 9.5 provides some information on the ways in which Republican amateurs who won open seats or who beat Democratic incumbents funded their campaigns.

Some aspects of this table stand out immediately. Of the 36 Republicans who won in open seats, 16 were experienced candidates and 6 others held relevant unelected offices. Of these only 4 funded more than 10 percent of their campaigns out of their own pockets. Of these 4, only 1, Sonny Bono of California, contributed more than $100,000 to his own campaign; Bono, of course, achieved fame as a singer and actor more than as the local official that he also was. The average personal contribution of these candidates was $23,953, but that amount is inflated by Bono's contribution of more than a quarter of a million dollars to his own campaign; if Bono is excluded, the average personal contribution by these experienced candidates or by those with other relevant experience was $13,567. Of the 22, 12 contributed $1,000 or less to their own campaigns, 10 making no donation at all.

By contrast, of the 14 amateurs winning in open seats, 7 contributed more than 10 percent of the total they individually spent winning seats in the House of Representatives (8 of 15, if one puts Bono into this category). The average contribution for these 14 amateur open-seat winners to their own campaigns was

$65,196 ($76,861 if Bono is included). Interestingly, the 7 who did not contribute more than 10 percent of their campaign treasury each gave $1,000 or less. Thus, it seems these amateurs fall into two categories—those who were financing much of their campaigns from their own pockets and those relying totally on other sources. Those who contributed heavily to their own campaigns included corporate lawyers, business executives, a physician, and former NFL wide receiver Steve Largent in Oklahoma. Those relying totally on others included a developer, a former comptroller, an insurance salesman, and J. C. Watts, the former University of Oklahoma quarterback who was touted as the kind of religious and economically conservative black who would be attractive to Republicans.

A similar pattern emerges if one examines the Republicans who beat Democratic incumbents in the general elections. Seventeen of these 34 winners were either experienced candidates or those who had held relevant unelected office. None of the experienced candidates contributed $100,000 to his or her own campaign; only 1 contributed more than 10 percent of the total receipts. One of those who had held appointive office (as a gubernatorial aide) contributed more than $1.5 million to her own campaign. If that large contribution is excluded, the average contribution by a candidate among this group to his or her own campaign among this group was slightly over $18,000.

Once again the nonexperienced candidates who won seats fall into two distinct groups. The average candidate contribution among these 17 winners was over $87,000; however, 7 of the 17 gave $1,000 or less to their own efforts. Six of these incumbent conquerors contributed more than $100,000 to their own campaigns; five of these and one other contributed more that 15 percent of total receipts reported by their reelection committees. The average contribution from these candidates was more than $200,000.

This brief examination of the ways in which Republican amateurs financed their campaigns raises an important research question. It seems important to note that a non-trivial percentage of Republican non-incumbent winners were inexperienced candidates with the means to fund large portions of their own campaigns. While some winners have fallen into this category in each of the most recent congressional elections, the 1994 cycle stands out because enough of these candidates won to move the Republicans into the majority. Moreover, if one assumes that many of those who contribute large sums to their own campaigns do so early in the election season, providing the seed money needed to prove themselves serious candidates so that additional money can be raised from other sources, it should be possible for analysts to identify these candidates by examining early FEC reports.

By contrast, of the Democrats who won in open seats, only 1, Patrick Kennedy of Rhode Island, the latest in the Kennedy family line to enter the Congress, contributed more than 10 percent of his campaign's receipts (and his contribution of just over $135,000 was only about one-eighth of what his campaign spent). If one looks at the Democratic losers in the open seat races, the differences between the parties are apparent. Of the 37 Democratic losers in open seats, 21 either held elective office or had other relevant experience; only 3 of those contributed more than 10 percent of their campaign's total receipts while most of the others gave less than 5 percent, and in 7 cases less than 1 percent, obviously a very low number for open seats. More to the point, of the 37 Democratic nominees in open seats, only 3 were inexperienced candidates who contributed more than 10 percent of their campaign's receipts and only 2 of those put more than $100,000 of their own money into their efforts—both losing efforts. The Democrats do not seem to have developed a second pool of challengers for congressional seats.

CONCLUSION

This review of the candidates who emerged or were recruited to run in the 1994 congressional elections allows us to reconsider a number of theories on which scholars studying congressional elections have been working.

First, the strategic-politician model remains robust on two counts. As predicted, experienced candidates did indeed run in districts in which they were more likely to be successful. Though the number of Republican experienced politicians who ran was not as large as one might have expected, the districts in which they ran were those in which their chances seemed strongest. Similarly, the number of experienced Democrats seeking congressional nominations declined in precisely the ways one would predict (see also Jacobson 1995).

Moreover, those experienced politicians who did run proved again that having successfully sought elective office is a good predictor of campaign ability. In every category the experienced politicians seeking congressional seats (and those who had other relevant experience but to a lesser extent) fared much better than did "amateur" candidates.

We did note, however, that those amateurs who were able to fund a significant portion of their own campaigns have become more prominent and were more successful, especially within the Republican party. The level of success of these candidates can be explained by the context of the election, but the difference in the Republican and Democratic candidate pools is important. The question then turns to whether the political ambition of these candidates can be predicted in a systematic way. The opportunity-cost model would lead one to predict that those who can fund their own campaigns would be deterred from doing so because the opportunity cost from winning would be too high and the benefits from winning too low to make the expected value of winning high enough to overcome. Were changes evident that would lead one to reevaluate this portion of the formula?

While the data from 1994 are suggestive at best, some obvious hypotheses present themselves. First, the theory has held that Republican potential candidates were deterred because the government was activist, and even if they won, they would not look forward to achieving their policy goals, which entailed curtailing government activity. The Contract with America, on the other hand, suggests a different approach. The implication of the contract is that individuals are running for Congress in order to cut back government. This direction provides a policy-oriented incentive that did not exist before for Republican ideologues.

One can add to this analysis that the anti-incumbent sentiment expressed in 1992 and the anti-Congress sentiment expressed in public opinion polls for many years but reaching its height during the 103rd Congress, each accentuated by the combative style of the new Republican leader, Gingrich, encouraged potential Republican candidates that they might emerge victorious if, not in the 1994 election, in one shortly thereafter. In some ways the 1994 recapturing of majority status was a bonus for those looking toward the future of Republican politics under Gingrich's influence. If this hypothesis has merit, one would expect more wealthy Republican ideologues to seek seats in Congress in 1996 and beyond.[17]

These conclusions hold largely for wealthy economic conservatives who desire to get the government off their backs and who, previously, have not sought elective office because of high personal costs and little opportunity for effective influence. But what about the other wing of the Republican party, the social conservatives, who have been increasingly influential in the party in recent years but whose agenda has also not moved very quickly in the Congress? While the data in this paper do not speak to those individuals, one could hypothesize—and one can find at least anecdotal supporting evidence in 1994—that some of those amateurs who won without large inputs of their own funds came from the religious right and were supported enthusiastically by those who agreed with their views and saw the opportunity, again under Gingrich, to have their views reflected by the Republican party in Congress.

In these cases the strategic decision making of potential candidates might well have been altered in 1994 from what it had been prior to that election. The Republican party has emerged as a potent political force throughout much of the South and other regions in which the religious right is influential. Republican candidates who in the past considered races against incumbent Democrats, or races in open seats that were traditionally held by Democrats, to be hopeless and thus not worth the personal costs now see these seats as winnable and providing a promising venue for pursuing their strongly felt political agenda.

That 1994 was a watershed election is beyond doubt (see Cook 1995). However, this analysis also implies that the experience of candidates in 1994 should cause us to look carefully at the 1996 candidate pool for continued evidence of new paths to Congress, particularly for Republicans. Only then can we see clearly how theories of recruitment and emergence fare in a new political order.

NOTES

1. An earlier version of this chapter was given as a paper at the 1995 Annual Meeting of the New England Political Science Association in Portland, Maine on May 6. The authors would like to thank Ann Camissa for her helpful comments at that time. We would also like to thank Gary Jacobson for his willingness to compare his dataset with ours, allowing us to clarify discrepancies caused by slight differences in definitions of terms.

2. The number 39 includes 3 Republicans who won in seats that became open became after the primary—New Jersey's 11th district, in which Rodney Freylinghuysen won the nomination after the incumbent Republican withdrew; New York's 4th, in which the in-

cumbent Republican was beaten in a primary by Daniel Frisa; and Oklahoma 2, in which incumbent Democrat Mike Synar lost a primary to Virgil Cooper, who in turn lost in the general election to Republican Tom Coburn. Throughout this paper, primary candidates for seats in which incumbents lost primaries are included among those challenging incumbents because that categorization reflects their perspective at the time they had to decide on running in congressional races.

3. If one excludes from this data the 5 seats that became open after incumbents lost primaries, 47 seats were open. The Democrats held 28 and the Republicans 19, and the Republicans won 21 of the Democratic seats and lost 4 of their own, showing a gain of 17. The also won one seat (Oklahoma's 2nd) in which a Democratic incumbent lost a primary and his conqueror lost the general election.

4. The three most prominent models for forecasting congressional elections are those put forth by James Campbell of Louisiana State University, Alan Abramowitz of Emory University, and Michael Lewis-Beck of the University of Iowa. On the eve of the 1994 election, these scholars met at a round table discussion at the Southern Political Science Association's Annual Meeting. None of their models predicted the Republican takeover of the House. None of their models predicted Republican gains that were within acceptable margins of error. At the Midwest Political Science Association's Annual Meeting in April, 1995, Campbell posited how his model could be modified to come up with better results, but no extant model predicted the 1994 outcome.

5. It is worth noting that the concept of "qualified" candidates, which is most often operationalized as those currently holding elective office and thus those who have demonstrated the ability to run successful campaigns, was first developed as a means to identify candidates who would do well in general elections *before* the fact. It is easy to identify quality candidates after an election; they are those who ran good races, and many measures exist to operationalize this variable—votes received, increment in votes received from a previous race, money raised and spent, and so forth. It is more difficult to predict in advance who will be a good candidate. The measure that Jacobson employs throughout his research (holding elective office) is most commonly used and has the advantage of ready replication. It has been criticized, however, because it misses many highly qualified candidates—prominent amateurs (Canon 1990) or others, such as party officials, former representatives, and those who have run races and done well in the past although losing, whose previous careers would lead one to think that they could run quality campaigns (see Bond, Covington, and Fleisher 1985; Fowler and Maisel 1991; Kazee 1983; Krasno and Green 1988). None of the measures developed by others differs significantly from Jacobson's in terms of results; his has the advantage of simplicity, while others seem to make more sense theoretically.

6. We remain aware of the limitations of any of these definitions. For instance, running successfully for a seat in the Maine State House involves running in a district with approximately 1.5 percent of the voters in a congressional district, while winning a state senate seat in California involves running in a district larger than, and often including all or most of, a congressional district. Obviously running in the latter is a better indication of the ability to run a quality campaign for Congress than the former. Much the same can be said of various appointive offices. Yet these remain the best predictors of "qualified" candidates that we have been able to induce from the data.

7. For comparative purposes, we also looked at the nonincumbent Democrats whom they defeated.

8. The one Independent incumbent, Bernie Sanders of Vermont, was included in our data set. The two Republicans who ran to oppose him are included as well.

9. The variety of these offices, as well as the differences among state legislative districts, particularly as they relate to congressional districts, highlights the problem noted in footnote 5.

10. Again, some of these seem to have had experience quite relevant for seeking seats in Congress. In other cases the relevance of the experience is less obvious. Our decision was to include all of them in our analysis but to recognize that the differences noted previously exist.

11. It is difficult to know how to classify Rodney Frelinghuysen, who won the nomination as the handpicked designee of the incumbent Republican who surrendered his renomination because of ill health. Frelinghuysen was by all accounts an experienced candidate, a former state legislator and twice-defeated candidate in a neighboring congressional district and heir to one of the best known and most respected political names in his state.

12. It should be noted that no Republicans sought the nomination in 17 of those districts.

13. Jacobson (1995) also notes that these experienced politicians were not randomly distributed among congressional districts in which incumbent Democrats sought reelection. Rather, they sought office disproportionately and were successful disproportionately in districts which leaned more toward the Republican party in presidential elections, further evidence of strategic decision making.

14. These numbers include the 7 districts in Louisiana in which all 7 incumbents (4 Democrats and 3 Republicans) were reelected in the state's unique open primary system because they each received more than 50 percent of the primary vote in their districts. Vermont's at-large seat is considered a district without a Democratic candidate, even though Independent Bernie Sanders was supported by most of his state's Democrats.

15. This number and this analysis excludes the 5 districts which became open after incumbents lost the primaries. Those districts are excluded because the districts were not open at the time potential candidates had to make their decisions concerning seeking office. See footnotes 2 and 3.

16. To our knowledge no data, controlling for the party previously holding the seat, has been gathered on differences in primary competition in open seats. Other variables, such as the reasons seats have been vacated, would have to be considered in any such analysis. We view this as a fruitful line for further study.

17. One could also add that the push for term limits, although unsuccessful at a national level, has reduced the opportunity costs for Republican officeholders. Using the 104th Congress as a model, Republican officeholders can see that they can have influence in the short run and leave office after a few years and have influence on policy on the ways in which they believe the country should be moving without giving up personal economic benefits for as long as one would have thought necessary in the past.

10

Innovative Midterm Elections

DAVID R. MAYHEW[1]

For a party out of the White House, there is an age-old way to conduct midterm elections: Talk retrospective and make vague promises. The Republicans' "Had Enough?" campaign against the Truman administration in 1946 is a classic instance. In midterms, a retrospective focus makes sense because it is so inviting to blame everything on an incumbent president's two-year record. Vagueness helps along a "coalition-of-disaffected-minorities" strategy at a time when not having presidential candidates on the ballot lets House and Senate candidates run on local issues; what works in Alabama may not work in Rhode Island.

All the more surprising, then, that the Republicans of 1994 should present a campaign appeal—the Contract with America—that was both prospective and specific. For a congressional party, it broke new ground to commit hundreds of candidates to an action program and then use that program as respectively a campaign theme, a lens for interpreting the election outcome and a centerpiece for a "hundred-days" legislative drive. Many presidential candidates have acted out this familiar mandate scenario—consider Ronald Reagan's use of the Kemp-Roth tax cut plan in the 1980 campaign and subsequently in his 1981 budget—as have U.S. national parties more generally by writing platforms every four years and then sometimes paying attention to them after winning. But it was a first for a congressional party—more specifically, for just a House-of-Representatives party.

Of course, election mandates are largely a matter of social construction (Hershey 1992): Who can be sure what voters intend when they vote or if their individual intentions can be successfully added up? But being socially constructed does not make a mandate any the less consequential. Believable electoral connections can be immensely consequential, as is evident in the records of William Gladstone, Woodrow Wilson, and others who pioneered in the genre of election programs and their governmental use. Perceived mandates can legitimize. Partly because presidents discovered this fact, the twentieth century presidency shot ahead of Congress in power. An intriguing question is whether congressional "contracts" like Newt Gingrich's, played out into the future, could serve as something of an institutional equalizer. Congress to president: "My mandate and hundred days are better than yours." Is this a possible future? We should stay tuned.

PLACING 1994 IN U.S. HISTORY

But if the apparatus of the contract is new, midterm elections that make a difference are not. My chief aim here is to develop this historical generalization, not to dwell on 1994's uniqueness. If the 1994 midterms turn out to have spurred a decisive long-term policy shift—we can't be sure yet that it has—this will not be the first time midterms have done that, contract or no contract. In fact, presidential elections, transfixing as they are for most of us, have had to compete with midterms as boundary events in U.S policy history. This is an important, largely untold story.

More specifically, I will try in this chapter to isolate and discuss a class of past midterms that meet the following four criteria: Each of them (1) elevated to power a new dominant congressional coalition that (2) anchored in place a new national policy agenda and (3) enjoyed considerable (though never complete) success in enacting that agenda, and (4) the coalition, the agenda, and the enacting capacity lasted for not just two years but eight or ten years or even longer. In short, these are midterms that triggered new policy eras. It is hard to imagine a more ambitious role for midterm elections, and the Gingrich Republicans will be delighted if theirs can eventually be said to have met this stiff standard. We cannot know if it will, but if it does, it will join an already-populated historical class.

The evidence to document midterms of the stipulated type will center on relevant innovativeness shown by post-midterm Congresses rather than on events inherent in the midterm elections themselves. What happens afterward is what counts. Just how the midterms may have engendered such innovativeness is another matter, and I will do the best I can with that question in a follow-up discussion, though without confidence that I have gotten anywhere near closure. The sources for this electoral and policy analysis are standard secondary works on U.S. political history, which I have been examining as systematically as I can for another project.

I will close the chapter on a different note. It is entirely possible, after all, that the 1994 midterms have engendered not a new policy era but a flash-in-the-pan. The "Age of Gingrich" may come and go in a hurry leaving little trace. I will take a look at a past flash-in-the-pan midterm victory that arguably approximates best some relevant properties of 1994—the Republican midterm victory of 1946.

INNOVATIVE MIDTERMS OF THE PAST

The ambitious criteria outlined above seem to be met by four past midterms, two from the nineteenth century and two from the twentieth.

1810

Here is a case we all learned about in elementary school but that later professional training in election analysis seems to have taught us to ignore. The election of

1810, at the midpoint of James Madison's first term in the White House, "swept in a new generation of Republicans" to power in the House of Representatives. This breath of fresh air came from within the dominant Jeffersonian Republican party rather than from the declining Federalist opposition. "War Hawks" was the familiar label given to the new faction of some 30 members who took the lead in organizing the new House in November 1811, electing freshman Henry Clay to the Speakership.

The War Hawks' new agenda featured nationalism, aggressive expansionism, economic development, and, in the short term, war against England. They got much of what they wanted. The new Congress led off with military legislation and nudged Madison toward requesting a declaration of war, which he did in mid–1812. Beyond that, House Republican pressure for such initiatives as a new national bank, internal improvements, higher tariffs, and admission of new states continued through the 1810s and into the 1820s, often winning success though often losing out to White House opposition (as with Madison's veto of an internal improvements bill on his last day in office). The House had become the center of initiative in the government. If today's media had operated back then, it is a good bet that more TV bytes per year would have gone to Clay, who served as Speaker most of the time between 1811 and 1825, than to Presidents James Madison (1809–1817) or James Monroe (1817–1825) (White 1951: 57–62; Peters 1990: 33–34; Smelser 1968: 208–13; Davidson et al. 1994: 325–26; Jordan 1994: 98–99; Boyer 1993: 267–68).

1866

This was the election that ushered in congressional Reconstruction. Elevated to veto-proof two-thirds majorities in both House and Senate, the dominant radical faction of the Republican party proceeded to seize the initiative from President Andrew Johnson and enact its own blueprint for the conquered South. Representative Thaddeus Stevens, though not Speaker, assumed a leadership role something like Henry Clay's earlier.

Following the election, in January 1867, the outgoing 39th Congress arranged a special session of the incoming 40th Congress for March 1867. (Without that, the new Congress wouldn't have met until November 1867, as was the norm before the 20th "Lame-Duck" Amendment was added to the Constitution in the 1930s.) In ambition, speed, and decisiveness, the legislative record of March 1867 resembles that of early 1933 under Franklin Roosevelt. On March 2, 1867, alone, three major acts were approved: the Tenure of Office Act restricting the president's control over executive personnel; the Command of the Army Act requiring the president to issue all military orders through the general of the army; and above all, the First Reconstruction Act dividing the South into five military districts to the end of writing new state constitutions and forming new governments based on enfranchisement of African-Americans but restricted suffrage for rebel whites (Cashman 1993: 211–12; Randall and Donald 1969: ch. 34).

In general, though with flagging commitment after the late 1860s, the Republicans' Reconstruction majority held in place on Capitol Hill until the midterm election of 1874. In the realm of lawmaking, three more Reconstruction Acts ensued during 1867 and 1868 (though the coalition fell one Senate vote short of evicting the impeached Johnson from office in 1868), the 15th Amendment enfranchising blacks cleared Congress in February 1869, and subsequent Congresses followed with the five Enforcement Acts of 1870 through 1872 and the era-closing Civil Rights Act of early 1875.

1910

No opening big bang this time, and no new leader as prominent as Clay or Stevens. At this midpoint of the William Howard Taft administration, the Republicans kept formal control of the Senate while losing the House. But in coalitional terms, the election gave decisive control of Capitol Hill to a cross-party coalition of Democrats and progressive Republicans who pursued a reform agenda until U.S. entry into World War I in 1917 (or perhaps until the 1918 midterm). Congressional conservatives had lost their ascendancy and largely their blocking power; as of 1910, the House's Cannon regime and the Senate's Allison-Aldrich regime came to an end.

Many notable laws were to win enactment during Woodrow Wilson's legislative drives of 1913–14 and 1916, but the Congress of 1911–13 compiled a busy record before that. It included the 17th Amendment requiring direct election of U.S. Senators, first voted by the House in 1892 and now finally endorsed by the Senate; an eight-hour day for workers on federal contracts, favored by the House against Senate opposition since 1896; a ban on phosphorus matches whose manufacture was said to cause a hideous disease; establishment of the federal Children's Bureau, championed by that era's women's movement; creation of the Department of Labor; and a campaign-finance measure placing a ceiling on candidate expenditures (Mowry 1958: 262–65; Kobach 1994: 1776–79; Moss 1994; Mutch 1988: 1–16). In 1912, the House broke new ground with its so-called Money Trust Investigation—"the first Congressional investigation conducted in the 'grand manner' of modern times, and geared to the avowed purpose of proving and publicizing the need for major legislative enactments in new fields." Wall Street received a major roasting (Taylor 1961: 81–84).

1938

"It was not the 1936 Roosevelt landslide, but the more ambiguous [in party terms] result of 1938, that set the pattern that was followed, with relatively minor variations until after World War II was over and Roosevelt was dead" (Barone 1990: 122). The 1938 midterm brought to dominance the so-called "conservative coalition" of Republicans and southern Democrats who now had the resolve, numbers, and institutional bases to block liberal initiatives, conduct investigations serving conservative ends, and sometimes enact their own laws. Special attention was to go to cutting back New Deal programs, hunting for alleged subversives, and curbing the then muscle-flexing labor movement. The coalition's major actors included Edward Cox (D.–Ga.), Howard Smith (D.–Va.), and Charles Halleck (R.–Ind.), a formidable trio on the House Rules Committee which served as a kind of cross-party headquarters; Martin Dies (D.–Tex.) as chairman of a special committee to investigate un-American activities; House Republican Minority Leader Joseph Martin of Massachusetts; and, as the years went on, Senator Robert Taft of Ohio (Patterson 1967: ch. 9).

No new major New Deal initiative won enactment after the 1938 election (Jeffries 1990; Amenta and Skocpol 1988). In 1939–40, Congress slashed relief spending, ended Roosevelt's prized undistributed-profits tax, and killed two key White House proposals in the areas of public works and housing. Congressman Clifton A. Woodrum (D.–Va.) ran a damaging investigation of the Works Progress Administration (WPA), Congressman Smith conducted a year-long probe of the National Labor Relations Board (NLRB), and the Dies committee targeted the left in general. Notable laws actually passed during those years included the Hatch Act of 1939 curbing executive use of patronage jobs and the Smith Act of 1940 requiring aliens to register and penalizing subversion of the Armed Forces (Patterson 1967: ch. 9). By the end of 1943, Congress had directly or indirectly killed such New Deal instruments as the Federal Theatre Project, the Civilian Conservation Corps, the WPA, the National Youth Administration, the Home Owners' Loan Corporation, and the National Resources Planning Board (Leuchtenberg 1963: 273; Brinkley 1995: 141, 255). Labor unions suffered constraints through the Smith-Connally Act of 1943 and later the Taft-Hartley Act of 1947.

Just how long the "conservative coalition" can be said to have prevailed on Capitol Hill is a slippery subject, partly because there were ups and downs. One account, using roll-call data, points to 1939 through 1955 as the era of particular coalition success in the House: On occasions during those years when most Republicans and most southern Democrats lined up against most northern Democrats, the conservative side won 92.8 percent of the time. A comparable Senate era, exhibiting a lag as the Senate, for staggered-election reasons, often does, was 1942 through 1958 (Shelley 1983: 29–41). Liberal Democrats reaching for power under Kennedy still found it necessary to "pack" the House Rules Committee with their own loyalists in a celebrated showdown in 1961.

Also-rans

Those are the four midterms that seem to stand out. In the nineteenth century, according to standard sources, no other midterm comes close to 1810 or 1866 in the stipulated kind of policy impact. As for more recent times, I gave serious consideration to the 1958 election during Eisenhower's second term, which elected immense Democratic majorities that contributed to party projects later in the 1960s. But 1958 doesn't work well. Eisenhower kept surprisingly good control of the national policy agenda in 1959 through 1960 by attacking government spending and promoting reform of labor unions—the latter coming to fruition in the Landrum-Griffin Act of 1959 (Evans and Novak 1966: ch. 10). The liberals had to wait. I considered the 1974 midterm, which elected the 75 famed "Watergate babies" who forced an overhaul of the House seniority system in the winter of 1974–75. But what did they do after that? What policy regime did they inaugurate? Not much on the socioeconomic front, and the era's chief Watergate-related procedural reforms—the War Powers Act, the Budget and Impoundment Act, and the Campaign Finance Reform Act—were enacted by the preceding Congress of 1973–1974.

Possibly the closest call was the midterm of 1930 under Hoover, which has much in common with that of 1910 under Taft. In March through June of 1932, a cross-party congressional coalition of Democrats and progressive Republicans erupted to enact important new statutes in the areas of taxation and relief. A New Deal reform impulse that would last into 1937–38 was investing Capitol Hill before Roosevelt reached Washington. But it is not easy to credit this eruption in any direct way to the 1930 midterm, notwithstanding the large seat shifts that year to the Democrats. The Congress of 1931–33 started out in a spirit of bipartisan cooperation. Perhaps this is surprising, given the background of the Depression, but the antiestablishment reform eruption came later and seems to have had later causes. It was one of those things—no doubt induced by the Depression getting worse. Unlike 1910, the 1930 midterm did not itself empower a new coalition bearing a new policy agenda (Schwarz 1970: chs. 4–6; Mayhew 1991: 154–56).

EXPLAINING INNOVATIVE MIDTERMS

What might account for midterm aftermaths as striking as those associated with 1810, 1866, 1910, and 1938? Four models come to mind. Each model will be discussed briefly here, with an eye for all past U.S. experience with midterms, innovative and noninnovative, insofar as that is possible. The recent 1994 midterms will be brought in where relevant. We know that 1994 elevated to power a new congressional coalition bearing a new policy agenda; as of this writing in May 1995, notwithstanding the House's remarkable early-year "one hundred-days" campaign, we cannot tell how much luck this coalition will finally have enacting its agenda into law during 1995–96, and we certainly can't tell whether the new regime will exhibit decade-long staying power. But it will be interesting to see whether midterm features associated with past exceptional innovativeness, insofar as those can be teased out of history, obtained in 1994.

Large Party Seat Swings

A simple and obvious idea is that new, aggressive, long-lasting policy regimes on Capitol Hill might have origins in midterm seat gains for the out-party that are abnormally large—whatever might cause those gains. It is a proximate explanation. This is unquestionably part of the story for 1910, when the Democrats gained 56 House seats and 10 Senate seats and took over the House (though not the Senate); for 1938 when the Republicans gained 80 House seats and 6 Senate seats (though still fell well short of capturing either body); and, to compare with the present, for 1994 with its Republican gains of 52 and 8 seats.

Unfortunately, as a general proposition, this seat-gain diagnostic is not much better than most of those offered by pre-modern medicine. The 1810 midterms don't help the discussion much, since they occurred before competition between mass-based parties kicked into place in the 1830s (though still: Those War Hawks weren't a Federalist party opposition). But note that the 1866 midterms brought scarcely any partisan seat change at all—3 House seats and 1 Senate seat to the Democrats, compared with the results for 1864. Moreover, a great many midterms have brought large partisan seat swings without generating aggressive, long-lasting new policy orders—for example, Democratic gains of 93 House seats in 1874, 70 in 1882, 75 in 1890, 75 in 1922, and (as previously discussed) 49 in both 1958 and 1974 and Republican gains of 120 in 1894, 66 in 1914, and 47 in 1966. Spot quiz: What was undertaken or achieved by that Congress of 1895–97 fortified by a record 120 new House Republicans? The history books are a blank. Large partisan seat swings may help, but on the evidence they have been neither a necessary nor a sufficient condition for an innovative post-midterm policy order.

Public Opinion Change

At a much more basic level, Capitol Hill policy change may be motored by ups and downs in public opinion. Politics may finally be that simple. Assume a universe in which U.S. public opinion is ordinarily stable but sometimes shows breaking points—"public moods," for example, may come and go—that the breaking points occur randomly across electoral cycles, and that both the stabilities and the breaking points are reflected on Capitol Hill. One result is that off-election-season "policy eruptions" will occasionally take place in Congress, as in, say, the Progressive-Democratic uprising of the spring of 1932 or the onset of McCarthyism in early 1950. But another result, given the stickiness inherent in electing politicians for terms, is that opinion breaking points will need to wait for the next even-year November to find full expression in Washington.

Nothing is particularly strange about this universe, though note one thing that it predicts: Elections that elevate new Capitol Hill policy coalitions will occur as often in midterms as in presidential years. And that may be a basic fact of U.S politics (though, yes, a freshly elected coalition may run into more enactment trouble after midterms than after a presidential election since it faces holdover politicians in both the White House and two-thirds of the Senate rather than just in two-thirds of the Senate). In this scenario, Clay or Stevens (or Gingrich), as leader of a new policy coalition, should be no more surprising than Franklin Roosevelt in that role.

I have a hunch that this model accounts for a good deal in general and helps to explain innovative midterms. Survey evidence for 1937–38, and moves by elite actors around 1810, in 1865–66, and in 1909–10 that admit inference of substantial underlying opinion shifts also at those junctures, help the model along—and for comparison, 1993–94 showed evidence of an opinion shift too. But this analysis has to stay in the realm of hunch. Most of U.S. history lacks opinion data, and at any rate, for recent times, assuming agreement on what kinds of data to look for, we would very likely find instances of sizable pre-midterm shifts of opinion that did not trigger new post-midterm policy regimes. Consider Truman's first two years or Reagan's. A hypothesized relation between large opinion shifts and new policy regimes would likely pan out across U.S. history, as a statistical matter, but there would be a lot of error.

Resolution of High-Stakes Conflict

To switch to an elite setting more easily documented and more proximate to the phenomenon being explained, consider the following scenario for the opening two years of a president's term. For a year or more, dramatic battles take place on Capitol Hill as Congress lines up for and against White House positions. The stakes are enormous as the future seems to be presenting itself for basic shaping; by historical standards, one of the opposing sides is pressing an exceptionally prodigious agenda. There are wins, losses, and standoffs. The overall outcome remains uncertain going into a midterm season where a self-conscious opposition confronts the White House in elections seen by many as showdowns. The opposition wins and stands ready with its own agenda.

Let me concede that this scenario misdescribes the lead-up to the midterm of 1810. Spectacular as the War Hawks may be as an instance of a post-midterm policy coalition, the early-nineteenth century politics surrounding their rise sometimes fits into the discussion here aptly, sometimes not so aptly. Part of the story of 1810 is that the House, for various reasons, was succeeding at that time in surging temporarily past the Presidency as a national representative institution (it still far surpassed the Senate). U.S. institutions, parties, and voters were all getting their sea legs back then.

But of 1865–66, 1909–10, and 1937–38, this resolution-of-conflict model provides a quite good description. From late 1865 through 1866, radical Republicans in Congress squared off against Andrew Johnson, winning some victories over his vetoes but not able to dominate yet. In 1909–10, aggressive Capitol Hill reformers went to the mat with Taft-backed conservatives over the tariff, taxation, conservation, and railroad regulation. It remained unclear who would prevail. In these Johnson and Taft instances the transformative agendas came from the Capitol Hill side, but in 1937–38 FDR bore that distinction with his post-landslide program to pack the Supreme Court, tighten presidential control of the executive branch, help along labor union organization, and press legislative initiatives in such areas as housing, minimum wage, public-works spending, and more river-valley developments like the Tennessee Valley Authority (TVA). Intense reaction to these aims brought a "conservative manifesto" by Senate dissidents in late 1937, landmark White House defeats on court packing and executive reorganization, a customizing of the House Rules Committee to serve as a base for congressional conservatism, and a first round of Dies committee hearings damaging to New

Deal interests in 1938. It was a warm-up for 1939, though until the 1938 midterms it wasn't certain which side would come out ahead (Randall and Donald 1969: ch. 33; Cooper 1990: 145–57; Patterson 1967: chs. 6–8).

These three Congresses were unquestionably among the most contentious in U.S. history. In the cases of 1865–66 and 1909–10, though not as clearly 1937–38 when congressional support for the White House plummeted during the recession of late 1937 through early 1938 but then rose again in mid–1938, elite-level events during the two-year intervals are consistent with a model of gradual underlying public-opinion drift away from the White House side. House insurgents, for example, failed in an attempt to cripple the conservative Cannon Speakership in March 1909 but succeeded a year later in March 1910.

All three Congresses discussed here may remind the reader of 1993–94. The Democrats are back! it was proclaimed at the start of 1993, and the Clinton administration's drive to rival the New Deal and Great Society ensued. Health care reform in 1994 raised the stakes about as high as they get in U.S. domestic politics, and the resulting coalitional combat up through the 1994 midterms does not need to be reviewed.

Leaving aside the circumstances of 1810, very-high-stakes, unresolved conflict before midterms looks like a necessary condition for a new policy regime after the midterms. The logic is good as are the facts; not least, it is important for an opposition to discover and steel itself through conflict before midterms so as to be ready with an agenda afterward. But a sufficient condition, it is probably not. Other relevant historical junctures seem to register fairly high on the "high-stakes-and-unresolved-conflict-before-midterms" scale, for example, the first two years of Theodore Roosevelt's second term (which brought wins and losses for the Square Deal), of Truman's second term (the Fair Deal's ups and downs, McCarthyism), of Kennedy's presidency (the stalemate over civil rights, the losing White House drives for education aid and medicare), of Nixon's first term (lots of conflict on many fronts), and of Carter's presidency (the close-fought stalemate over energy policy). Still, to be fair to the idea being pressed here, most beginnings of presidential terms do *not* seem to exhibit such unresolved high-stakes conflict—some examples (when the presidents all got what they wanted, more or less) are Woodrow Wilson's first two years in 1913–14, Franklin Roosevelt's in 1933–34, Lyndon Johnson's in 1965–66, and Reagan's 1981–82; Eisenhower's in 1953–54 (low-temperature politics); and (when the presidents didn't want much) Reagan's in 1985–86 and Bush's in 1989–90.

Majority-Party Factionalism

The fourth model is compatible with the public-opinion and conflict-resolution accounts presented previously but makes a distinctive claim. It is this: The decisive lead-up to a new post-midterm policy regime is a fundamental, take-no-prisoners conflict over an era's central policy issues *within* the ruling majority party during the preceding midterm-election season, from which an anti–White House faction emerges victorious and then constitutes or joins a dominant new policy regime on Capitol Hill.

I have not found evidence of such intraparty conflict during the 1810 election season, which hasn't been written up all that much. Perhaps the War Hawks of 1811–12—who were certainly a prime instance of a party faction—emerged from such election-related conflict within the dominant Jeffersonian Republican party of that era, perhaps not. But for U.S. history after, say, 1860—this gets past the confusing reconfiguration of parties during the 1850s—the factionalism model works very well. There seems to be a one-to-one relation between exceptional factionalism within the majority party and the advent of new long-lasting policy regimes.

Here is the evidence. In the post–Civil War election year of 1866, beyond the usual contesting between Republicans and Democrats, much hinged on which kinds of Republicans managed to get nominated and elected. Nominating showdowns took place at the district level between radicals and conservatives. President Andrew Johnson, a deposit of the Lincoln-led Union ticket of 1864 but now well distanced from the Republican median on Reconstruction policy, undertook an extraordinary speaking tour across the North during the late summer of 1866 aimed at electing a cross-party coalition of "Douglas Democrats" and conservative Republicans to Congress. No president before that time had intruded so boldly into electoral politics, and none would do so again during the nineteenth century; Johnson's campaign was "the stark exception." The radicals won; the opposing cross-party coalition lost. On balance, radicals triumphed over conservatives in the Republican party's nominating processes that year; later, the party kept virtually all its congressional seats in a general election lacking conventional "in-party" versus "out-party" dynamics; and Johnson ended the election season discredited (Tulis 1987: 87–93; Powell 1973; Stampp 1970: 114–18; Randall and Donald 1969: 589–91).

In 1910 President Taft and his allies undertook the first great midterm party purge of the twentieth century—an effort to aid Republican party regulars and defeat progressive insurgents in Republican primaries in the Midwest and West. Disloyal incumbents were targeted. Statewide networks of "Taft Republican clubs" appeared and were answered by "progressive Republican clubs." The result was a disaster for the White House—"an almost unbroken string of reverses" as some 40 incumbent Republican regulars lost their House nominations (mostly to progressives), anti-Taft incumbents held their seats, and aggressive reform factions led by Robert La Follette and Hiram Johnson won eye-catching complete victories in Wisconsin and California (Mowry 1958: 266–68, 272–73; Cooper 1990: 157; Patterson 1967: 270–87).

And in 1938 Franklin Roosevelt, exasperated by a growing faction of anti–New Deal Democrats on Capitol Hill, undertook the second and last great midterm party purge of the twentieth century. The result was another White House disaster, or at least it was seen as such: In three of the best-known confrontations, conservative Senators Walter George of Georgia, "Cotton Ed" Smith of South Carolina, and Millard Tydings of Maryland easily won their primaries against FDR-backed challengers (Patterson 1967: 270–87). In fact, more seems to have gone on in the 1938 Democratic primaries than we see in the conventional

Roosevelt-centered accounts. (Both the 1910 and 1938 primary seasons could use more scholarly attention.) Through random reading, for example, I have come across instances of incumbent liberal Democrats losing House nominations in 1938 in San Antonio, where the defeat of Maury Maverick was a major blow to the left, and in Norfolk, Virginia. A nationwide grinding of party teeth seems to have occurred, not always involving the White House (Koeniger 1982: 878, 884; Weiss 1971).

In short, the majority-party factional showdowns of 1866, 1910, and 1938 stand out as distinctive; no other midterm season since 1860 has exhibited such dynamics. Certainly the three presidential intrusions at those times are distinctive. And in all three cases an anti–White House faction that won out overall (the radical Republicans in 1866) or in a substantial section of the country (the progressive Republicans in 1910, the conservative Democrats in 1938) went on to constitute or join a new Capitol Hill policy coalition that prevailed for a long time.

What might explain this apparent cause-and-effect relationship? One answer is that such factional showdowns do not do anything more than efficiently index emerging conflicts in U.S. society that are particularly severe and lasting. New societal cleavages are the real causal factor; that loud noise you hear is just a new issue cutting the political sector at a new joint. But another plausible answer is that such showdowns between party factions, whatever their origins, have causal power of their own: They may generate a psychology that something basic has been "settled" in a whole party or a large geographic region within one party (those Walter George types just can't be beaten); they may stir lasting animosities among elite actors, convert historical opponents into friends and old comrades-in-arms into enemies, and result in blocs of voters being cued by factional leaders once old party images and signals become muddled. Whichever way, the effect on the system as a whole is to permanently weaken one actual or potential governing coalition (the anti-Reconstructionists, the Taft-Cannon-Aldrich Republicans, the New Dealers) and strengthen another (the radical Republicans, the progressives/Democrats, the "conservative coalition").

There is no easy way to choose between these two accounts, but it may be illuminating to note that intraparty conflict can play a large and analogous role in other settings. Consider the factional showdowns that occasionally occur in U.S. nominating conventions with the result of ushering in a new durable policy coalition within a presidential party and affecting the national balance between the parties—the 1896 Democratic convention that elevated the Silverite faction led by William Jennings Bryan and alienated the more conservative Gold Democrats; the 1964 Republican convention that nominated Barry Goldwater, jarred that party toward conservatism of a southwestern variety, and ostracized the Rockefeller moderates; and the 1972 Democratic convention that nominated George McGovern and shifted that party's base toward candidate organizations catering to race, gender, and age categories at the expense of the old establishment of labor unions, regular state organizations, and city machines. In British politics, to cite another analogy, nothing has been more productive of dominant, long-lasting coalitions in the

House of Commons than having one major party hive off a faction through serious internal policy conflict and thus improve the competitive position of the other major party—as did the Tories over repeal of the Corn Laws in 1846, the Liberals over Irish Home rule in 1886 and again over conduct of World War I in 1916, and the Labor Party over policy toward the Depression in 1931 and again through defection of its centrist Social Democratic faction in 1981.

But obviously, nothing even faintly resembling the midterm factional showdowns of 1868, 1910, and 1938 took place within the Democratic party during the 1994 election season. Imagine a counterfactual scenario in which the Clinton White House, fed up with less than 100 percent Democratic support for the President's budget and health care programs, stage-manages a party purge in mid-1994. "Clinton Clubs" sprout up around the country. Disloyalists are listed and denounced. Liberal money cascades out from New York and California. In a whirlwind speaking tour through the relevant states and districts, the president appeals in person to Democratic primary voters to nominate unabashed liberals to replace Senators Richard Bryan of Nevada and Bob Kerrey of Nebraska; Congressmen Gary Condit of California, Bill Brewster of Oklahoma, Charles Stenholm of Texas; and others. House members Sam Gejdenson and David Obey are tapped by the White House to enter primaries against two other Senators of uncertain reliability—Joseph Lieberman of Connecticut and Herb Kohl of Wisconsin. In the event, virtually all the White House–backed candidates lose out to a now-angry collection of party veterans who have taken to calling themselves "The True Democratic Center." Nothing like this happened in 1994.

Back to 1994

In general, then, where does this analysis of past "innovative midterms" leave us as regards 1994? For one thing, it throws a comparative light on Gingrich. Followers as we are of the twentieth century presidency, we tend to forget that House leaders elevated by elections—such as Clay and Stevens—can sometimes seize the policy initiative too. It may be just historical accident that no congressional leader has assumed this role in recent times. (Senator Robert Taft may be the closest twentieth century approximation until now—see the following discussion.)

For another thing, in *some* background respects 1994 bears resemblance to some or all of the past innovative midterm years: Witness the year-long drift of public opinion against the Clinton White House, the exceptionally high-stakes conflict over health care, the impressive November seat gains for the opposition. This is food for thought. Yet, in the final analysis, the trademark characteristic of relevant past midterms—the no-holds-barred conflict between factions of the majority party—was entirely missing in 1994. The new Republican policy coalition of 1995 is not propelled by any such explosion. Yes, the Democrats suffered a major election loss in 1994, but they did not tear themselves apart in that year's election processes and thus they remain a formidable instrument. The normal gyrations of politics can bring them back. The implication: We may be witnessing not the start of a long-lasting new policy regime but rather the start of conventional toss-up politics in which Congress goes back and forth between the parties and key policy options stay up for grabs.

THE ANALOGY OF 1946

If 1810, 1866, 1910, and 1938 are high rungs to reach for, 1946 is a very low rung—at least in terms of the durability of the new policy coalition produced by that midterm. The analogy is haunting to today's Republicans since 1946 looks so much like 1994. Then, Harry Truman, a first-term Democratic president floundering in his job and low in the polls, saw his party lose control of both houses of Congress as Republicans gained 58 House members and 13 Senators and surged to 54.7 percent of the national major-party House vote. The comparable statistics for 1994 are 52 House members, 9 senators, and some 53.8 percent of the House popular vote. Between the two dates, the Republicans never captured control of the House or Senate at midterms (they did *keep* the Senate in 1982) or won a decisive edge in the House popular vote at any time.

Yet, of course, the party majorities of 1946 hemorrhaged away two years later. Besides re-electing Truman in 1948, the Democrats gained 75 House members, 9 Senators, and formal control of both houses that lasted with one brief interlude (1953–54) for three decades. In hindsight, the Republican 80th Congress of 1947–48 proved to be a classic instance of up the hill and down again. It didn't begin a long-lasting new policy regime; instead it just offered a sort of local peak experience for the cross-party "conservative coalition" that reigned during those times anyway. From the Republican long-term perspective, 1946 is an awful precedent for 1994.

But how about a more modest perspective in which short-term slogging is the norm in politics and can make a difference? With that standard in mind, it is worth closing with a brief look at the Republicans' last exercise in post-midterm rule. They didn't employ a "contract" or a hundred-days script in 1947, but they did have a program of sorts and a talented leader in Robert Taft.

What was the result? (Hartmann 1971; Witte 1985: ch. 7; Meier 1985: 142, 159). The phrase "do-nothing 80th Congress" has echoed down through the years, but that was largely Democratic campaign propaganda. It meant that, no surprise, a Republican Congress refused to enact Truman's Fair Deal program. (As it happens, the ensuing 81st Congress, run by Democrats, enacted a major housing bill but balked as the 80th did at Truman's education, health insurance, river-valley, and civil rights proposals and wouldn't support the President on agriculture or labor-management relations; the conservative coalition lived on.)

Otherwise, there was considerable legislative motion in 1947–48. In the area of foreign and defense policy, teamwork across party lines generated the Truman Doctrine authorizing aid to Greece and Turkey, the Marshall Plan, and the National Security Act unifying the armed services under one cabinet secretary. The 80th's domestic initiatives that remained influential long afterward included the Federal Insecticide, Fungicide, and Rodenticide Act (FIFRA) of 1947, inaugurating federal control of pesticides, and the Water Pollution Control Act of 1948, the federal entry into that policy realm; it was still a program-building era, even if many initiatives failed.

As for the Taft Republicans' distinctive policy agenda, three enactments deserve mention. The 22nd Amendment limiting presidents to two terms—the "term-limits" formula of those times—cleared Congress easily in early 1947. A sizable tax cut lost out twice to Truman vetoes in 1947, but a third version attracted the needed votes for an override in the spring of 1948. Most important by far, the promanagement Taft-Hartley Act, which rolled back the Wagner Act and has regulated labor relations for the last half century despite energetic union efforts to repeal it under Truman (in 1949), Johnson, and Carter, won passage over Truman's veto in mid-1947.

By conservative standards, that was quite a successful two years. It is not entirely clear that the current 104th Congress will surpass it, though probably it will.

At any rate, long-term electoral prospects for the Republicans are scarcely as grim today as they must have looked back in 1947–48. Republican winners in 1946 included no Senators and only 2 House members from the still solidly Democratic South, which meant that the GOP needed to win immense—and, after the New Deal realignment, unlikely—victories outside the South to organize Congress. House delegations from the North in 1947–48 had Republican edges as extreme as 8–1 in Minnesota, 10–0 in Wisconsin, 14–3 in Michigan, 20–6 in Illinois, 9–2 in Indiana, 19–4 in Ohio, 12–2 in New Jersey, and 28–5 in Pennsylvania. All 6 Philadelphians were Republicans. Numbers like these were not likely to last very long. Today, given the Republican surge in the South, they are no longer needed.

And beyond this, we now have Gingrich and the Contract with America. The 80th Congress's Robert Taft, for all his pugnacity and energy, his analytic capacity, his encyclopedic knowledge of policy areas, his ability to bore in day after day with telling critiques, amendments, and counterproposals, never made much of a mark as a dramatizer, stage manager, or salesman—as witness his failed presidential drives. Gingrich, like some Presidents, possesses exactly those merchandising capabilities—as witness the contract and the programmatic House drama built on it in early 1995. At the least, this should guarantee that we won't hear a great deal about a "do-nothing 104th Congress."

NOTES

1. I would like to thank Joseph LaPalombara and Eric Schickler for their helpful comments on an early draft.

References

Abramowitz, Alan I. 1975. "Name Familiarity, Reputation, and the Incumbency Effect in a Congressional Election." *Western Political Quarterly* 28:668–84.
———. 1980. "A Comparison of Voting for U.S. Senator and Representative in 1978." *American Political Science Review* 74:633–640.
———. 1988. "Explaining Senate Election Outcomes." *American Political Science Review* 82:385–403.
———. 1991. "Incumbency, Candidate Spending, and the Decline of Competition in U.S. House Elections." *Journal of Politics* 53:34–56.
Abramowitz, Alan I., Albert D. Cover, and Helmut Norpoth. 1986. "The President's Party in Midterm Elections: Going from Bad to Worse." *American Journal of Political Science* 30:562–76.
Abramowitz, Alan I., and Jeffrey A. Segal. 1986. "Determinants of the Outcomes of U.S. Senate Elections." *Journal of Politics* 48:433–439.
———. 1992. *Senate Elections.* Ann Arbor: University of Michigan Press.
Abramson, Jill, and David Rogers. 1995. "Shifting Fortunes: As GOP Tries to Shrink Government, Coffers Grow with New Money. *Wall Street Journal,* 9 February, A1.
Abramson, Paul R., John H. Aldrich, David W. Rohde, eds. 1995. *Change and Continuity in the 1992 Elections.* rev. ed. Washington, D.C.: CQ Press.
Alesina, Alberta, and Howard Rosenthal. 1989. "Partisan Cycles in Congressional Elections and the Macroeconomy." *American Political Science Review* 83:373–398.
Amenta, Edwin, and Theda Skocpol. 1988. "Redefining the New Deal: World War II and the Development of Social Provision in the United States." Ch. 2 in Margaret Weir, Ann Shola Orloff, and Theda Skocpol, eds. *The Politics of Social Policy in the United States,* Princeton, N.J.: Princeton University Press.
Apple, R.W. 1994a. "Democrats See Only Negative Numbers." *New York Times,* 2 October.
———. 1994b. "For Clinton, A Sharp Rebuff at the Polls." *New York Times,* 9 November, A1.
Armey, Dick. 1994a. "Freedom's Choir." *Policy Review* 67 (winter):27–34.
———. 1994b. Transcript of remarks at Contract with America Rally, Washington, D.C., Federal News Service, 27 September.
Arnold, R. Douglas. 1990. *The Logic of Congressional Action.* New Haven: Yale University Press.
Baer, Denise L. 1993. "Who Has the Body? Party Institutionalization and Theories of Party Organization." *The American Review of Politics* 14:1–38.
Balz, Dan, and Thomas B. Edsall. 1994. "As South Goes, So Goes the Democratic Majority?" *Washington Post National Weekly Edition,* 30 May–5 June, 15.
Banning, Lance. 1978. *The Jeffersonian Persuasion: Evolution of a Party Ideology.* Ithaca, N.Y.: Cornell University Press.

Barnes, Fred. 1995. "Politically Incorrect. The Emerging Faith Factor in American Politics." *The American Spectator*, March.

Barone, Michael. 1990. *Our Country: The Shaping of America from Roosevelt to Reagan.* New York: Free Press.

Barone, Michael, and Grant Unifusa. 1993. *The Almanac of American Politics: 1994.* Washington, D.C.: National Journal.

Bendar, Nancy L., and Allen D. Hertzke. 1995. "The Christian Right and Republican Realignment in Oklahoma," *PS: Political Science and Politics* 37:11–15.

Benedetto, Richard. 1994. "Once Possible 'Blowout Now Contest.'" *USA Today*, 27 October, 1A–2A.

Bennett, Stephen Earl, Alfred J. Tuchfarber, Andrew E. Smith, and Eric W. Rademacher. 1995. "Americans' Opinions about Affirmative Action." Cincinnati: Institute for Policy Research. Manuscript.

Berke, Richard L. 1995a. "Christian Coalition Unveils Suggestions." *New York Times*, 18 May.

———. 1995b. "G.O.P. Seeks Foes' Donors, and Baldly." *New York Times*, 17 June, A1.

Bernstein, Robert. 1977. "Divisive Primaries Do Hurt: U.S. Senate Races, 1956–1972." *American Political Science Review* 71:540–5.

Black, Earl, and Merle Black. 1992. *The Vital South.* Cambridge: Harvard University Press.

Bond, Jon R., Gary Covington, and Richard Fleisher. 1985. "Explaining Challenger Quality in Congressional Elections." *Journal of Politics* 47:510–29.

Box-Steffensmeier, Janet, and Charles H. Franklin. 1995. "The Long Campaign: Senate Elections in 1992." In Herbert F. Weisberg, ed. *Democracy's Feast*, Chatham House, N.J.: Chatham House.

Boyer, Paul S., et al. 1993. *The Enduring Vision.* Lexington, Mass.: D.C. Heath.

Boyer, Peter J. 1994. "Whip Cracker." *The New Yorker*, 5 September.

Brady, David W., John F. Cogan, and Douglas Rivers. 1995. *How the Republicans Captured the House: An Assessment of the 1994 Midterm.* Stanford, Calif.: Hoover Institution.

Brady, David W., and Bernard Grofman. 1991. "Sectional Differences in Partisan Bias and Electoral Responsiveness in U.S. House Elections, 1850–1980." *American Journal of Political Science* 21:247–56.

Brady, David W., L. Sandy Maisel, and Kevin M. Warsh. 1994. "An Opportunity Cost Model of the Decision to Run for Congress: Another Contributor to Democratic Hegemony." Paper presented at the Annual Meeting of the American Political Science Association, 1–4 September. New York.

Brinkley, Alan. 1995. *The End of Reform: New Deal Liberalism in Recession and War.* New York: Alfred A. Knopf.

Brinkley, Wilfred E. 1947. *President and Congress.* New York: Alfred A. Knopf.

Broder, David S. 1980. "Capitol Steps Theatrical." *Washington Post*, 10 September.

Brownsein, Ronald. 1995. "Robertson Cites Abortion Rights Peril to GOP Ticket." *Los Angeles Times*, 26 April.

Bullock, Charles S., III. 1995. "The Impact of Changing the Racial Composition of Congressional Districts on Legislator's Roll Call Behavior." *American Politics Quarterly* 23:141–158.

Burnham, Walter Dean. 1975. "Insulation and Responsiveness in Congressional Elections." *Political Science Quarterly* 90:411–35.

———. 1987. "The Turnout Problem." In A. James Reichley, ed. *Elections American Style*, Washington, D.C.: Brookings Institute, 97–133.

Cain, Bruce, Morris P. Fiorina, and John Ferejohn. 1987. *The Personal Vote*. Cambridge, Mass., Harvard University Press.

Calmes, Jackie. 1994. "Candidates of Change in 1992 Find Congress Reforms Them Instead." *Wall Street Journal*, 6 May.

———. 1995. "House GOP Freshmen, Unafraid of Sacred Cows, Face Moment of Truth in Balanced-Budget Talks." *Wall Street Journal*, 11 May, A18.

Campbell, Angus. 1960. "Surge and Decline: A Study of Electoral Change." *Public Opinion Quarterly* 24:397–418.

Campbell, James E. 1993. *The Presidential Pulse of Congressional Elections*. Lexington, Ky.: University Press of Kentucky.

Cannon, Carl M. 1995. "'Thank You, God, for Newt Gingrich.'" *Forbes Media Critic*, Spring.

Canon, David T. 1990. *Actors, Athletes, and Astronauts: Political Amateurs in the United States Congress*. Chicago: University of Chicago Press.

Canon, David T., and David J. Sousa. 1992. "Party System Change and Political Career Structures in the U.S. Congress." *Legislative Studies Quarterly* 17 (3):347–63.

Carmines, Edward G., and James A. Stimson. 1990. *Issue Evolution: Race and the Transformation of American Politics*. Princeton, N.J.: Princeton University Press.

Cashman, Sean Dennis. 1993. *America in the Gilded Age: From the Death of Lincoln to the Rise of Theodore Roosevelt*. New York: New York University Press.

Ceaser, James W. 1990. *Liberal Democracy and Political Science*. Baltimore: Johns Hopkins University Press, 1990.

Clawson, Dan, Alan Neustadtl, and Denise Scott. 1992. *Money Talks*. New York: Basic Books.

Clinton, Bill, and Al Gore. 1992. *Putting People First: How We Can All Change America*. New York: Times Books.

Cloud, David S. 1995. "Industry, Politics Intertwined in Dole's Regulatory Bill" [on-line document]. *Congressional Quarterly Weekly Report*, 6 May. Available from gopher://gopher.cqalert.com:70/0F-1%3A40101%3A18WR_MAY95%20gopher.

Cohen, Richard E. 1994. "Hot Seats." *National Journal*, 9 July, 1618–22.

———. 1995. "Team Gingrich." *National Journal*, 14 January.

Committee on Political Parties of the American Political Science Association. 1950. *Toward a More Responsible Two-Party System*. New York: Rinehart and Company.

Congressional Budget Office. 1994. *Green Book*. Washington, D.C.

Congressional Record. 1980. 96th Cong., 2nd sess. Vol. 126, pts. 14, 19.

Connelly, William F., Jr. and John J. Pitney, Jr. 1994. *Congress's Permanent Minority? Republicans in the US House*. Lanham, Md.: Rowman and Littlefield.

Connolly, Ceci. 1994. "Campaign '94: A Volatile Season as Voter Discontent Lingers." *Congressional Quarterly Weekly Report*, 23 April, 937–40.

Conover, Pamela Johnston. 1988. "Feminists and the Gender Gap." *Journal of Politics* 50:985–1010.

Cook, Elizabeth Adell, and Clyde Wilcox. 1991. "Feminism and the Gender Gap—A Second Look." *Journal of Politics* 53:1111–22.

Cook, Rhodes. 1995. "Rare Combination of Forces May Make History of '94." *Congressional Quarterly Weekly Report*, 15 April, 1076–81.

Cooper John Milton, Jr. 1990. *Pivotal Decades: The United States, 1900–1920*. New York: W.W. Norton.

Cooper, Joseph, and David W. Brady. 1981. "Institutional Context and Leadership Style: The House from Cannon to Rayburn." *American Political Science Review* 75 (June): 411–25.

Curran, Tim. 1994. "On Stump, Republicans Quick to Make an Issue Out of Rosty." *Roll Call*, 23 June.
Davidson, James West, et al. *Nation of Nations*. Vol. 1. New York: McGraw-Hill.
Davidson, Roger H., and Walter J. Oleszek. 1984. "Changing the Guard in the U.S. Senate." *Legislative Studies Quarterly* 9:635–63.
Democratic Leadership Council. 1994. *Third Force: Why Independents Turned against Democrats—And How to Win Them Back*. Washington, D.C.: Democratic Leadership Council.
Dewar, Helen. 1980. "Party with Reagan: Republicans Gather for a Show of Unity." *Washington Post*, 16 September.
Dionne, E. J., Jr. 1991 (HC), 1992 (PB). *Why Americans Hate Politics*. New York: Touchstone.
Drew, Elizabeth. 1994. *On the Edge: The Clinton Presidency*. New York: Simon and Schuster.
Duncan, Philip D., and Christine C. Lawrence. 1995. *Congressional Quarterly's Politics in America: 1995, the 104th Congress*. Washington, D.C.: Congressional Quarterly.
Edsall, Thomas Byrne, and Mary D. Edsall. 1992. *Chain Reaction: The Impact of Race, Rights and Taxes on American Politics*. New York: Norton.
Ehrenhalt, Alan. 1991. *The United States of Ambition*. New York: Times Books.
Eismeier, Theodore J., and Philip H. Pollock III. 1986. "Strategy and Choice in Congressional Elections: The Role of Political Action Committees." *American Journal of Political Science* 30 (1): 197–213.
Elkins, Stanley, and Eric McKitrick. 1993. *The Age of Federalism*. New York: Oxford University Press.
Ellis, Steven, ed. 1989. *Republican Almanac, 1989*. Washington, D.C.: Republican National Committee.
Erikson, Robert S. 1988. "The Puzzle of Midterm Loss." *Journal of Politics* 50:1011–29.
———. 1989. "Why the Democrats Lose Presidential Elections." *PS: Political Science and Politics* 22:30–34.
Erikson, Robert S., Gerald C. Wright, and John P. McIver. 1993. *Statehouse Democracy. Public Opinion and Policy in the American States*. Cambridge: Cambridge University Press.
Evans, Rowland, and Robert Novak. 1966. *Lyndon B. Johnson: The Exercise of Power*. New York: New American Library.
Faucheux, Ron. 1995. "The Grassroots Explosion." *Campaigns and Elections*, December/January, 20–30.
Federal Election Commission. 1995. "PAC Activity in 1994 Elections Remains at 1992 Levels." 31 March. Press release.
Fenno, Richard F., Jr. 1978. *Home Style: House Members in their Districts*. Boston: Little, Brown.
Ferejohn, John A. 1977. "On the Decline of Competition in Congressional Elections." *American Political Science Review* 71:166–76.
Ferguson, Thomas. 1994. "GOP Money Talked: Did Voters Listen?" *The Nation*, 26 December, 792–98.
Fine, Terri Susan. 1993. "Social Position and Commitment to Core Values: Grappling with the (Non)Impact of Gender." *Women & Politics* 13:53–72.
Fingerhut, Eric D. 1994. "A Democrat Throws Stones." *New York Times*, 17 December.
Fiorina, Morris P. 1977. *Congress: Keystone of the Washington Establishment*. New Haven: Yale University Press.

———. 1978. "Economic Retrospective Voting in American National Elections: A Micro Analysis." *American Journal of Political Science* 22:426–43.

———. 1992a. *Divided Government*. New York: Macmillan.

———. 1992b. "An Era of Divided Government." *Political Science Quarterly* 107:387–410.

———. 1996. *Divided Government*. Rev. ed. Boston: Allyn and Bacon.

Fiorina, Morris P., and Douglas Rivers. 1989. "Constituency Service, Reputation, and the Incumbency Advantage." In Morris P. Fiorina and David W. Rohde, eds., *Home Style and Congressional Work*, Ann Arbor: University of Michigan Press.

Fowler, Linda L., and L. Sandy Maisel. 1991. "The Changing Supply of Competitive Candidates in House Elections, 1982–1990." Revised version of a paper presented at the 1989 Annual Meeting of the American Political Science Association, Atlanta.

Frankovic, Kathleen A. 1993. "Public Opinion in the 1992 Campaign." In Gerald M. Pomper et al., *The Election of 1992*, Chatham: Chatham House.

Freeman, Jo. 1986. "The Political Culture of the Democratic and Republican Parties." *Political Science Quarterly*. 101:327–56.

Frymer, Paul. 1994. "Ideological Consensus within Divided Party Government." *Political Science Quarterly* 109:287–311.

Frymer, Paul, Thomas P. Kim and Terri L. Bimes. 1995. "Party Cleavage, Ideological Voters, and Divided Party Government." Unpublished manuscript.

Fuerbringer, Jonathan. 1985. "House Republicans Propose Wide Range of Policy Goals." *New York Times*, 15 January.

Gelman, Andrew, and Gary King. 1990. "Estimating the Incumbency Advantage without Bias." *American Journal of Political Science* 34:1142–64.

Germond, Jack W., and Jules Witcover. 1993. *Mad As Hell: Revolt at the Ballot Box, 1992*. New York: Warner Books.

———. 1994. "A Showdown in the 'Show Me' State." *National Journal*, 8 October, 2363.

Gilbert, Christopher P. 1995. "Christians and Quistians in Minnesota." *PS: Political Science and Politics* 37:20–23.

Gillespie, Ed, and Bob Schellhas, eds. 1994. *Contract with America: The Bold Plan by Rep. Newt Gingrich, Rep. Dick Armey and the House Republicans to Change the Nation*. New York: Times Books.

Gilmour, John B., and Paul Rothstein. 1993. "Early Republican Retirement: A Cause of Democratic Dominance in the House of Representatives." *Legislative Studies Quarterly* 18 (August): 345–65.

Gingrich, Newt. 1984. *Window of Opportunity*. New York: TOR Books.

Gingrich, Newt, and Marianne Gingrich. 1981. "Post-Industrial Politics: The Leader as Learner." *The Futurist*, December.

Glasser, Susan B. 1994. "Dems Unleash on 'Radical Right.'" *Roll Call*, 20 June.

"GOP Platform: Groups Weigh In on Abortion Plank." 1995. *Hotline Weekly Report*, 10 March.

Gosselin, Peter G. 1994. "GOP Planning Campaign on Rostenkowski." *Boston Globe*, 2 June.

Green, John C. 1995. "The Christian Right and the 1994 Elections: A View from the States." *PS: Political Science and Politics* 28:5–8.

Green, John C., and James L. Guth. 1991. "The Bible and the Ballot Box," In James L. Guth and John C. Green, eds., *The Bible and the Ballot Box*, 207–26, Boulder, Colo.: Westview.

Green, John C., James L. Guth, and Kevin Hill. 1993. "Faith and Election: The Christian Right in Congressional Campaigns, 1978–1988." *Journal of Politics*. 55:80–91.

Greenberg, Stanley B. 1995. *Middle Class Dreams: The Politics and Power of the New American Majority*. New York: Times Books.

Greider, William. 1992. *Who Will Tell the People: The Betrayal of American Democracy*. New York: Simon and Schuster.

Grove, Lloyd. 1994. "A Good Ol' Boy Going In for the Kill." *Washington Post National Weekly Edition*, 22–28 August, 13.

Guth, James L. 1995. "The Christian Right Wins One." *PS: Political Science and Politics* 37:8–11.

Guth, James L, and John C. Green. 1990. "Salience: The Core Concept." In David C. Leege and Lyman A. Kellstedt, eds., *Rediscovering the Religious Factor in American Politics*, 157–74, Armonk, New York: M. E. Sharpe.

———, eds. 1991. *The Bible and the Ballot Box*. Boulder, Colo.: Westview Press.

Guth, James L., John C. Green, Lyman A. Kellstedt, and Corwin E. Smidt. 1993. "God's Own Party: Evangelicals and Republicans in the '92 Election." *The Christian Century*. 17 February.

Hartmann, Susan. 1971. *Truman and the 80th Congress*. Columbia, Mo.: University of Missouri Press.

Hedges, Michael. 1994. "White House Finally Moves to Put Out Liberal Fire." *Washington Times*, 10 December.

Herrnson, Paul S. 1995. *Congressional Elections: Campaigning at Home and in Washington*. Washington, D.C.: CQ Press.

Hershey, Majorie Randon. 1992. "The Constructed Explanation: Interpreting Election Results in the 1984 Presidential Race," *Journal of Politics* 54:943–76.

Hertzke, Allen, D. 1993. *Echoes of Discontent*. Washington, D.C.: Congressional Quarterly Press.

Hill, Kevin A. 1995. "Does the Creation of Majority Black Districts Aid Republicans? An Analysis of the 1992 Congressional Elections in Eight Southern States." *Journal of Politics* 57:384–401.

Hinckley, Barbara. 1980. "House Re-elections and Senate Defeats: The Role of the Challenger." *British Journal of Political Science* 10:441–60.

Holmes, Geoffrey. 1987. *British Politics in the Age of Anne*. Rev. ed. London: Hambledon Press.

Horowitz, David Alan. 1988. "White Southerners' Alienation and Civil Rights: The Response of Corporate Liberalism, 1956–1965." *Journal of Southern History* 54:173–200.

House Republican Research Committee. 1985. *Ideas for Tomorrow, Choices for Today: Policy Initiatives of the Committee on the First One Hundred Days*. Washington, D.C.: House Republican Research Committee.

Houston, Paul. 1986. "Political Gifts, Fueled by PACs, Continue to Soar." *Los Angeles Times*, 8 April.

Huckfeldt, Robert, and Carol Weitzel Kohfeld. 1989. *Race and the Decline of Class in American Politics*. Champaign, Ill.: University of Illinois Press.

Hugick, Larry, and Andrew Kohut. 1994. "The 1994 US Elections: Taking the Nation's Pulse." *Public Perspective*, November/December.

Jacobson, Gary C. 1980. *Money in Congressional Elections*. New Haven: Yale University Press.

———. 1989a. "Parties and PACs in Congressional Elections." In Lawrence C. Dodd and Bruce I. Oppenheimer, eds., *Congress Reconsidered*, 4th ed., Washington, D.C.: Congressional Quarterly.

———. 1989b. "Strategic Politicians and the Dynamics of U.S. House Elections, 1946–1986." *American Political Science Review* 83:773–93.

———. 1990a. *The Electoral Origins of Divided Government: Competition in U.S. House Elections, 1946–1988*. Boulder, Colo.: Westview Press.
———. 1990b. "The Effects of Campaign Spending in House Elections: New Evidence for Old Arguments." *American Journal of Political Science* 34:334–62.
———. 1992. *The Politics of Congressional Elections*. 3rd ed. New York: HarperCollins.
———. 1993a. "Deficit Cutting Politics and Congressional Elections." *Political Science Quarterly* 108:375–401.
———. 1993b. "Congress: Unusual Year, Unusual Election." In Michael Nelson, ed., *The Elections of 1992*, Washington, D.C.: CQ Press.
———. 1995. "The 1994 House Elections in Perspective." Paper presented at the 1995 Annual Meeting of the Midwest Political Science Association, Chicago, 6–8 April.
Jacobson, Gary C., and Samuel Kernell. 1983. *Strategy and Choice in Congressional Elections*. 2nd ed. New Haven: Yale University Press.
Jeffries, John W. 1990. "The 'New' New Deal: FDR and American Liberalism, 1937–1945." *Political Science Quarterly* 105:397–418.
Johannes, John R. 1984. *To Serve the People: Congress and Constituency Service*. Lincoln, Nebr.: University of Nebraska Press.
Jones, Charles O. 1981. "The New, New Senate." In Ellis Sandoz and Cecil V. Crabb Jr., eds. *A Tide of Discontent*. Washington, D.C.: CQ Press.
Jones, J. R. 1978. *Country and Court: England, 1658–1714*. Cambridge: Harvard University Press.
Jordan, Winthrop D. 1994. *The United States*. Englewood Cliffs, N.J.: Prentice Hall.
Kazee, Thomas A. 1983. "The Deterrent Effect of Incumbency on Recruiting Challengers in U.S. House Elections." *Legislative Studies Quarterly* 8:469–80.
Kelly, Michael. 1994. "Clinton's Escape Clause." *The New Yorker*, October 24.
Kellstedt, Lyman A., John C. Green, James L. Guth, and Corwin E. Smidt. 1994. "Religious Voting Blocs in the 1992 Election." *Sociology of Religion* 55:307–26.
Kenney, Patrick J., and Tom W. Rice. 1984. "The Effect of Primary Divisiveness in Gubernatorial and Senatorial Elections." *Journal of Politics* 46:904–15.
Kernell, Samuel. 1977. "Presidential Popularity and Negative Voting." *American Political Science Review* 71:44–66.
Klinkner, Philip A. 1994. *The Losing Parties: Out-Party National Committees, 1956–1993*. New Haven: Yale University Press.
Kobach, Kris W. "Rethinking Article V: Term Limits and the Seventeenth and Nineteenth Amendments." *Yale Law Journal* 103:1971–2007.
Koeniger, A. Cash. 1982. "The New Deal and the States: Roosevelt versus the Byrd Organization in Virginia." *Journal of American History* 68:876–96.
Koopman, Douglas L. 1994. "The 1994 House Elections: A Republican View." *APSA Legislative Studies Newsletter: Extension of Remarks*. December 1994, 4–5, 15.
Kranish, Michael. 1994. "Gingrich Tries to Build Himself Political Empire." *San Jose Mercury News*, November 25.
Krasno, Jonathan S. 1994. *Challengers, Competition, and Reelection: Comparing Senate and House Elections*. New Haven: Yale University Press.
Krasno, Jonathan S., and Donald Philip Green. 1988. "Preempting Quality Challengers in House Elections." *Journal of Politics* 50:920–36.
Krehbiel, Keith. 1993. "A Theory of Divided and Unified Government." Graduate School of Business, Stanford University. Unpublished manuscript.
Kristol, William. 1994. "The Democratic Strategy to Demonize Religious Conservatives." Washington, D.C.: Project for the Republican Future. Fax.

Ladd, Everett Carll. 1991. "Like Waiting for Godot: The Uselessness of 'Realignment' for Understanding Change in Contemporary American Politics." In Byron E. Shafer, ed., *The End of Realignment,* 24–36, Madison: University of Wisconsin Press.

———, ed. 1995a. *America at the Polls, 1994.* Storrs, Conn.: The Roper Center for Public Opinion Research.

———. 1995b. "The 1994 Congressional Elections: The Postindustrial Realignment Continues." *Political Science Quarterly* 110:1–23.

Langer, Gary. 1994. "'94 Vote: Republicans Seize the Reins of Discontent." *ABC News Analysis,* 11 November.

Lapham, Lewis H. 1994. *The Wish for Kings: Democracy at Bay.* New York: Grove Press.

Leege, David C., and Lyman A. Kellstedt, eds. 1990. *Rediscovering the Religious Factor in American Politics.* Armonk, N.Y.: M. E. Sharpe.

Lesher, Dave. 1995. "Political Winds Driving Wilson's Shift to the Right." *Los Angeles Times,* 28 January.

Leuchtenberg, William E. 1963. *Franklin D. Roosevelt and the New Deal, 1932–1940.* New York: Harper Torchback.

Lewis-Beck, Michael S., and Tom Rice. 1992. *Forecasting Elections.* Washington, D.C.: CQ Press.

Lewis-Beck, Michael S., and J. Mark Wrighton. 1994. "A Republican Congress?" Forecasts for 1994." *Public Opinions* 1:14–16.

Lind, Michael. 1995. "The South, the GOP and America: The Southern Coup." *The New Republic,* 19 June, 20–30.

Lowi, Theodore J., and Benjamin Ginsberg. 1995. *Embattled Democracy: Politics and Policy in the Clinton Era.* New York: W. W. Norton.

Lubell, Samuel. 1956. *The Future of American Politics.* 2d ed., rev. Garden City, N.Y.: Doubleday Anchor.

McCormick, Richard L. 1982. "The Realignment Synthesis in American History." *Journal of Interdisciplinary History* 13 (summer): 85–105.

Madonna, G. Terry, and Berwood A. Yost. 1995. *Pennsylvania Voters at the Polls, 1994: Why Rick Santorum is U.S. Senator.* Millersville, Pa.: Center for Politics and Public Affairs, University of Pennsylvania—Millersville.

Maisel, Sandy L. 1992. "Quality Candidates in House and Senate Elections, from 1982 to 1990." In Allen D. Hertzke and Ronald M. Peters Jr., eds., *The Atomistic Congress: An Interpretation of Congressional Change,* Armonk, N.Y.: M. E. Sharpe.

Maisel, L. Sandy, and Joseph Cooper, eds. 1981. *Congressional Elections.* Beverly Hills, Calif.: Sage Publications.

Maisel, L. Sandy, Linda L. Fowler, Ruth S. Jones, and Walter J. Stone. 1988. "Collaborative Research on Congressional Candidate Emergence." Proposal to the National Science Foundation.

———. 1994. "Nomination Politics: The Roles of Institutional, Contextual, and Personal Variables." In L. Sandy Maisel, ed., *The Parties Respond: Changes in American Parties and Campaigns,* Boulder, Colo.: Westview Press.

Maisel, L. Sandy, and Walter Stone. 1994. "Competition in Congressional Elections: Why More 'Qualified' Candidates Do Not Seek Office." Paper presented at the 1994 Annual Meeting of the American Political Science Association, September 1–4, New York.

Mann, Thomas E. 1978. *Unsafe at Any Margin.* Washington, D.C.: American Enterprise Institute.

Mann, Thomas E., and Norman J. Ornstein. 1981. "The Republican Surge in Congress." In Austin Ranney, ed., *The American Elections of 1980,* Washington, D.C.: American Enterprise Institute.

———. 1983. "Sending a Message: Voters and Congress in 1982." In Thomas E. Mann and Norman J. Ornstein, eds., *The American Elections of 1982*, Washington, D.C.: American Enterprise Institute.
Mann, Thomas E., and Raymond E. Wolfinger. 1980. "Candidates and Parties in Congressional Elections." *American Political Science Review* 74:617–32.
Mayhew, David R. 1974a. *Congress: The Electoral Connection*. New Haven: Yale University Press.
———. 1974b. "Congressional Elections: The Case of the Vanishing Marginals." *Polity* 6:295–317.
———. 1986. *Placing Parties in American Politics*. Princeton: Princeton University Press.
———. 1991. *Divided We Govern: Party Control, Lawmaking, and Investigations, 1946–1990*. New Haven: Yale University Press.
Meier, Kenneth J. 1985. *Regulation: Politics, Bureaucracy, and Economics*. New York: St. Martin's Press.
Merida, Kevin. 1994. "Running Away from Bill Clinton." *Washington Post National Weekly Edition*, 26 September–2 October, 12.
Milkis, Sidney M., and Michael Nelson. 1994. *The American Presidency: Origins and Development*. 2nd ed. Washington, D.C.: CQ Press.
Mishel, Lawrence, and Jared Bernstein. 1994. *The State of Working America 1994–1995*. Armonk, N.Y.: M. E. Sharpe.
Moen, Matthew C. 1994. "From Revolution to Evolution." *Sociology of Religion*. 55:345–58.
Mondak, Jeffrey J. 1993. "Presidential Coattails and Open Seats: The District-Level Impact of Heuristic Processing." *American Politics Quarterly* 21:307–19.
Morin, Richard. 1994. "Bill Clinton: He's There for the Whacking." *Washington Post National Weekly Edition*, 7–12 November, 37.
Moss, David A. "Kindling a Flame under Federalism: Progressive Reformers, Corporate Elites, and the Phosphorus Match Campaign of 1909–1912," *Business History Review* 68: 244–75.
Mowry, George E. 1958. *The Era of Theodore Roosevelt, 1900–1912*. New York: Harper and Brothers.
Murrin, John M. 1980. "The Great Inversion, or Court versus Country: A Comparison of the Revolution Settlements in England (1688–1721) and America (1776–1816)." In J. G. A. Pocock, ed., *Three British Revolutions: 1641, 1688, 1776*, Princeton: Princeton University Press.
Mutch, Robert E. 1988. *Campaigns, Congress, and Courts: The Making of Federal Campaign Finance Law*. New York: Praeger.
Neibuhr, Gustav. 1995. "The Religious Right Readies Agenda for Second 100 Days." *New York Times*, 17 May.
"Number of People Living in Poverty Edged Up in '93." 1994. *Wall Street Journal*, 7 October, A2.
O'Leary, Brad. 1995. "Fire Power." *Campaigns and Elections*, December/January.
Ornstein, Norman J. 1985. "The Elections for Congress." In *The American Elections of 1984*, edited by Austin Ranney, Washington, D.C.: American Enterprise Institute.
Ornstein, Norman J., Thomas E. Mann, and Michael Malbin. 1994. *Vital Statistics on Congress 1993–1994*. Washington, D.C.: American Enterprise Institute.
Owen, John B. 1974. *The Eighteenth Century: 1714–1815*. London: Nelson.
Patterson, James T. 1967. *Congressional Conservatism and the New Deal: The Growth of the Conservative Coalition in Congress, 1933–1939*. Lexington, Ky.: University Press of Kentucky.

Pear, Robert. 1994. "Health Insurance Percentage is Lowest in 4 Sunbelt States." *New York Times*, 7 October 1994, A16.

Perot, Ross. 1992. *United We Stand: How We Can Take Back Our Country.* New York: Hyperion.

Persinos, John F. 1994. "Has the Christian Right Taken Over the Republican Party?" *Campaigns and Elections.* 21–24 September.

Peters, John G., and Susan Welch. 1980. "The Effects of Charges of Corruption on Voting Behavior in Congressional Elections." *American Political Science Review* 74:697–708.

Peters, Ronald M., Jr. 1990. *The American Speakership.* Baltimore, Md.: Johns Hopkins Press.

Petrocik, John R. 1991. "Divided Government: Is It All In the Campaigns?" In Gary W. Cox and Samuel Kernell, eds., *The Politics of Divided Government*, Boulder, Colo.: Westview Press.

Peyton, Jeffrey M. 1994. "GOP Promises Change." *Christian American*, October.

Phillips, Kevin. 1990. *The Politics of Rich and Poor: Wealth and the American Electorate in the Reagan Aftermath.* New York: Random House.

———. 1993. *Boiling Point: Democrats, Republicans and the Decline of Middle-Class Prosperity.* New York: Harper.

———. 1994. *Arrogant Capital: Washington, Wall Street, and the Frustration of American Politics.* Boston: Little Brown.

Pocock, J. G. A. 1975. *The Machiavellian Moment: Florentine Political Thought and the Atlantic Republican Tradition.* Princeton, N. J.: Princeton University Press.

"Portrait of the Electorate: Who Voted for Whom in the House." 1994. *New York Times*, 13 November.

Powell, Lawrence N. "Rejected Republican Incumbents in the 1866 Congressional Nominating Conventions: A Study in Reconstruction Politics." *Civil War History* 5:219–37.

President. 1995. *Economic Report of the President.* Washington, D.C.: GPO.

Ragsdale, Lyn. 1981. "Incumbent Popularity, Challenger Invisibility, and Congressional Voters." *Legislative Studies Quarterly* 6:201–18.

Randall, J. G., and David Donald. 1969. *The Civil War and Reconstruction.* Lexington, Mass.: D.C. Heath.

Rauch, Jonathan. 1994. *Demosclerosis: The Silent Killer of American Government.* New York: Times Books.

Reed, Ralph. 1993. "The Religious Right Reaches Out." *New York Times*, 22 August.

Reichley, A. James. 1994. "Get Ready for 60 Years of GOP Rule." *Wall Street Journal*, 5 December.

Republican National Committee. 1994. "Why Participate?" Washington, D.C.: Republican National Committee. Photocopy.

Rohde, David W. 1991. *Parties and Leaders in the Postreform House.* Chicago: University of Chicago Press.

Rosenbaum, David E. 1994. "GOP Unleashes Its New Weapon: Winning Candidates." *New York Times*, 13 November.

Rosenstiel, Thomas B. 1994. "Gingrich's Power Play 10 Years in the Making." *Los Angeles Times*, 19 December.

Rosenstone, Steven J., and John Mark Hansen. 1993. *Mobilization, Participation, and Democracy in America.* New York: Macmillan.

Salisbury, Robert H. 1990. "The Paradox of Interest Groups in Washington—More Groups, Less Clout." In Anthony King, ed., *The New American Political System.* 2nd ed., Washington, D.C.: American Enterprise Institute.

Schlesinger, Joseph A. 1966. *Ambition and Politics: Political Careers in the United States.* Chicago: Rand McNally and Co.
Schneider, William. 1994. "Clinton: The Reason Why." *National Journal,* 12 November.
Schwarz, Jordan A. 1970. *The Interregnum of Despair: Hoover, Congress, and the Depression.* Urbana, Ill.: University of Illinois Press.
Seelye, Katharine Q. 1994. "Clinton and Allies Rediscover Their Voice in Writing Epitaph for Congress." *New York Times,* 9 October.
Shafer, Byron, ed. 1991. *The End of Realignment.* Madison, Wisc.: University of Wisconsin Press.
Shalit, Ruth. 1995. "The Undertaker: Tony Coelho and the Death of the Democrats." *The New Republic,* 2 January 1995, 17–25.
Shelly, Mack C., II. 1983. *The Permanent Majority: The Conservative Coalition in the United States Congress.* University, Ala.: University of Alabama Press.
Simpson, Glenn R. 1994. "Republicans Step Up Pressure on PACs as November Gains Look More Certain." *Roll Call,* 6 October.
Smelser, Marshall. 1968. *The Democratic Republic, 1801–1815.* New York: Harper & Row.
Soper, J. Christopher. 1994. *Evangelical Christianity in the United States and Great Britain.* New York: New York University Press.
Sorauf, Frank J. 1992. *Inside Campaign Finance.* New Haven: Yale University Press.
Squire, Peverill. 1989. "Challengers in U.S. Senate Elections." *Legislative Studies Quarterly* 14:531–47.
Stampp, Kenneth M. 1970. *The Era of Reconstruction, 1865–1877.* New York: Alfred A. Knopf.
Stanley, Harold W., and Richard G. Niemi. 1994. *Vital Statistics on American Politics.* 4th ed. Washington, D.C.: CQ Press.
Steeper, Fred. 1995. "This Swing Is Different." Southfield, Mich.: Market Strategies, Inc. Photocopy.
Stokes, Donald. E. 1965. "A Variance-Component Model of Political Effects." In John M. Claunch, ed., *Mathematical Applications in Political Science,* Dallas: Arnold Foundation.
Stone, Peter H. 1995. "All Aboard!" *National Journal,* 25 March, 744–47.
Sundquist, James L. 1983. *Dynamics of the Party System.* 2nd ed. Washington, D.C.: Brookings Institute.
———. 1988. "Needed: A Political Theory for the New Era of Coalitional Government in the United States." *Political Science Quarterly* 103:613–35.
Taylor, Paul. 1995. "Behind the '94 Broom: Wealthy, Educated Voters." *Washington Post,* 8 June.
Taylor, Telford. 1961. *Grand Inquest: The Story of Congressional Investigations.* New York: Ballantine.
Toner, Robin. 1995. "Quarrels and Sour Memories Fuel a Hostility to Gingrich." *New York Times,* 24 January.
Tuchfarber, Alfred J., Andrew E. Smith, Eric W. Rademacher, and Stephen E. Bennett. 1995. "Interpreting the 1994 Election Results: A Direct Test of Competing Explanations." Paper presented at the Annual Meeting of the American Association for Public Opinion Research, Ft. Lauderdale, Florida.
Tufte, Edward R. 1973. "The Relationship between Seats and Votes in Two-Party Systems." *American Political Science Review* 67:540–54.
———. 1975. "Determinants of the Outcomes of Midterm Congressional Elections." *American Political Science Review* 69:812–26.
———. 1979. *The Political Control of the Economy.* Princeton, N.J.: Princeton University Press.

Tulis, Jeffrey K. 1987. *The Rhetorical Presidency*. Princeton, N.J.: Princeton University Press.
U.S. Department of Commerce. Bureau of the Census. 1994. *Statistical Abstract of the United States*. Washington, D.C.: GPO.
U.S., Bureau of Labor Statistics. 1995. "BLS Daily Report." 23 June.
Vogel, David. 1989. *Fluctuating Fortunes*. New York: Basic Books.
Von Drehle, David. 1994. "For the GOP, the Magic Number is 47." *Washington Post National Weekly Edition*, August 1–7, 15.
"Voter Turnout Falls Sharply Among the Less Affluent." 1995. *New York Times*, 11 June, A16.
Wald, Ken D. 1992. *Religion and Politics in the United States*, 2nd ed. New York: St. Martins Press.
Walker, Jack L. 1991. *Mobilizing Interest Groups in America*. Ann Arbor: University of Michigan Press.
Waterman, Richard W., Bruce I. Oppenheimer, and James A. Stimson. 1991. "Sequence and Equilibrium in Congressional Elections: An Integrated Approach." *Journal of Politics* 53:372–93.
Wattenberg, Martin P. 1990. The *Decline of American Political Parties: 1952–1988*. Cambridge: Harvard University Press.
Webb, R. K. 1980. *Modern England: From the Eighteenth Century to the Present*. 2nd ed. New York: Harper & Row.
Weiss, Stuart L. 1971. "Maury Maverick and the Liberal Bloc." *Journal of American History* 57:880–95.
Westlye, Mark C. 1991. *Senate Elections and Campaign Intensity*. Baltimore, Md.: Johns Hopkins University Press.
White, Leonard. 1951. *The Jeffersonians: A Study in Administrative History, 1801–1829*. New York: Macmillan.
Wilcox, Clyde. 1992. *God's Warriors*. Baltimore, Md.: Johns Hopkins University Press.
———. 1995. *The Latest American Revolution? The 1994 Elections and Their Implications for Governance*. New York: St. Martin's Press.
Wilcox, Clyde, Mark J. Rozell, and J. Bradford Coker 1995. "The Christian Right in the Old Dominion." *PS: Political Science and Politics* 37:15–18.
Wilhelm, David. 1994. "Health Is 'Litmus Test' for Change in 1994." *Roll Call*, 8 August.
Wills, Garry. 1995. "The Visionary." *New York Review of Books*, 23 March.
Witte, John F. 1985. *The Politics and Development of the Federal Income Tax*. Madison, Wisc.: University of Wisconsin Press.
Woodward, Bob. 1993. *The Agenda: Inside the Clinton White House*. New York: Simon and Schuster.
Wuthnow, Robert. 1983. *The New Christian Right*. New York: Aldine Press.
Yiannakis, Diana Evans. 1981. "The Critical Electorate: Casework and Congressional Elections." *American Journal of Political Science* 25:568–80.

About the Book

By all accounts, 1994 represents sweeping electoral and policy change rarely seen in any American election, let alone a midterm. This book puts 1994 in context with other significant midterm elections, from 1810 to the present. It also captures the very contemporary concerns unique to 1994: the role of the religious right, the "angry white male," the Contract with America, and the overall tenor of antipathy as voters turned out (or not) to show the Clinton administration what they thought of its first two years. This collection of original essays by noted political scientists gives us the first thoughtful analysis of the 1994 election results and prepares us to anticipate the certain drama and import of the election of 1996.

About the Editor and Contributors

Philip A. Klinkner is an Assistant Professor of Government at Hamilton College in Clinton, New York. He received his B.A. from Lake Forest College in 1985 and his Ph.D. from Yale University in 1992. During 1990–91 he was a Governmental Studies Research Fellow at the Brookings Institution in Washington, D.C. From 1991 to 1995, he taught at Loyola Marymount University in Los Angeles. He is the author of *The Losing Parties: Out-Party National Committees, 1956–1993*. In 1995 he received the Emerging Scholar Award from the Political Organizations and Parties Section of the American Political Science Association.

Joseph Cammarano is an Assistant Professor of Political Science at Syracuse University's Maxwell School of Citizenship and Public Affairs. He has conducted research and published articles in political communication and political campaigning. His current research focuses on political accountability in an era of candidate-centered politics.

William F. Connelly, Jr. is an Associate Professor of Politics at Washington and Lee University in Lexington, Virginia. With John J. Pitney, Jr., he coauthored *Congress' Permanent Minority?: Republicans in the U.S. House*. He was an American Political Science Association Congressional Fellow in 1985–86 and Guest Scholar at the Brookings Institution during 1991–92.

Theodore J. Eismeier is the James L. Ferguson Professor of Government at Hamilton College. He is the author with Philip H. Pollock of *Business, Money, and the Rise of Corporate PACs in American Politics*, and is currently completing a book on political leadership.

Paul Frymer received his Ph.D. from Yale University in 1995. He is currently a visiting professor at the University of California, Los Angeles. He has written on divided government, political parties, and the politics of race in America.

Elizabeth Ivry is a government major at Colby College, Waterville, Maine.

Gary C. Jacobson is Professor of Political Science and Chair of the department at the University of California, San Diego, where he has taught since 1979. He received his A.B. from Stanford in 1966 and his Ph.D. from Yale in 1972, both in political science. From 1970 to 1979 he taught at Trinity College in Hartford, Connecticut. During 1990–91 he was a Fellow at the Center for Advanced Study in the Behavioral Sciences. Jacobson is the author of *Money in Congressional Elections* (1980), which won the Gladys E. Kammerer Award (1981) and the Leon Epstein Award (1991), *The Politics of Congressional Elections* (3rd ed., 1992), *The Electoral Origins of Divided Government* (1990), and coauthor of *Strategy and Choice in Congressional Elections* (2nd ed., 1983). He has served on the advisory council of the American Political Science Association and is a fellow of the American Academy of Arts and Sciences.

Charles O. Jones is the Hawkins Professor of Political Science, University of Wisconsin-Madison and was the Douglas Dillon Visiting Fellow, The Brookings Institution (1994–1995). He is a former Managing Editor of the *American Political Science Review* and President of the American Political Science Association. His most recent books include *The Presidency in a Separated System* and *Separate But Equal Branches: Congress and the Presidency*.

Benjamin D. Ling is a government major at Colby College, Waterville, Maine.

L. Sandy Maisel is the William R. Kenan, Jr. Professor and Chair of the Department of Government at Colby College, Waterville, Maine. He is the immediate past chair of the Political Organizations and Parties Organized Section of the American Political Science Association. Among his published works are *Parties and Elections in America, The Parties Respond: Changes in American Parties,* and the encyclopedia, *Political Parties and Elections in the United States.*

Franco Mattei is an Assistant Professor of Political Science at the State University of New York at Buffalo. He teaches courses on parties, elections, public opinion and voting behavior, and research methodology. His work has been published in the *American Political Science Review,* the *British Journal of Political Science,* the *Journal of Politics,* as well as in other journals.

David R. Mayhew is the Alfred Cowles Professor of Government at Yale University. Among other works, he is the author of *Congress: The Electoral Connection* and *Divided We Govern: Party Control, Lawmaking, and Investigations, 1946–1990.*

Stephanie G. Pennix received her B.A. in government from Colby College in Waterville, Maine and is currently a paralegal in the office of Arnold and Porter in Washington, D.C.

John J. Pitney, Jr. is an Associate Professor of Government at Claremont McKenna College, in Claremont, California. He has a bachelor's degree from Union College and a Ph.D. in political science from Yale University. He has been a Congressional Fellow of the American Political Science Association, senior domestic policy analyst for the House Republican Research Committee, and acting director of the Republican National Committee's Research Department. He is coauthor with William F. Connelly, Jr., of *Congress's Permanent Minority? Republicans in the U.S. House* (1994).

Philip H. Pollock, III received his Ph.D. in political science from the University of Minnesota in 1979. He is currently a Professor of Political Science at the University of Central Florida. Among other works on American politics, he is author with Theodore J. Eismeier of *Business, Money, and the Rise of Corporate PACs in American Elections.* His current research investigates the role of individual contributors in congressional elections.

Grant Reeher is Assistant Professor of Political Science at Syracuse University's Maxwell School of Citizenship and Public Affairs, and is the author of *Narratives of Justice: Legislators' Beliefs About Distributive Fairness.* His present research projects include studies of beliefs about distributive justice as they relate to health care policy, and the determinants of legislative activism at the individual level. In 1993 he received the American Political Science Association's William Anderson Prize, for the best dissertation in state and local politics, federalism, or intergovernmental relations. For 1995–1997, he will be at the University of Michigan as a Robert Wood Johnson Foundation Scholar in Health Policy.

Christopher Soper is an Assistant Professor of Political Science at Pepperdine University. He received his Ph.D. from Yale University in 1992. His most recent book is *Evangelical Christianity in the United States and Great Britain: Religious Beliefs, Political Choices* (1994).

Index

ABA. *See* American Bankers Association (ABA), PAC of
Abdnor, James, 38
Abortion issue, 118, 119–120, 123
Abraham, S., 36
Abramowitz, Alan I., 24, 37, 38, 39, 139, 154(n2)
Abramson, Jill, 92
Abramson, Paul R., 61, 71, 72, 78(n3)
Activism, Christian right, 8–9, 116–118, 123
ADA score. *See* Americans for Democratic Action (ADA) scores
Advocacy explosion, nationalization of, 90
  See also Interests
Affirmative action, views on, 129–130, 131
AFL-CIO COPE. *See* American Federation of Labor-Congress of Industrial Organizations Committee on Political Education (AFL-CIO COPE)
African-American representatives, 110–111
  See also Race(s)
Age, mobilization and, 127, 130–132
Agenda for the Republican Majority, 46(n11)
Akaka, Daniel, 28
Alabama, lack of Republican opposition before 1994 in House elections in, 106
Aldrich, John H., 61, 71, 72, 78(n3)
Alesina, Alberta, 99
Alexander, Bill, 106, 107
Alexander, Lamar, 45(n2)
Alienation of voters, 5–7, 53
Alignment of district-level presidential and House results, 7–8
Alternative media, use of, 50–51, 67–68
Amateurs, Republican, 11–12, 37, 143, 149–152
  identifying quality challengers among, 150–152
  self-financed, 87, 150–151
Ambition theory, 139
Ambivalence
  with parties, voter turnout and, 132–136
  from women, 127, 133, 134
Amendments, constitutional
  15th, 160
  17th, 160
  20th, 159
  22nd, 170
Amenta, Edwin, 161
American Bankers Association (ABA), PAC of, 95
American Federation of Labor-Congress of Industrial Organizations Committee on Political Education (AFL-CIO COPE), 33
American National Election Study (ANES), 139
  angry white males thesis and data from, 127, 128–132
  data on southern voters, 101, 104, 106, 108
  on gender, age and mobilization, 127, 130–132
American Political Science Association, Committee on Political Parties of, 48
Americans for Democratic Action (ADA) scores, 31–36, 107–108, 109
Analogy of 1946, 169–170
Andrews, Thomas, 34, 40
ANES. *See* American National Election Study (ANES)
Anger with Democrats, voter turnout and, 132–136
Angry public, 3–5
Angry white male, phenomenon of, 5–6, 125–136
  factors motivating, 126–127
  findings from 1994 elections on, 127
  locating emergence of, 128–130
  turnout of, factors in, 127, 130–136
Anthony, Beryl, 57
Apple, R.W., 45, 51

189

Armey, Dick, 50, 53
Arnold, R. Douglas, 19
Ashcroft, John, 34, 44, 115
Aspin, Les, 69
Attitudinal influences on turnout, 132–136

Bacchus, Jim, 106
Baer, Denise L., 123
Baltimore Sun, 138
Banning, Lance, 64, 78(n5)
Barbour, Haley, 23–24
Barlow, Tom, 106
Barnes, Fred, 123
Barone, Michael, 20(n3), 160
Baseler, Scotty, 53
Beasley, David, 115
Begala, Paul, ix, 25
Bendar, Nancy L., 117
Bennett, Stephen Earl, 127, 128, 129, 130, 132, 136
Bennett (senator from Utah), 36
Bentsen, Lloyd, 24, 69, 108
Berke, Richard, 77, 122
Bernstein, Jared, 136(n3)
Bernstein, Robert, 38
Bevill, Tom, 106
Bimes, Terri L., 103, 107, 110
Black, Earl, 101
Black, Merle, 101
Bond, Jon R., 139, 154(n5)
Bono, Sonny, 150
Boren, David, 35, 46(n13)
Box-Steffensmeier, Janet, 31
Boyer, Paul S., 159
Boyer, Peter J., 52
Boyle, Mary, 44
Bradley, B., 36
Brady, David W., 57, 93, 139, 140
Bredesen, Phil, 30
Brinkley, Alan, 161
British politics. See England
Brock, Bill, 42, 43
Broder, David, 49
Brooks, Jack, 108, 138
Brown, Jerry, 66
Brown, Ron, 69, 70
Brownstein, Ronald, 123
Bryan, Richard, 28
Bryan, William Jennings, 167
Buchanan, Pat, 66
Buckley v. Valeo, 86, 90
Bullock, Charles S., III, 110

Bureau of Labor Statistics, 71
Burleson, Omar, 105
Burnham, Walter Dean, 99, 139
Bush, George, 3, 9, 19, 46(n4), 54, 65, 105, 116
Business, mobilization of, 90
   See also Corporate PACs
Byrd, Robert, 28–29, 40

Cain, Bruce, 139
California, politics of pragmatism in, 117–118
Calmes, Jackie, 56, 87
Campaign, House Republican, 48–58
   ideas in, role of, 48–51
   individuals in, role of, 56–58
   institutions and, role of, 54–56
   interests in, role of, 51–54, 58
Campaign intensity in Senate elections, 38, 43–44
Campaign spending
   for House elections, 12–17, 20(n10), 82–86, 150–152
   in Senate elections, 42–43, 81, 82, 83–84
   See also Money in 1994 elections
Campbell, Ben Nighthorse, 31, 45(n2), 78(n1)
Campbell, James E., 22, 154(n2)
Candidate-centered election system, 2–3
Candidate contributions to campaign, 86–87, 150–152
   of Republican amateur winners, 87, 150–151
Candidate pools (1994), 137–155
   backgrounds of, 144
   challenging incumbents in primaries, 144–146
   contesting in open seats, 148–149
   methodology of study of, 141–144
   Republican "amateurs" winning seats in House, 37, 143, 149–152
   seeking nomination to challenge incumbents in general election, 146–148
   theories of candidate emergence and, 139–141
Candidate recruitment, 57
Cannon, Carl M., 50
Cannon, Howard, 38
Cannon, Joseph (Uncle Joe), 19
Canon, David T., 36, 37, 87, 139, 154(n5)

Carlson, Arne, 117
Carmines, Edward G., 127
Carter, Jimmy, 45, 62, 87, 101, 165
Carville, James, 70
Cashman, Sean Dennis, 159
Castro, Bernadette, 43
CBS/New York Times polls, 28
Ceaser, James W., 54
Chafee, John, 32, 40
Challengers
  campaign spending by, 81, 82, 85–86
  PAC contributions to, 82–86, 92
  quality of: in House elections, 11–12, 57; in primaries, 38–40; in Senate elections, 40–41; *See also* Experience, political
  Republican, in southern House elections, 105–106
  weak-challenger hypothesis, 139–141
  See also Candidate pools (1994)
Change, public desire for, 3–4
Chapman, Jim, 105
Christian Coalition, 20(n5), 32, 53, 115, 116–119, 122–124
  Contract with the American Family, 122, 123
Christian right, 53–54, 115–124
  activism, 8–9, 116–118, 123
  Contract with America and, 115, 122
  future prospects of, in Republican party, 122–124
  GOP-evangelical alliance, emergence of, 116–118
  1994 midterm elections and, 8–9, 115–116, 118–121
  politics of pragmatism and, 117–118, 122–124
Cisneros, Henry, 70
Citizen groups, 90
Civil Rights Act
  of 1875, 160
  of 1964, 101
Civil rights movement, 64
Clark, Joseph, 29
Class skew in 1994 election, 73
Clawson, Dan, 90
Clay, Henry, 159
Clinton, Bill, x, 66, 107, 126
  alienation of swing voters, 5–7, 53
  co-optation of Republican ideas, 49–50
  Court-versus-Country politics and administration of, 68–71
  divided government continuing under, 3–4
  election campaign, 66, 68
  election of, 4, 61–62, 100
  grassroots financial mobilization and antipathy toward, 93
  health care plan, failure of, 29, 52, 71, 126
  lack of coattails, 62
  party pressure on conservative Democrats from, 108
  popularity/unpopularity of, 6, 24–25, 28, 30, 45, 46(nn 5, 7)
  reelection prospects of, 76, 136
  response to Republican victory, 48
Clinton, Hillary Rodham, 5
Cloud, David S., 77
Coburn, Tom, 145, 154(n2)
Coehlo, Tony, 25, 51, 56, 58, 69, 92
Cogan, John F., 93
Cohen, Richard E., 58
Coker, J. Bradford, 56
Cold War, end of, 65
Command of the Army Act (1867), 159
Committee organization in Congress, 54
CompuServe, Contract of America on, 50
Congress
  80th, 169–170
  81st, 169
  40th, 159
  97th, comparing experience of 104th with, 37
  99th, 49
  104th. *See* House of Representatives, Republican victory in; Senate, Republican takeover of
  103rd, 5, 13, 36, 42
  organization along two conflicting lines, 54
  public contempt for members of, 3–5
Congressional Black Caucus, 110–111
Congressional elections
  distinction between Senate and House elections, 37–38
  midterm penalty in, 22–23, 61
  national conditions affecting, 22–25
  similarity between 1980 and 1994 results, 45
  theories of, 139–141
Congressional Quarterly Weekly Report, 21, 43
Connelly, William F., Jr., 48, 50, 55

Index

Connolly, Ceci, 21
Conover, Pamela Johnston, 128
Conservatism, increase in, 31–36, 62
Conservative coalition
    continued prominence of, in South, 106–110
    in 1938, 160–161
Conservatives
    Christian right, 8–9, 53–54, 115–124
    support of Republican candidates, 29–30, 99–100
    turnout of, 8–9
Contract with America, ix, 48–51, 95, 152, 170
    Christian right and, 115, 122
    Country themes in, 71–72
    covenant between party and electorate, 48, 49
    Democrats and analysts' criticism of, ix, 25, 51
    elements of, 50
    impact on voters, 6–7
    innovation of, 157
    reactions to unveiling of, 50–51
    Republican commitment to, 1996 elections and, 19–20
    roots of, 49–50
    unity of Republicans under, 55
    vision of conservative governance in, 48–49
Contract with the American Family, 122, 123
Cook, Elizabeth Adell, 128
Cook, Rhodes, 47, 152
Cooper, Jim, 40
Cooper, John Milton, Jr., 165, 166
Cooper, Joseph, 57, 139
Cooper, Virgil, 145, 154(n2)
Co-optation of Republican ideas by Clinton, 49–50
Coppersmith, Sam, 40, 43, 44
Corporate lobbyists, 77
Corporate PACs, 88, 91–92
Court-versus-Country politics, 61–79
    Clinton administration and, 68–71
    decline of Democratic party and, 65–68, 69
    in England, 63–64, 78(n5)
    in 1994 elections, 71–73
    rise of, 61–65
    themes of, 63
Covenant, Contract with America as, 48, 49
Coverdell, Paul, 24, 117

Covington, Gary, 139, 154(n5)
Cox, Edward, 161
Crime bill, 13, 15, 52, 108
C-SPAN, 57
Cultural decline, perception of, 4
Curran, Tim, 56
Cynicism toward government, 64–65

Danforth, John, 33–34
Dannemeyer, William, 38, 117
Darden, Buddy, 106, 108
Davidson, James West, 159
Deal, Nathan, 110, 113(n2)
Dealignment, 99–100, 101
    See also Realignment
DeConcini, Dennis, 35, 43
Deficit reduction, Clinton's focus on, 70
Democratic incumbents
    contributions of Republican amateur winners in races against, 151
    House, impact of campaign spending on, 14–17
    PAC contributions to, 92, 94
    Republicans seeking nominations to challenge, 146–147
    Senate, performance of, 29–31
Democratic Leadership Council, 66, 108
Democratic National Committee (DNC), 66
Democratic party
    Court-versus-Country politics and decline of, 65–68, 69
    end of hegemony in House, 137–139
    erosion of support for, 25
    evangelical opposition to, 119
    factors motivating defections from, 126
    impact of 1994 elections on, 73–77
    organizational decline over last three decades, 66–67, 68, 73, 76
    rebuilding of, 1994 losses forcing, 77
    secular left in, 121
Democrats
    alienation of Christian right, 53
    anger with, voter turnout and, 132–136
    candidates challenging incumbents in primaries, 145–146
    error in reading public mood in 1994, 51
    "farm system" supplying experienced candidates, 11
    House majority until 1994, reasons for, 2–3
    loss of majority status, altered strategic environment due to, 18–19

as party of government, 6, 68
in primaries for open seats, 148–149
prospects in 1996 elections, 18, 136
response to Contract, ix, 25, 51
retirements, 10, 17, 31, 57, 73, 76
scandals involving, 4–5, 56, 69, 70
seeking nominations to oppose
 incumbent Republicans, 147–148
strategic behavior of, 10–17
Dewar, Helen, 49
DeWine, Michael, 34, 36, 44, 115
Dies, Martin, 161
Dionne, E.J., Jr., 64
Direct-mail fund-raising operation,
 Republican, 67
District voting patterns, impact on House
 Democratic incumbents, 14–17
Divided government, politics of, 3–4
Dixon, Alan, 39
DNC. *See* Democratic National Committee
 (DNC)
Dole, Bob, 3, 25, 59
Donald, David, 159, 165, 166
Drew, Elizabeth, 56, 69
Dukakis, Michael, 62, 100
Duncan, Philip D., 73, 74, 75
Du Pont, Pete, 57
Durenberger, David, 32

Economic policy, Clinton administration's
 failure in, 70, 71, 73
Economy
 Court-versus-Country politics
  overlapping transformations in, 78(n6)
 identification of government with
  stagnant, 64
 role in 1994 campaign, 4, 52
 whites' views about affirmative action and
  concerns about, 130
Edsall, Mary D., 64, 126
Edsall, Thomas Byrne, 64, 126
Ehrenhalt, Alan, 87, 140, 149
Eikenberry, Ken, 123
Eisenhower, Dwight D., 101, 161–162
Eismeier, Theodore J., 91
Elders, Joycelyn, 5
Election mandates, 157
 See also Contract with America
Electorate, mood of, 23–25, 62
Elkins, Stanley, 64, 78(n5)
Ellis, Steven, 47
Enforcement Acts (1870–1872), 160

England
 Court-versus-Country politics in, 63–64,
  78(n5)
 intraparty conflict in British politics,
  167–168
Erikson, Robert S., 9, 28
Espy, Mike, 69, 70
Ethical scandals, 69, 70
Evangelical Christians. *See* Christian right
Evans, Rowland, 162
Expectations, Democrats' strategic responses
 to, 10–12
Expected value of losing (EVL), 140
Expected value of running (EVR), 140
Expected value of winning (EVW), 140, 152
Experience, political
 advantage of, 147, 148–149, 152
 amateurs, Republican, 37, 87, 143,
  149–152
 of candidates for House, 14–17, 36
 of candidates for Senate, 36–37, 40–42
 qualified candidates and, defining, 140,
  143–144, 154(nn 5, 6)
 strategic-politician model and, 152
Exposure in Senate, seat, 23

Fabrizio/McLaughlin post-election poll, 53
Factionalism model of innovative midterms,
 majority-party, 165–168
Falwell, Jerry, 116
Family values, 119–120, 124
"Farm system" of experienced candidates,
 11, 149
Fattah, Chaka, 145
Faucheux, Ron, 52
Fazio, Vic, 53, 119
Federal Election Campaign Act (FECA), 90
 amendments of 1974, 87, 89, 90
Federal Election Commission (FEC), 43, 52,
 81, 93, 150
 1975 SunPAC decision, 90
Federal Insecticide, Fungicide, and
 Rodenticide Act (FIFRA, 1947), 170
Feinstein, Dianne, 38, 40, 41, 42, 43
Fenno, Richard F., Jr., 6
Ferejohn, John, 139
Ferguson, Thomas, 81
FIFRA. *See* Federal Insecticide, Fungicide,
 and Rodenticide Act (FIFRA, 1947)
15th Amendment, 160
Finance, campaign. *See* Campaign spending;
 Money in 1994 elections

Fine, Terri Susan, 128
Fingerhut, Eric D., 56
Fiorina, Morris P., 99, 139, 140
First Reconstruction Act, 159
Fisher, Richard, 43
Fleisher, Richard, 139, 154(n5)
Flippo, Ronnie, 106
Foley, Tom, 56, 94, 138
Folsom, Jim, Jr., 39
Fontenot, Eugene, 87
Fowler, Linda L., 139, 143, 144, 149, 154(n5)
Fowler, Wyche, Jr., 24
Fox, Jon, 138–139
Franklin, Benjamin, 22
Franklin, Charles H., 31
Frankovic, Kathleen A., 125
Freeman, Jo, 118
Frelinghuysen, Rodney, 145, 153(n2), 155(n11)
Freneau, Philip, 64
Freshmen Republicans, 138–139
  amateurs winning House seats, 37, 87, 143, 149–152
Friction and fission in political system, 54
Frisa, Daniel, 145, 154(n2)
Frist, Bill, 30, 36, 41, 43, 82, 87
Frymer, Paul, 100, 103, 107, 110
Fuerbringer, Jonathan, 49
Futurist, The, 59

Gay rights, 123
Gelman, Andrew, 20(n8)
Gelman-King index, 10, 20(n8)
Gender
  ambivalence from women, 127, 133, 134
  mobilization and, 127, 130–132
  probit estimates of vote choice by, 134–136
  probit estimates of voter turnout by, 133, 134
  views on affirmative action by, 129–130, 131
  views on racial issues by, 128
  See also Angry white male, phenomenon of
Gender gap, 125, 127
George, Walter, 166
Gephardt, Richard, 48
Germond, Jack W., 44, 62, 66
Gibbons, Sam, 94
Gilbert, Christopher P., 117
Gillespie, Ed, 50, 72, 77
Gilvour, John B., 57

Gingrich, Marianne, 59
Gingrich, Newt, ix, 9, 19, 25, 47, 56, 59, 92, 94, 122, 153, 168
  crime bill and, 52
  House Democrats' efforts against, 59
  as House GOP whip, 50
  as leader, 57–58, 59
  merchandising capabilities of, 170
  PACs and, 51
  power of speakership and, 59
  on realignment, 59–60
  recognition of freshmen Republicans, 138–139
  religious conservatives and, 53
  speech foreshadowing Contract (1980), 49
  unity of Republicans and, 55, 56
Ginn, Bo, 106
Gladstone, William, 157
Glasser, Susan B., 53
Glickman, Dan, 138
Goldwater, Barry, 101, 167
Goode, Virgil, Jr., 40
GOP. *See* Republican party
GOPAC, 57–58
Gore, Al, Jr., 46(n13), 66
Gorton, S., 40
Gosselin, Peter G., 56
Governing Team Day (September 15, 1980), 49
Government
  cynicism toward, 64–65
  proper role of, issue of, 48
Governorship as primary stepping stone to Senate, 36–37
Grams, Rod, 32
Grassroots volunteer labor, Christian right as, 53
Green, Donald Philip, 154(n5)
Green, John C., 67, 116, 117, 121, 122
Greenberg, Stanley B., 24, 47, 62, 68, 72, 79(n10)
Greenberg Research, 108
Greenspan, Alan, 70
Greider, William, 62, 66, 79(n8)
Grofman, Bernard, 139
Guinier, Lani, 5, 111
Gunter, William, 38
Guth, James L., 116, 117, 121, 122

Halleck, Charles, 161
Hamiltonians and Jeffersonians, conflict between, 64

Hansen, John Mark, 67, 132
Hartmann, Susan, 169
Hatch, O., 36
Hatch Act (1939), 161
Hatcher, Charles, 106
Hatfield, Mark, 32
Health care reform, failure of, 29, 52, 71, 126
Health Insurance Association of America (HIAA), 52
Hedges, Michael, 53
Herrnson, Paul S., 36
Hershey, Majorie Randon, 157
Hertzke, Allen D., 117
HIAA. *See* Health Insurance Association of America (HIAA)
Hill, Kevin A., 19, 110, 117
Hinckley, Barbara, 31, 37, 139
Holmes, Geoffrey, 63, 64, 78(n5)
Horowitz, David Alan, 64
House Bank controversy, 56
House elections
　distinction between Senate and, 37–38
　PAC contributions in (1978–1994), distribution of, 91
　Republican opposition in southern, 105–106
House of Representatives, election to Senate and service in, 36–37
House of Representatives, Republican victory in, 1–20, 47
　campaign for, elements in, 48–58
　campaign spending and, 12–17, 20(n10), 82–86
　candidate experience and, 14–17, 36
　candidate pools in. *See* Candidate pools (1994)
　Christian right and, 118–121
　end of Democratic hegemony, 137–139
　end of "permanent minority" status, 47–48, 58
　future elections and, impact on, 18–20
　previous Democratic majority, reasons for, 2–3
　reasons for, 2–9: angry public, 3–5; Clinton problem, 5–7; nationalization of vote, 1, 7–9, 24, 55
　sources of House vote by issue, 119
　strategic behavior reflecting and magnifying election year trends, 10–17
　variables affecting incumbents in, 13–17
Houston, Paul, 51
Houston Post, 138

Hubbard, Carroll, 106
Huckfeldt, Robert, 127
Huffington, Michael, 41, 42, 43, 81, 82, 117–118, 119, 122
Hugick, Larry, 51
Humphrey, Hubert, 62
Hutchison, Kay Bailey, 24, 28, 40, 117
Hutto, Earl, 106
Hyatt, Joel, 44

Ideas, role in House Republican campaign, 48–51
Ideas for Tomorrow, Choices for Today, 49
Ideology, political
　by religious group, 121
　shift in ideological orientation of Senate, 31–36
　state, correlation between Senate election results and, 28
　See also Court-versus-Country politics
Incumbency
　alignment of district-level presidential and House results and, 7–8
　electoral value of, 10, 20(n8), 139
Incumbents
　campaign spending by: in House, 12–17, 82, 85–86; in Senate, 42–43, 82
　PAC contributions to, 82–86, 92, 94
　in primaries, 38–40, 144–146
　strategic retirements of, 10, 17, 31, 32–33, 57, 73, 76
　See also Democratic incumbents; Republican incumbents
Independent expenditures, 86, 88
Individual contributions, increase in, 92–94
Individuals, role in House Republican campaign, 56–58
Inhofe, James, 36
Innovative midterm elections, 157–170
　analogy of 1946, 169–170
　criteria for, 158
　explaining, 162–169: large party seat swings, 162–163; majority-party factionalism, 165–168; 1994 election, 165, 168–169; resolution of high-stakes conflict, 164–165
　of the past, 158–162: also-rans (1930, 1958, 1974), 161–162; of 1810, 158–159, 163, 164, 166; of 1866, 159–160, 163, 164, 165, 166; of 1910, 160, 162–163, 164, 165, 166; of 1938, 160–161, 163, 164–165, 166–167

Institutions
  appearance of failure of public, 4
  composing Democratic party, demise of, 66–67, 68
  role in House Republican campaign, 54–56
Interest groups
  contribution from, as mixed blessing, 96
  system of, 90
Interests
  Republican links with organized, 76–77
  role in House Republican campaign, 51–54, 58
Internet, Contract of America on, 50–51

Jacksonian Democratic party, 68
Jacobson, Gary C., 2, 3, 9, 10, 11, 12, 15, 18, 21, 45, 73, 99, 105, 107, 139, 140, 141, 143, 149, 152, 154(n5), 155(n13)
Jeffersonian Republican party, 159
  conflict between Hamiltonians and, 64
Jeffords, Jim, 28, 32
Jeffries, John W., 161
Johannes, John R., 139
Johnson, Andrew, 159, 160, 164, 166
Johnson, Don, 108
Johnson, Hiram, 166
Johnson, Lyndon, 101, 165
Jones, J.R., 64
Jones, Ruth S., 139
Jontz, Jim, 41
Jordan, Winthrop D, 159

Karnes, David, 38
Kazee, Thomas A., 139, 154(n5)
Kellstedt, Lyman A., 116, 121, 122
Kelly, Michael, 51
Kennedy, John F., 62, 101, 165
Kennedy, Patrick, 151
Kennedy, Ted, 43
Kenney, Patrick J., 38
Kernell, Samuel, 10, 12, 73, 105, 139, 143
Kerrey, Bob, 29
Kim, Thomas P., 103, 107, 110
King, Gary, 20(n8)
Klinkner, Philip A., 68, 118
Kobach, Kris W., 160
Koeniger, A. Cash, 167
Kohfeld, Carol Weitzel, 127
Kohl, Herb, 28, 40
Kohut, Andrew, 51

Koopman, Douglas L., 50
Kranish, Michael, 58
Krasno, Jonathan S., 30, 38, 154(n5)
Krehbiel, Keith, 3
Kristol, William, 53
Krueger, Bob, 28
Kyl, Jon, 36, 43–44

Labor PACs, 87–88, 89, 91, 94, 95
Ladd, Everett Carll, 29, 51, 52, 54, 99
La Follette, Robert, 166
Lancaster, Martin, 107
Landrum-Griffin Act (1959), 162
Langer, Gary, 4, 5, 6
Largent, Steve, 115, 151
Lautenberg, Frank, 29, 36, 40
Lawrence, Christine C., 73, 74, 75
Leaders, House Republican, 57–58
Leath, Marvin, 105
Lee, Shiela Jackson, 145
Lesher, Dave, 124
Leuchtenberg, William E., 161
Levy, David, 145
Lewis, Jerry, 49
Lewis, John, 59
Lewis, Ron, 115
Lewis-Beck, Michael S., 24, 154(n2)
Liberalism, racial, 64
Liberals
  Court tradition of, 63
  support of Democrats, 29
Lieberman, Joe, 28
Limbaugh, Rush, 51, 64
Lind, Michael, 62
Lobbyists, corporate, 77
Los Angeles Times poll (October 1994), 4
Lubell, Samuel, 48
Lugar, Richard, 41

McCormick, Richard L., 97
McGovern, George, 62, 101, 106, 167
McIver, John P., 28
Mack, Charles, 94–95
McKitrick, Eric, 64, 78(n5)
McMillan, Colin, 43
Madison, James, 64, 159
Madonna, G. Terry, 30
Mahoney, Richard, 43
Maisel, L. Sandy, 38, 46(n16), 139, 140, 141, 143, 144, 149, 154(n5)
Majority-party factionalism model of innovative midterms, 165–168

Malbin, Michael, 23
Male voters, Clinton's alienation of white, 5–6
　See also Angry white male, phenomenon of
Mandates, election, 157
　See also Contract with America
Mann, Thomas E., 23, 28, 37, 45, 139
Margolies-Mezvinsky, Marjorie, 139
Marshall Plan, 169
Martin, Joseph, 161
Mathews, Harlon, 35
Mathis, Dawson, 106
Mattingly, Mack, 39
Maverick, Maury, 167
Mayhew, David R., 19, 117, 139, 162
Media, use of alternative, 50–51, 67–68
Meier, Kenneth J., 169
Merida, Kevin, 24
Metzenbaum, Howard, 34
Michel, Bob, 50, 53
Middle class, economic growth from 1973–1992 and, 4
Midterm penalty, 22–23, 61
Milkis, Sidney M., 66
Miller, Zell, 39
Mishel, Lawrence, 136(n3)
Mitchell, George, 30, 34
Mitofsky International, 118
Mobilization. See Voter turnout
Moderates, support of Democrats by, 29
Moderation, politics of pragmatism and, 118
Moen, Matthew C., 118
Mondak, Jeffrey J., 9
Mondale, Walter, 62, 106
Money in 1994 elections, 81–97
　campaign finance reforms and, 88–90
　candidate contributions, 86–87, 150–152
　changes in flows and realignment of, 81, 92–94, 95–96, 97
　Democratic party organization and, demise of, 67
　future impact of, 94–97
　gravitation toward power, 94–95, 96
　independent expenditures, 86, 88
　individual contributions, 92–94
　inertia of campaign economy and, 81
　overview of flows of, 82–87
　PACs and, 18, 51–52, 82–92, 94, 95
　total spent, 81
Money Trust Investigation, 160

Monroe, James, 159
Montgomery, Sonny, 106
Mood of electorate, 23–25, 62
Moral issues, 4, 119, 124
　See also Christian right
Moral Majority, 116
Moss, David A., 160
Mowry, George E., 160, 166
Moynihan, Daniel Patrick, 40
Murrin, John M., 63, 78(n5)
Mutch, Robert E., 160

NAFTA. See North American Free Trade Agreement (NAFTA)
Natcher, William, 113(n2)
National conditions forecasting Republican takeover, 22–25
National Federation of Independent Businesses (NFIB), 52
National issues, electoral effect of, 16–17
Nationalization of advocacy explosion, 90
Nationalization of vote, 1, 7–9, 24, 55
National Journal, 33
National Republican Congressional Committee (NRCC), 55
National Rifle Association (NRA), 52–53, 108
　Political Victory Fund, 52
National Security Act, 169
Neal, Stephen, 106
Neibuhr, Gustav, 123
Nelson, Bill, 106
Nelson, Michael, 66
Neustadtl, Alan, 90
New Deal, 161
New Democrats, 50
New York Times/CBS News poll (October 19-November 1 1994), 6–7
NFIB. See National Federation of Independent Businesses (NFIB)
Nichols, Bill, 106
Niemi, Richard G., 62, 65, 77
Nixon, Richard M., 65, 101, 106, 165
Nomination to challenge incumbents in general election, seeking, 146–148
Nonconnected PACs, 88, 89, 91
North, Oliver, 40, 42, 43, 81, 82, 93, 115
North American Free Trade Agreement (NAFTA), 5, 15, 70
North American Free Trade Agreement (NAFTA) Implementation Bill (HR 3450), 13

Novak, Robert, 162
NRA. *See* National Rifle Association (NRA)
NRCC. *See* National Republican Congressional Committee (NRCC)

O'Leary, Brad, 53
Omnibus Anti-Crime Bill of 1994 (HR 3355), 13
Omnibus Reconciliation Bill of 1993 (HR 2264), 13
O'Neill, Tip, 2–3, 45, 48
Open seats
   desirability of running for, 142, 143
   House, 17, 138: campaign spending for, 82–84, 85, 150–152
   primaries for, 40, 148–149
   Senate, 23, 41–42: campaign intensity for, 38, 43–44; spending on, 82
Opportunity-cost model, 140, 152–153
Organized labor, 70
Ornstein, Norman J., 23, 28, 45
Owen, John B., 78(n5)

PAC. *See* Political action committees (PACs)
Panetta, Leon, 69
Party affiliation, switch in, 31, 45(n2), 76, 78(n1), 111
Party identification by religious group, 121
Party loyalty or support, 8
   district presidential partisanship and, 16
   on key votes, impact on Democratic incumbents, 13–17
   pressure from Clinton on conservative Democrats for, 108
Party organization in Congress, 54
Patterson, James T., 161, 165, 166
Pear, Robert, 71
Pennsylvania, Wofford race in, 29–30
Percy, Charles, 38
Perot, Ross, 63–64, 66, 92
Perot constituency, 5, 6, 24
   Country sentiments of, 72
   influence on Democratic losses, 72–73, 74, 75
Persinos, John F., 117
Peters, John G., 39
Peters, Ronald M., Jr., 159
Petrocik, John R., 107
Peyton, Jeffrey M., 53
Phillips, Kevin, 46(n7), 62, 64, 65, 68, 70, 96
Pitney, John J., Jr., 48, 50, 55
Place Acts, 64, 78(n5)

"Pluralist" school, 54
Pocock, J.G.A., 78(n5)
Political action committees (PACs)
   contributions of, 18, 51–52, 82–92, 94, 95
   history of campaign finance reforms and, 88–90
   impact in 1994, 87–92
   population dynamics of, 90–91
   Republicans and, 77, 87
   rise of, 90
   types of, 87–88, 89, 91–92, 94, 95
Political experience. *See* Experience, political
Political system, friction and fission in, 54
Pollock, Philip H., III, 91
Populist, use of term, 62
Post Office controversy, 56
Powell, Lawrence N., 166
Power
   gravitation of money in elections toward, 94–95, 96
   of speakership of House, 59
   temptations of, 59
Pragmatism, Christian right and politics of, 117–118, 122–124
Presidential elections
   district presidential partisanship in: alignment of House results and, 7–8; party support and, 16
   after major losses in midterm elections, 76
   of 1980, 87
   of 1992, 4, 61–62, 65–66, 100
   Republican dominance of, 2
   Southern voting patterns in, 101
Price, David, 106, 137
Primaries
   candidate contributions in, 86
   challenging incumbents in, 38–40, 144–146
   data on candidates in, 141–143
   decision to enter, 141
   for open seats, 40, 148–149
Progressive Era, Court-and-Country politics during, 78(nn 5, 6)
Project on the First One Hundred Days, 49
Public institutions, appearance of failure of, 4
Public opinion change, innovative midterms due to, 162–164
Public sentiment in 1994, related waves of, 3–7
   anger at politics, politicians, and government, 3–5

economic discontent, 4
rejection of Clinton by swing voters, 5–7

"Qualified" candidates, defining, 140, 143–144, 154(nn 5, 6)
See also Candidate pools (1994)
Quist, Allen, 117

Race(s)
    affirmative action opinions by, 129–130, 131
    political gap between, 127
    racial issue opinions by, 128
Racial liberalism, 64
Racially-based redistricting, 19, 110–111
Rademacher, Eric W., 127, 128, 129, 130, 132, 136
Ragsdale, Lyn, 37
Randall, J.G., 159, 165, 166
Rauch, Jonathan, 69
Reagan, Ronald, 49, 54, 87, 105, 106, 107, 116, 126, 157, 165
Reagan Democrats, 5
Reagan Revolution, 95
Realignment, 48
    Gingrich on, 59–60
    money in 1994 elections and, 81, 92–94, 95–96, 97
Realignment in South, 99–113
    conservative coalition and, continued prominence of, 106–110
    dealignment vs., 99–100, 101
    delay of, 100–105
    realignment nationwide and, factors in, 111, 112
    Republican opposition in Southern House elections and, 105–106
Reapportionment, effects of, 19
Reconstruction, congressional, 159
Reconstruction Acts (1867 and 1868), 159, 160
Recruitment, candidate, 57
    See also Candidate pools (1994)
Redistricting, 18–19, 110–111, 144
Reed, Ralph, 115, 117, 122–123
Reforms
    campaign finance, 88–90
    Clinton administration's abandonment of political, 68–69
Regional distribution of Senate seats, 31, 35
Religiosity, likelihood of voting Republican and, 54

Religious conservatives. *See* Christian right
Religious groups
    party identification and ideology by selected, 121
    party vote by selected, 120–121
    See also Christian right
Republican incumbents, 31
    Democrats seeking nominations to oppose, 147–148
    support for, 137
Republican National Committee, 95
Republican party
    future prospects of Christian right in, 122–124
    GOP-evangelical alliance, emergence of, 116–118
    organizational renaissance, 8–9, 67–68
    PACs and, 77, 87
Republicans
    amateurs, 11–12, 37, 87, 143, 149–152
    candidates challenging incumbents in primaries, 144–145
    House, status as party of government and opposition under Reagan and Bush, 54–55
    links with organized interests, 76–77
    in primaries for open seats, 40, 148–149
    seeking nominations to challenge incumbent Democrats, 146–147
    See also House of Representatives, Republican victory in; Senate, Republican takeover of
Resolution-of-conflict model of innovative midterms, 164–165
Responsible-party school of political science, 48, 54
Retirements, strategic, 10, 17, 31, 32–33, 57, 73, 76
Rice, Tom W., 24, 38
Richter, Paul, 20(n2)
Riegle, Don, 34
Rivers, Douglas, 93, 139
RJR Nabisco, PAC of, 95
Robb, Charles, 29, 39–40, 42
Robertson, Pat, 123
Robinson, Tommy, 107
Rogers, David, 92
Rohde, David W., 61, 71, 72, 78(n3), 107
Rollins, Ed, 46(n4)
Romney, Mitt, 43
Roosevelt, Franklin D., 164, 165, 166

Roosevelt, Theodore, 165
Rosenbaum, David E., 57
Rosenstiel, Thomas B., 58
Rosenstone, Steven J., 67, 132
Rosenthal, Howard, 99
Rostenkowski, Dan, 56, 58, 70, 94
Roth, William, 28
Rothstein, Paul, 57
Rozell, Mark J., 56

Salisbury, Robert H., 90
Sanders, Bernard, 20(n1), 154(n8), 155(n14)
Santorum, Rick, 30, 34, 41, 82, 115
Sarbanes, Paul, 29, 40, 42
Sarpalius, Bill, 108, 138
Sasser, Jim, 29, 30, 35
Scandals, 4–5, 56, 69, 70
Schellhas, Bob, 50, 72, 77
Schlesinger, Joseph A., 139
Schneider, William, 45
Schwarz, Jordan A., 162
Scott, Denise, 90
Seat swings, innovative midterms due to large party, 162–163
Secular left, 121
Seelye, Katharine Q., 25
Segal, Jeffrey A., 24, 38, 39
Self-financed races (candidate contributions), 86–87, 150–152
Senate, Republican takeover of, 1, 21–46
    campaign intensity and, 38, 43–44
    campaign spending in, 42–43, 82, 83–84
    candidate experience and, 36–37, 40–42
    compared with 1992 elections, 22
    election results, overview of, 26–37
    ideological change with, 31–36
    incumbents, reelection rate of, 30–33
    member and party turnover, 29–33, 34
    midterm penalty and, 22–23
    mood of electorate and, 23–25
    national conditions forecasting, 22–25
    in 1980, 28
    party primaries and, 38–40
    regional distribution of seats, 31, 35
    relationship between House and Senate Republicans, 59
    seat exposure and open seats, risks of, 23
Senate elections, distinction between House and, 37–38
Separation of powers, 54
17th Amendment, 160
Sex. *See* Gender

Seymour, John, 38
Shafer, Byron, 112
Shalit, Ruth, 69
Shapiro, Isaac, 71
Sharpe, Mark, 94
Shays, Christopher, 58
Shelby, Richard C., 1, 31, 45(n2), 78(n1)
Shelly, Mack C., II, 160
Shepherd, Karen, 56
Simpson, Glenn R., 51
Skocpol, Theda, 161
Smelser, Marshall, 159
Smidt, Corwin E., 116, 121, 122
Smith, Andrew E., 127, 128, 129, 130, 132, 136
Smith, "Cotton Ed," 166
Smith, Howard, 161
Smith Act (1940), 161
Smith-Connally Act (1943), 161
Snowe, Olympia, 34
Soper, J. Christopher, 116
Sorauf, Frank J., 86, 91, 96
Sousa, David J., 87
South, the
    Democrat's loss of special influence in, 18
    impact of incumbent House Democrat's roll-call record in, 16
    split-ticket voters in, 100, 101–104, 111
    See also Realignment in South
Southern Democrats, 3
    ability to differentiate selves from national Democrats, 107–108
    change in perception of, in 1994, 108–110
Southern whites
    Clinton's reputation among white southern males, 5, 6
    ongoing transformation in voting behavior of, 110–111
    party identification of (1952–1994), 102, 103
    realignment of, 101–105
Soviet Union, fall of, 65
Speakership of House, power of, 59
Special elections (1992 and 1993), 23, 24
Split-ticket voters in the South, 100, 101–104, 111
Squire, Peverill, 38
Stampp, Kenneth M., 166
Stanley, Harold W., 62, 65, 77
State ideology, correlation between Senate election results and, 28
Steeper, Fred, 54

Stenholm, Chuck, 105
Stephanopoulos, George, 51
Stevens, Thaddeus, 159
Stewart, Donald, 39
Stimson, James A., 127
Stockman, Steve, 138
Stokes, Donald E., 9
Stone, Peter H., 95
Stone, Richard, 38
Stone, Walter J., 139, 141
Strategic behavior, election year trends reflected and magnified in, 10–17
Strategic environment, alteration of, 18–19
Strategic-politician model, 152
Strategic retirements, 10, 17, 31, 32–33, 57, 73, 76
Sullivan, Mike, 40
Sundquist, Don, 30
Sundquist, James L., 100, 104
SunPAC decision (1975), 90
Supreme Court, on racially-based redistricting, 111
Swing voters, 5–7, 24, 53, 132
Synar, Mike, 106, 145, 154(n2)

Taber, Ron, 123
Taft, Robert, 161, 168, 169, 170
Taft, William Howard, 160, 164, 166
Taft-Hartley Act (1947), 161, 170
Talk radio shows, 8, 51, 126
Talmadge, Herman, 38–39
Taylor, Paul, 52
Taylor, Telford, 160
Tenure of Office Act (1867), 159
Term limits, 64, 155(n17)
Texas, lack of Republican opposition in House elections in, 105
Theories of congressional elections, 139–141
Thomas, Clarence, 111
Thomas, Craig, 33
Thomas, Linsey, 106
THOMAS website system, 59
Thompson, Fred, 36
Thornberry, "Mac," 138
Thornburg, Richard, 29
Thurmond, Strom, 101
Tiahrt, Todd, 138
Toner, Robin, 59
Trade PACs, 88, 91–92
Truman, Harry, 165, 169–170
Truman Doctrine, 169
Tsongas, Paul, 65–66

Tuchfarber, Alfred J., 127, 128, 129, 130, 132, 136
Tulis, Jeffrey K., 166
Turnout, voter. *See* Voter turnout
Turnover in Senate, member and party, 29–33, 34
20th "Lame-Duck" Amendment, 159
22nd Amendment, 170
Tydings, Millard, 166

Uncontested House seats, distribution of, 11, 12
Unified government in 1992, 44
Unifusa, Grant, 20(n3)
U.S. Chamber of Commerce, 33
Unity of House Republicans, 55–56, 58

Veto strategy, x
Vietnam, cynicism toward government and, 65
Vogel, David, 90, 95
Voinovich, George, 44
Von Drehle, David, 24
Vote choice, effects of anger and ambivalence on, 133–136
Voter guides issued by Christian Coalition, 118–119
Voter News Service, 28
Voters
 split-ticket, 100, 101–104, 111
 swing, 5–7, 24, 53, 132
Voter turnout, 8–9, 130–136
 age and, 127, 130–132
 of angry white males, 127, 130–136
 attitudinal influences on, 132–136
 demise of Democratic party as mobilizing institution for, 67
 gender and, 127, 130–132
 by income and race in 1994, 73, 75
 probit estimates of (1994), 133, 134
Voting patterns
 district, impact on House Democratic incumbents, 14–17
 religiosity and voting Republican in 1994, 54
 by religious groups, 120–121
 southern split-ticket 101–4, 100, 111
Voting Rights Act, 110, 111

Wagner Act, 170
Wald, Ken D., 116
Walker, Jack L., 90

Wallop, Malcolm, 32–33
Wamp, Zach, 138
War Hawks, 159, 163, 164, 166
Warsh, Kevin M., 140
Washington Post, 138
Watergate, cynicism toward government and, 65
Water Pollution Control Act (1948), 170
Wattenberg, Martin P., 99
Watts, J.C., 115, 151
Weak-challenger hypothesis, 139–141
  See also Candidate pools (1994)
Webb, R.K., 78(n5)
Weiss, Stuart L., 167
Welch, Susan, 39
Westlye, Mark C., 38, 40, 41
Wheat, Alan, 40, 44
White, Leonard, 159
White southern males. *See* Angry white male, phenomenon of; Southern whites
Whitewater affair, 70
Whitten, Jamie, 106
Wilcox, Clyde, 56, 71, 72, 78(n3), 116, 117, 128
Wilder, Douglas, 39–40
Wilhelm, David, 51
Wills, Garry, 57
Wilson, Pete, 117, 118, 119, 124
Wilson, Woodrow, 157, 165
Window of Opportunity (Gingrich), 57
Witcover, Jules, 44, 62, 66
Witte, John F., 169
Wofford, Harris, 29–30, 34, 41
Wolfinger, Raymond E., 37, 139
Women, ambivalence from, 127, 133, 134
Woodrum, Clifton A., 161
Woodward, Bob, 70
Wright, Gerald C., 28
Wright, Jim, 56, 58, 59
Wuthnow, Robert, 116

Yost, Berwood A., 30